NORTH KOREA UNDERCOVER

NORTH KOREA UNDERCOVER

INSIDE THE WORLD'S MOST SECRET STATE

John Sweeney

PEGASUS BOOKS
NEW YORK LONDON

NORTH KOREA UNDERCOVER

Pegasus Books LLC
80 Broad Street, 5th Floor
New York, NY 10004

ISBN: 978-1-60598-802-3

10 9 8 7 6 5 4 3 2 1

Printed in the United States of America
Distributed by W. W. Norton & Company, Inc.

To the forgotten of the gulag

The woman was paper-thin
A sign hung from her neck:
'Selling my daughter, 100 won'
[100 won is roughly 73 US cents or 47p]
    Jang Jin Seong, 'Selling My Daughter'

The Leader is the supreme brain of a living body, the Party is the
nerve of that living body, and the masses are only endowed with
life when they offer their absolute loyalty
    Juche, the guiding philosophy of the North Korean
    regime, set out in Kim Jong Il's *Ten Principles*

Life, in the abstract, in its great coach – how nice;
But amidst vomit and outrage the real thing triumphs,
It flows, sewage and decay . . .
I suffer moons, hungers, cruel Christs of pus . . .
I give in bone the explanation of this, my misfortune.
    'Pieta' by North Korean gulag inmate 1967–74,
    Ali Lameda

Preface to the American Edition

North Korea is mad, bad and dangerous to mock. Kim Jong Un may appear a fat clown but when his tyranny bites its venom, like a cobra's, blackens flesh. In 2013 I went undercover to the dark state for BBC Panorama. Pyongyang feels like the set of some weird version of The Hunger Games. North Korea's go-between kicked up a great fuss about our documentary and, to cut a long story short, the BBC apologised and I ended up losing my job.

So I feel great sympathy for the makers of *The Interview*, Seth Rogen and James Franco, who came up with a bold comedy idea about two dumb-ass American journalists getting an interview with Kim Jong Un. Along comes the CIA and they're ordered to assassinate Kim. The movie has too many butt jokes but it is funny and good. There is a show-stopping moment when the hitherto entirely moronic celebrity interviewer asks a simple question of Kim Jong Un: 'why don't you feed your people?' The North Koreans called *The Interview* 'an act of war.' There followed a massive hack of the almighty Sony Picture Corporation.

The North Koreans denied hacking Sony but nevertheless called it a 'righteous deed.' When the film wasn't shelved, a peculiar outfit calling itself 'The Guardians of Peace' made more threats: 'We will clearly show it to you at the very time and places *The Interview* be shown, including the premiere, how bitter fate those who seek fun in terror should be doomed to . . . The world will be full of fear. Remember the 11th of September 2001.'

The idiom is pure North-Korglish, hate-speak with clunky English grammar boiler-plated in Pyongyang. Despite their denials of being responsible for the hacking, North Korea remains the prime suspect. The leaks show how the Japanese boss of the parent company, the Sony Corporation, worked hard to tone down the satire's sting. Kazuo Hirai, the chief executive of Sony proper, instructed the Sony Pictures boss, Amy Pascal, and she emailed the film's director, Rogen, to enfeeble the scene which culminates with Kim Jong Un's head exploding. Pascal requested: 'no face melting, less fire in the hair, fewer embers on the face.'

Rogen replied: 'This is now a story of Americans changing their movie to make North Koreans happy.' But in time chunks of the film, including 'the entire secondary wave of head chunks,' were deleted. Then Sony killed the movie, pulling it from release on Christmas Day 2014. The bad news for North Korea was that this was widely seen as a cave-in to a mad dictatorship. President Obama diplomatically rebuked Sony and on Twitter one wit replaced the famous 'HOLLYWOOD' sign with one boasting 'NORTH KOREA.' Sony reversed its decision and *The Interview* was watched in a small number of independently owned picture houses across the States but by millions more on the internet.

Kim Jong Un's minions should have been more wary of the Barbara Streisand effect, that if you try and suppress something in the West, you may end up giving it a far wider publicity. The great virtue of the *Interview* affair is that it has shone a light on the darkest government in the world and for that we have reasons to cheer Rogen and Franco. North Korea is a clown state but it is also evil. The simple aim of this book is to set out to Americans the nature of that evil and how it might be ended.

The European who has known North Korea the longest is Izidor Urian, who first went to the newly Stalinized state in 1948. The journey from his native Romania to Pyongyang by train took the best part of 14 days. Izidor ended up being Ceausescu's interpreter when he visited the founder of the state, Kim Il Sung, in the early seventies. On YouTube you can see Izidor, a real-life Zelig, crouching in the back of the massive limousine carrying the two despots when Ceausescu went to Pyongyang: https://www.youtube.com/watch?v=qd3H9X-Yl2k

I tracked Izidor, now a very old man in his late eighties, to his home in Bucharest. How long has the regime got? Izidor and I both agreed that Kim Il Sung's grandson, Kim Jong Un, was making a hash of power: openly bloody, reckless, foolish. 'Forty years?' said Izidor.

My take? Kim Jong Un could fall in forty months. How is that possible in a society whose people know next to nothing about the outside world? For example, the average North Korean doesn't know that the Americans have landed on the moon, that Michael Jackson lived and died, and that Elvis lives again. For the vast majority of people, there is no internet. The regime shoves propaganda down people's throats all the livelong day, telling them they live in the most perfect – and most racially pure – society in the world.

The good news is that I suspect more and more North Koreans are beginning to realise that that claim is a stinking lie. The reason is simple. North Korea's information lockdown is no longer possible in the digital age. Just as the tyranny of Libya fell because people who hated the moronic, botoxed rule of Muammar Gaddafi realised via the internet and social media that they were not alone, North Koreans are beginning to understand that too. The most powerful moment of optimism I felt in North Korea was the day when we visited the DMZ – the very south of the country – and one of the very bright LSE students I was with, an American, realised that his iPhone would work, piggy-backing off the signal from mobile phone masts in the very north of South Korea. If we could do that, then so could a North Korean with a smuggled Chinese-manufactured phone. Likewise, North Koreans who live in the very north of the country can piggy-back signals from the very south of China. We met people who had seen *Homeland, Mission Impossible* – the complexity of explaining Tom Cruise's devotion to the Church of Scientology to a North Korean was beyond me – and even, I suspected, *Team America* in which Kim The Second, Kim Jong Il, sings: 'I'm so ronery and sadry arone' while the skeleton of Hans Blix swims in the shark tank, his suitcase full of nuclear secrets still handcuffed to his hand.

I sang 'I'm so ronery' in Pyongyang – to myself, very quietly – because I was, am, and always will be confident that the Kim regime is a force for evil in the world and evil should be challenged, not accommodated. That challenge is all the more difficult because the North Koreans have now exploded three nuclear devices below ground. Making a nuclear bomb is one thing. Delivering it is quite different. Thus far, the North Koreans have not been able to shrink a nuke so that it can sit on top of one of their rockets. Thus far, their best bit of rocketry has been to fire a missile over the waist of Japan, splashing into the Pacific on the eastern seaboard of that country. That is a very, very long way from Los Angeles. The other thought to bear in mind is that any military challenge to the United States or its ally South Korea will be regime suicide. If North Korea dares strike, Kim Jong Un and his merry men will die, very quickly. Common sense tells us that threats of nuclear war from Pyongyang are empty bluster, but the hate-speak masks a human rights tragedy on an immense scale. The evidence of defectors, which numbers more than 25,000 people, points to the gulag being as hellish as Nazi concentration camps. That is the clear message from the United Nations Commission of Inquiry into human rights abuses in North Korea.

Calls to have Kim Jong Un hauled up in front of the International Criminal Court will be frustrated by China and Russia. The Kremlin is currently happy to back a regime that does not threaten it but does irritate the West. Beijing is vastly more powerful. If China wanted to crush the Kim tyranny, it could do so very easily. But the ultra-conservative security and military complex that runs China to this day fears an American ally, South Korea, moving up to its borders, so better, in its view, to put up with a tricky and occasionally obnoxious neighbour than have a US proxy there instead. The other regional stake-holders, South Korea, Japan, and the United States, fear any sudden transition from the status quo. War is not an option with an adversary with nuclear weapons tucked away somewhere underground. Stasis is better than a mob armed, not with pikes, but nukes.

For the moment the key to unlocking the poor, wretched people of North Korea from their prison-cell state lies in the hands of the Chinese government, and there is little sign of Beijing lifting a finger. On the contrary, there is powerful evidence that the Chinese routinely break international laws they have signed up to and send back refugees from North Korea, causing the victims fresh misery.

That picture could change. The Japanese right is pressing the Americans, by asking: 'why should we abjure nuclear weapons if the North Koreans have them?' That question causes unease in Beijing. The Stalinist show-trial of Kim Jong Un's uncle, Jang Sung Taek, and his execution in 2013, reportedly by being bitten to death by savage dogs although most likely by the traditional method of nine grams of lead to the back of the head, conveyed a message to China. Uncle Jang was China's man in Pyongyang and the message from Kim Jong Un was don't mess with me. For the moment, the subterranean pressures in Beijing favour toleration of the North Korean tyrant. That, too, could change.

Regime change in North Korea is most likely to happen when a general, perhaps head of the rocket division, realises that he may soon die because his toys won't work properly. Rather than accepting his fate, he may realise that killing Kim Jong Un is the better solution. The thing which could easily tilt it is someone powerful in China telling that North Korean general: 'if you shoot Kim Jong Un, we won't mind.'

As some point, the regime will get crushed by its own internal contradictions. The land is poor and mountainous and unless North Korea trades with the rest of the world is cannot feed its own people; if it trades, people will mix with the outside world and realise that the regime has been telling them a great big lie. The great famine of the late nineties, in which maybe four millions died out of a population of 20-odd million, was a shearing point. From the famine onwards, people knew in their hearts that the regime could not feed its subjects. I write that but am continually drawn to the internet. On YouTube you can watch videos of mass weeping at the death of Kim Jong Il in 2011, a man who presided over the famine. Do they mean it? Or are they mucking about?

The answer to that is tricky and conflicted. Yes, it seems, many, many millions of North Koreans continue to be brainwashed – and I use that word deliberately – but a much smaller number are beginning to become sceptical. The point is that the sceptics, the people who watch South Korean videos showing the good life, the food, the cars, the clothes that ordinary people in the world's 11th most successful economy enjoy, smuggled in on thumb-sticks, are growing in number. We in the West should do more to help that.

I believe that my former employer, the BBC – by the way, still a great thing – should broadcast into North Korea as it broadcast into Nazi-occupied Europe during the Second World War. I believe that American broadcasters, such as Voice of America, should boost their output.

Charles Robert Jenkins was an American GI who made the long mistake of crossing the DMZ and defecting to North Korea in 1965. One of the best moments of his 40 years in the dungeon state was listening to a dramatization of *Of Mice And Men* on Voice of America, beamed from Japan.

The West's broadcasters should pump out the work of great organisations, like the Committee for Human Rights in North Korea, based in Washington DC, but also the froth and giddy sillinesses of Western culture, in English and in North Korean. They should broadcast *Baywatch* and *Miami Vice* and *Star Trek* from the sixties, eighties, and nineties – remember, no North Korean has ever seen these shows – and report the saga of *The Interview*, warts and all, and show the North Koreans that a society or a company or a culture that can admit that it can get things wrong is far better than one that denies the very possibility of failure.

Information is light and the people of the dark state of North Korea need more of that than anything else. America: use your power to switch on the light.

John Sweeney

Contents

A Note on the Text

Translating text from one alphabet to another is always fraught. Koreans write their names, to us, backwards, so the surname comes first. The South Koreans hyphenate the forenames, making the second name lower case; thus I would be Sweeney John-paul. But North Korean practice, according to former British ambassador John Everard, is to write 'each syllable with a capital letter and without a hyphen between the last two. Thus I write Kim Il Sung rather than Kim Il-sung.' I follow that advice.

Where necessary, I have disguised the identity of people on the trip and North Koreans.

NORTH KOREA UNDERCOVER

Introduction

The Air Koryo jet floated down to earth, the ground below tree-less, bleak. The plane landed smoothly enough, but then we wobbled down an immensely long and bumpy runway, past banks of earth, sinister watchtowers and threadbare sprigs of barbed wire, straight out of *The Spy Who Came in from the Cold*. Down the plane's steps, one small leap and on to North Korean concrete. I thought to myself: What in Pyongyang do we do now?

The longer you spend in North Korea, the less fearful you become. Fear is fuelled by ignorance. The simple goal of this book is to make the world's most secretive state a little less unknown, to map this terra incognita that loves to tell us: Be afraid. It ain't easy.

Understanding North Korea is like figuring out a detective story where you stumble across a corpse in the library, a smoking gun beside it, and the corpse gets up and says that's no gun and it isn't smoking and this isn't a library. It is like nowhere else on earth. No ads burble. No traffic dragon roars. No birds sing. Kim Il Sung and his son Kim Jong Il smile down at you from a giant diptych hoarding. No one smiles back.

Kim Il Sung is Kim the First, but in the regime's iconography he comes across as an *über*-effeminate God-the-Mother, all mumsy and 1950s, a celestial Doris Day. Kim Jong Il, aka Kim the Second, is God-the-Lousy-Elvis-Impersonator in bouffant hairdo and elevator heels, creepy, beyond weird. Kim Jong Un is Fat Boy Kim, threatening thermo-nuclear war against the United States one day, reportedly having his ex-girlfriend machine-gunned the next.

Our frog-green tourist coach kicks into life and our black-suited minder, Mr Hyun, breathes into the mike: 'At the moment the situation is very tense. Nobody knows when the war will be provoked but we will be safe. Our bus has the mark of the Korean International Travel Company so the Americans won't strike our bus. Ha ha . . .'

Is the threat of nuclear war real? Has it ever been? Three words: I don't know. What I do know is this: they took us along a vast motorway. There were no cars. They took us to a university. There were no students. They took us to a library. There were no books, at least no books worth reading and certainly no George Orwell's *1984* – I did ask; a bottling plant, no bottles; an electricity-generating machine factory, no electricity; a children's camp, no children; a farm, no animals; a hospital, patients, but only in the morning. Then the lights went out. The dictatorship tells lies about ordinary things.

The evidence from our eight days inside North Korea, when Kim Jong Un's threats of thermo-nuclear war were at their most frenzied, suggests – how to put this diplomatically? – that the regime is full of dross. If North Korea launches a nuclear strike, the regime and everybody in it will die. The working hypothesis of *North Korea Undercover* is that Kim Jong Un's talk of nuclear war is a confidence trick and that the Pyongyang bluff is blinding us to a human rights tragedy on an immense scale.

To make the confidence trick work, the regime keeps everybody – outsiders and its own people – in the dark. Understanding what happens in front of your eyes is beyond strange. You are left wondering at your own grip on reality, like the moment in *The Matrix* when Neo sees a black cat walk by, and then another black cat walks by just like the first one, causing Trinity to warn him: 'A déjà vu is usually a glitch in the Matrix. It happens when they change something.' During our trip we saw no cats and one dog.

Time and again a glitch in the North Korean matrix has you scratching your head. Did I see that? Is that for real? It is, of course, deliberately crepuscular, an exquisitely constructed fog machine. North Korea feels like Kafka written in an alphabet no one can read. But in the murk, the regime hides its cunning.

Kim the Third's hysterical threat of nuclear war is part of a bleak but clever logic that has kept the dynasty in power long past its two great benefactors – Soviet Russia and Communist China – are dead and gone or mutated beyond all recognition.

The madness shines so bright it's hard to make out the survivalist logic lurking in the dark. Go see Kim Il Sung. The Great Leader, the Sun of the Nation, the Iron All-Victorious General, the Marshal of the Mighty Republic, the Eternal President is the subject of total love from his nation of 23 million people – or is it three million less? – and grants them an audience, every day of the year.[1] Accessible, yes, but you can't talk to the nation's head of state because Kim the First has not been alive these past nineteen years. This makes the Democratic People's Republic of North Korea the world's only necrocracy. That is: government by zombie.

The living-dead god lies in warmth and light in a glass box, a waxwork. The hideous goitre or growth the size of a grapefruit on his neck so artfully airbrushed out of all photographs in later life has been, in death, surgically removed. But be wary of mocking the zombie-god too much: in 1945 this thing in the glass box created the most successful tyranny in modern times, a hereditary gangsterism whose lock on power is still strong.

In life, Kim Il Sung was a thug, hand-picked by Stalin's gang to

[1] Andrei Lankov: *From Stalin to Kim Il Sung: The Formation of North Korea 1945–1960*, Hurst, London, 2002, p70.

3

take over the half-nation which emerged from Japanese occupation in the wake of the second world war. In 1950 Kim One, convinced that the people of the South would flock to his banner, started the Korean Civil War in which around three million died. Three years later the boundaries of his state were back to where they had been when he started the killing. At the De-Militarized Zone or DMZ, the colonel in charge told us that the Americans had started the war, a lie so big every North Korean appears to believe it. Kim the First created a personality cult that has brainwashed his people for three generations, and a gulag system for anyone who questions that brainwashing. At Pyongyang's Kumsusan Memorial Palace our minders – good people, zombie master – made it clear that we must bow to Kim the First, and we did, three times.

In a second chamber, the Great Leader's son, the Dear Leader, lies in a second glass box. The story goes that the son had the father murdered after a bitter row in which the ailing and flatulent old man finally woke up to the starvation afflicting his people.[2] Funnily enough, they whisper, all the doctors and security agents attending the dying Father of the Nation died mysteriously or vanished into the gulag.[3] True? False? Who knows? The best book about North Korea, someone said, was written in 1592 and it is called *Richard III*.

Kim Jong Il in death still looks like Bad Elvis. His image to the rest of the world was nailed by *South Park*'s brilliant puppet show film, *Team America*, in which he sings:

> I'm So Ronery
>
> So ronery
>
> So ronery and sadry arone.

[2] Peter Carlson: 'Sins of the Son', *Washington Post*, 11 May 2003, quoting defector Hwang Jang Yop.
[3] Victor Cha: *The Impossible State*, Bodley Head, London, 2012, p89.

I dared to sing that in North Korea while no one was listening, and even so it scared the pants off me. The puppet-masters appear to have got the *roneriness* wrong. Kim Two reportedly pleasured a human bed of hand-picked North Korean beauties and when he got bored with them, busty whores from Sweden and Bavaria were flown in for his entertainment.[4] For a long time, the West wondered whether he was a monosyllabic halfwit with only one sentence ever uttered in public: 'Glory to the people's heroic military!' But the real man was smarter than that. Defectors report that K2 was a sly, thoughtful Bond-villain-without-the-white-pussy-cat, a man of some charm and a self-deprecating wit. At one of his lavish parties for the elite, he told the beautiful South Korean actress whom he'd had kidnapped, Choi Un Hee: 'I'm as small as a midget's turd, aren't I?'

When a group of dancing girls started screaming: 'Long live the Great Leader!' Kim Two told Choi's husband, the South Korean film director Shin Sang Ok, also kidnapped, 'All that is bogus. It's just a pretence.'[5] He could say that, but no one else would dare.

And how can you satirize this? That during the 1990s Kim Jong Il presided over a man-made famine in which as many as three million people died. Zeros dull the mind. A North Korean defector told me the story of why he got out. The decision was forced on him, he said, after his three-year-old niece, at the height of the famine, gorged herself on dried corn, and then her stomach burst. They call the famine the 'Arduous March'. Orwell's great insight into the totalitarian mind-set was to point out how Big Brother took over language and rendered it his servant, and that people

[4] Jasper Becker: *Rogue Regime: Kim Jong Il and the Looming Threat of North Korea*, Oxford University Press, Oxford, 2005, p138.
[5] Shin Sang Ok, Choi Un Hee, *The Kingdom of Kim*, Tonga Ilbosa, Seoul, 1988.

with free minds had to push back against this insidious linguistic trick. North Korean Newspeak may call the March Arduous but it was also wholly unnecessary, an indictment of the regime's failure to feed its own people. This malfunction is even more dark when you consider that just on the other side of the DMZ lies one of the most successful societies on earth. South Korea is rich and, these days, democratically handsome. (It has its own troubles too. South Korea has one of the highest suicide rates in the world, with it being the most common cause of death for those under forty.) Part of North Korea's tragedy is that it cannot evolve into a tyranny less harsh. All it can do is stay the same, or die and be swallowed up by its southern twin, which is, according to some estimates, around thirty-eight times richer, its citizens on average three inches taller than their northern brothers and sisters. As regime death is not an option for the Kim dynasty and the Pyongyang elite, the nation lurches on, zombie-like, pitiable, blackly comic and scary in equal measure.

The United Nations estimates that one in four of the country's children is currently suffering from hunger and malnutrition – and 4 per cent are severely malnourished.[6] These figures may well understate the true horror. Faking statistics in a country with no journalism is easy. But even if we take these figures at face value, it's likely several thousand infants and children, in the poorest parts of the land, far away from the Pyongyang Belt, are starving to death as you read this book. Had we seen them out of our tourist coach, our minders would have said: 'No photos.'

And then there is the suffering of the invisibles in the gulag. The North Korean regime runs a system of concentration camps in the burning cold of the mountains in which the best estimate is one

[6] http://www.bigstory.ap.org/article/un-more-14-nkorean-children-malnourished

million people have died over the three generations the Kim dynasty has been in power.

Prisoners inside the gulag suffer 'unspeakable atrocities', according to a preliminary report by a United Nations Commission of Inquiry (COI) into Human Rights in the DPRK. North Korea blanked an invitation to take part, but once hearings in Seoul began, the DPRK's official news agency, KCNA, described them as slanderous and labelled the hearing participants as 'human scum'.

The head of the inquiry, Australian judge Michael Kirkby, said: 'Truth is a defence against "slander". If any of the testimony the COI has heard on political prison camps, international abductions, torture, starvation, inter-generational punishment and so forth can be shown to be untrue, the Commission invites the Democratic People's Republic of Korea to produce evidence to that effect. An ounce of evidence is worth far more than many pounds of insults and baseless attacks. So far, however, the evidence that the COI has heard has largely pointed in one direction – and evidence to the contrary is lacking.'[7]

Do the maths: three million dead in the war Kim Il Sung started; add three million dead from the famine under Kim Jong Il; add one million dead in the gulag and other fatal consequences of political and economic oppression and that equals: seven million people.[8]

Kill seven million people and you would think everyone in North Korea lives in gibbering fear. But Zombie and Sons are adored. People are happy, joking, witty, full of fun. I've been to a dozen or so dictatorships, more often than not undercover: Communist Romania, Czechoslovakia, Albania, Iran, Iraq under

[7] http://www.ohchr.org/EN/NewsEvents/Pages/Unspeakableatrocitiesreport byCoIinNorthKorea.aspx
[8] Becker gives high numbers for the famine's death toll in *Rogue Regime*, p209. Lankov gives low numbers in *The Real North Korea*, Oxford University Press, 2013, p80.

Saddam, Libya under Gaddafi, Syria, Chechnya, Zimbabwe, Serbia under Milošević, Cuba, Belarus and North Korea. The latter was the tyranny in which I felt the least sense of personal threat. You can get mugged in Cuba.

Ordinary tyrants demand devotion. In North Korea, the devotion comes pre-programmed. Our minders suggested we bow to Kim Jong Il, too, and we did, three times. On the way out of the Mausoleum, two women were weeping. Nothing compared to the mass mourning which took place after he was announced dead in 2011. Watch it on YouTube. It is a terrifying exhibition of mass grief for a man who must be judged by rational minds as a monster. Do they mean it? Or is this mass fakery in the twenty-first century?[9]

The regime began with Kim Il Sung, a streetwise guerrilla fighter gifted a state by Stalin's generals. Japanese occupation had been a great national insult, and for many in the North it was good to have a Korean ruler, however authoritarian. The bloodshed of the civil war followed, after which peace was a blessing. That Kim Il Sung started the war, no one in North Korea can say. In the mid-1950s, as de-Stalinization began to pick up speed in the Communist world, North Korea galloped off in the opposite direction. Kim the First's propagandists first developed a powerful and vicious national Stalinism. This mutated into Jucheism, home-baked Jabberwocky plus a Brobdingnagian cult of personality. As the old man's powers weakened, his son Kim Jong Il built up the Juche cult, rebaptizing it Kimilsungism. Bits of national Stalinism, Jucheism and Kimilsungism are all spouted by the regime when it suits, but the real belief system of the DPRK, the one aggressively fired at its people through television, propaganda posters, the radio and loudspeakers dotted across the nation, is that old black magic:

[9] https://www.youtube.com/watch?v=pSWN6Qj98Iw

racial purity. There is a subtle difference from Nazi ideology proper: the Koreans of the North are not a master race who must overlord other races, but pure children who must be protected by the Leaders, Great, Dear and Fat, sorry, Young.

Like Hitler's Third Reich, the regime is depressingly popular with masses of North Koreans. They are joyfully in thrall to a political religion. The slavishness of its adherents reminds one of America's death cults, but in North Korea they don't have Kool-Aid. They have nuclear bombs.

The regime's race cult chimes with popular but dark tropes in Korean history. The Nazi-style ideology equates racial purity with human goodness. The impure have no right to life, which is why the evidence suggesting that the regime commits infanticide is profoundly disturbing. The UN Human Rights inquiry reported: 'A North Korean woman testified how she "witnessed a female prisoner forced to drown her own baby in a bucket".'[10] In my eight days in North Korea, I saw two people who were disabled, and they were both adults. In Africa and Asia and Latin America, you see crippled beggars all the live-long day. The absence of North Korean disabled babies, infants or children raises one troubling question: where are they?

Under Kim Three, it has been goodbye to the last echoes of Communism. In the spring of 2012, giant pictures of Marx and Lenin adorned a building on Kim Il Sung Square; on our trip, one year on, Karl and Vlad had vanished.

Kim Jong Un is now the third generation Kim to lead the dark state. At thirty years of age, he is a fat young man in a very thin nation. He was educated in a fancy school in Switzerland, so he

[10] http://www.reuters.com/article/2013/09/17/us-korea-north-crimes-idUSBRE 98G0B920130917

knows the truth about North Korea, even if no one else does. Footage shown on North Korean television shows him visiting a rocky beach on a gunboat. Soldiers crowd around. Kim the Third retreats to the gunboat, which slowly backs away from the beach. The soldiers plunge into the freezing sea, in a state of religious ecstasy. It is beyond bonkers.[11]

On the day Kim the Third threatened to use his nukes in a thermo-nuclear war against the United States, we visited the De-Militarized Zone (or the DMZ or the Zee) where the two halves of Korea meet. The colonel in charge said: 'Don't worry about it,' and patted me on the back. We drove back to Pyongyang and rocked up at a karaoke bar where our minder, Mr Hyun, sang 'My Way'. Thermo-nuclear regrets? Too few to mention. Was this talk of Armageddon for real? Or a shadow game directed at Kim Three's own people, to make them line up behind him?

The government of North Korea tells big lies: about killing and famine and power. But the regime cannot lie about the darkness. Salute, reader, the Outer Space Treaty of 1967.[12] In space, there is freedom of movement and freedom of speech, two things not available in the Kims' utopia. The iconic image of North Korea taken from deep space was captured in 2011 by a satellite launched by NASA and NOAA, the American equivalent of the Met Office. The satellite boasts an instrument called the Visible Infrared Imaging Radiometer Suite, which you can think of as a very sensitive digital camera, producing images of the light emitted by human activity. This gives you the view you might get if you peeked out of the window of the International Space Station, around 500 miles up.

The weather satellite looks down on the face of the earth and

[11] Watch at 8 mins, 45 secs: https://www.youtube.com/watch?v=OzerbXJqzZc
[12] UN Outer Space Treaty: http://www.unoosa.org/oosa/SpaceLaw/outerspt.html

shows the world at night, the great cities sparkling with light: New York, London, Moscow, Beijing, Seoul. The capital of North Korea, Pyongyang, emits a feeble glow-worm but the rest of the country lies in darkness so deep you could easily make the mistake of thinking that this land does not exist. And about the truth of the darkness, Kim the Third can do nothing.

In this book are the stories of witnesses to this dark state, among them seven defectors from the North; an IRA man from West Belfast who spent two months in North Korea learning to make bombs; Ceausescu's translator; an American soldier who ran away to the North and, forty years later, managed to get out; an Italian senator; an Italian chef; two translators who endured 'cruel Christs of pus' in the gulag; and a sculptress who vanished from Italy and died unknown to her family, two decades later in Pyongyang.

But locked inside the dictatorship, the people of North Korea do not know how dark their government is. Brainwashing, according to the world's great authority on the subject, Professor Robert Lifton, an American military psychiatrist who treated US servicemen captured in North Korea, requires constriction of information.[13] The less people know, the more they put up with. From the outside, the less we know, the more our fears grow.

The regime tells big lies about itself, about history. To nail its quintessential dishonesty, I went to North Korea for BBC *Panorama* posing as a history professor. I told a lie to the dictatorship. I did so because the regime ordinarily bans journalists or minds them so tightly that they see next to nothing. The one exception is Associated Press, which boasts an office in Pyongyang. However, AP Pyongyang has been accused of running 'chirpy,

[13] Robert Jay Lifton: *Thought Reform and the Psychology of Totalism: A Study of 'Brainwashing' in China*, Norton, New York, 1961.

upbeat stories rather than real news', effectively, to paraphrase Basil Fawlty, of having a tacit policy of 'Don't mention the gulag.'[14] AP dispute the argument that they self-censor as 'erroneous'.

Going to North Korea undercover sometimes felt like being inside the movie *Argo* but readers should be aware of a strange paradox: although it treats its own people cruelly, the DPRK treats foreign guests with almost comic deference. So long as you do not proselytize Christianity, especially if you are a Korean-American missionary, no harm will come to a foreign tourist. North Korea is not Torremolinos. It is much safer.

As a group of students and a fake professor, we were honoured guests of the regime. The best – least bad – comparison I can think of is travelling around Nazi Germany in 1936 during the Munich Olympics. Michael Breen, Kim Jong Il's biographer, also went undercover to North Korea, pretending to be something other than a journalist: 'As foreigners, we felt safe. The worst that could happen was that we would be expelled.'[15] Nothing happened to him. Nothing happened to us.

Inside North Korea, we were accompanied pretty much for every single moment by 'tourist guides' Mr Hyun and Miss Jun. By filming inside North Korea without the regime's blessing, we were accused of endangering the guides. We did not, according to Simon Cockerell of Koryo Tours, generally a critic of our *Panorama*: 'The guides in the tour shown on the programme are fine. They are still working and I saw them personally when I visited North Korea last week [April 2013]. They were not shown saying anything out of the ordinary and the reporter – other than the raw fact of being

[14] Donald Kirk: 'The AP Plays Defense on North Korea', *38 North*, 22 March 2013, http://38north.org/2013/03/dkirk032213/
[15] Michael Breen: *Kim Jong Il: North Korea's Dear Leader*, John Wiley, Singapore, 2012, p145.

a reporter – didn't get up to anything wildly illegal in North Korea.'[16] Cockerell, who has visited North Korea 119 times, says that North Korea is safe for foreign tourists: 'We have run thousands of tours over twenty years and we have never had anyone detained, questioned, molested, ejected or arrested.'

Of President George W. Bush's three axes of evil, Saddam's Iraq, the Ayatollah's Iran and North Korea, the latter is by far and away the safest to visit but also the worst place to live in. Sergeant Charles Robert Jenkins of the US Army defected to North Korea in 1965. Thanks to extraordinary luck and the power of love, he got out after forty years inside what he calls 'a giant demented prison'.[17] He is right, but prisons have guards, not guides. Behind the question: 'Did you endanger the guides?' lies an assumption that North Korea is a normal place to visit.

North Korea is not normal. No ordinary person is free to move around inside the country. No ordinary person can leave it, ever. No free speech. No rule of law. No parliament, worthy of the name. Brainwashing for three generations. The guides work hard to present as normal a picture of North Korea as possible. To push back against the raising of difficult questions, the regime, subtly, pressures foreign visitors to comply with its world view. Obey the guides or they will suffer – that is the message. That pressure is effective.[18] But should it be complied with? The guides, of course, are real flesh-and-blood people. So, too, are the 100,000 political prisoners in the gulag. But they are invisible. By not 'endangering

[16] http://thediplomat.com/2013/04/25/debunking-panorama-paranoia-north-korea-tour-leader-simon-cockerell/?all=true
[17] See Chapter 17: 'The American Who Went to North Korea and Stayed'.
[18] One travel writer was asked, prior to being let into North Korea by a tour company, to promise not to 'write about North Korea's human rights record or in any way insult the Dear Leader'. Carole Cadwalladr: 'The strange innocence of the "axis of evil"', *Observer*, 14 February 2010.

the guides', is it possible that you are doing a greater disservice to the invisible victims of the regime? When our guides showed us nonsense – for example a hospital with patients, but only in the morning – I mentally imagined the 100,000 or so souls in the gulag cheering us on. But those cheers, and even more their screams, are silent to us. Just because we cannot see or hear them does not mean they do not exist, as Chapter 19: 'The Gulag Circus' sets out.

The human factor kicks in, as ever. Our guards or minders were sweet people but also agents of a dark regime. Richard Lloyd Parry of *The Times* put it bluntly: 'They are privileged, well educated, and (by North Korean standards) well-informed servants of a totalitarian dictatorship. As human beings, they are as various as the rest of us. But putting aside their friendliness, curiosity or the lack of it, their job is to lie, bamboozle and obfuscate.'

There has been a lot of controversy about the mechanics of the trip. My own position is that the people invited to come to North Korea were LSE students and alumni, but it wasn't an LSE trip. The students were told, twice, that a journalist was coming, and they were warned that there was a risk of arrest, detention and the possibility they might not be able to go on a return trip. On the day the group met, the North Koreans carried out a nuclear test. It was all over the news. Anyone who wanted to drop out could have done so. Long before we left London my name was on the paperwork. Again, from my perspective, there was no intention to deceive the students.

We went as part of a tourist trip, arranged through the KFA, the Korean Friendship Association, which has been described as being 'like one of the more improbable cults'.[19] The KFA's President is

[19] John Everard: *Only Beautiful, Please: A British Diplomat in North Korea*, Stanford University, Stanford, 2012, p139.

Alejandro Cao de Benós or, to use his Korean honorific, Zo Sun Il, which means 'Korea is One'. The Spanish IT consultant, who likes dressing up in North Korean uniform, has been criticized by the *Independent* as an 'ideological brown-noser'. The newspaper cited anonymous critics, describing him as 'the perfect example of the useful idiot'. Another said: 'In my view, he's a narcissist. And he loves the power and control he has over there. He does have real influence. People are frightened of him, and he likes that power. I think his primary motivation is that he's special there.' A third said: 'You can't possibly believe that stuff if you've been there. To come back and tell North Korean people that everything they hear is correct – that the rest of the world is evil, out to cut each other's throats, that war and oppression is everywhere . . . he perpetuates that. He's not forced to; he does that for personal gain and power and prestige. It's horrible.'

In his defence, Cao de Benós told the *Independent*: 'I will take this as a type of jealousy from people who have no goals in their life. I have lived a life of big things. I didn't want to dedicate my life to be a slave in the capitalist system. My dream was to be a part of the revolution.'[20]

Once our party was back from Pyongyang, safe and sound, I went on BBC World News, and said the regime was 'mad and sad and bad and silly, all at the same time'.[21]

The North Koreans saw my interview, and Cao de Benós, writing as the Special Delegate for the Committee for Cultural Relations with Foreign Countries of the DPRK, fired back: 'I am now in communication with LSE representatives . . . To obtain a

[20] Tim Hume, 'His dear leader: Meet North Korea's secret weapon – an IT consultant from Spain', *Independent*, 21 January 2012, http://www.independent.co.uk/news/world/asia/his-dear-leader-meet-north-koreas-secret-weapon--an-it-consultant-from-spain-6291303.html
[21] 'Inside North Korea: "It's a mad, sad and bad place"', http://www.bbc.co.uk/news/world-asia-22003715

visa without declaring the real purpose of the visit is against the law . . . We will ignore this incident if Mr. Sweeney stops his journalistic activities regarding the LSE–DPRK visit. Otherwise if the related programme is broadcasted, I will be left with no choice but to expose all the real story and data. And the only one to blame for this will be Mr. Sweeney . . . You decide.'

Cao de Benós made good on his threat. The London School of Economics, my old university, was supplied with the information we'd given to the North Korean embassy in Beijing. The LSE's director, Craig Calhoun, had been in Beijing at the same time that we were.[22]

The LSE went public with North Korea's information on us, condemned what we had done and called for the programme not to be broadcast. The BBC stood firm, and our documentary was aired. A row started which has yet to be resolved.

The story splashed in *The Times* and there were questions in Parliament. On Twitter, I was compared to Jimmy Savile, and to Saif Gaddafi, someone who really has a doctorate from the LSE.

[22] Craig Calhoun: Director, LSE, Beijing, 20 March 2013: 'What Threatens Global Capitalism Now?', LSE China Lecture Series. http://www.lse.ac.uk/intranet/LSEServices/ERD/LSEChina/LSE-China-Lecture-Series/LSE-China-Lecture-Series.aspx

These days my old university gets money from China in return for teaching Chinese senior government officials. LSE-China: 'Executive Public Policy Training Programme for high level Chinese Government officials has been developed and delivered by LSE and PKU'. This sets out: 'contributions from alumni, friends, trusts and corporations in and from China have supported scholarships, innovative learning and research programmes and developed teaching facilities on campus at LSE.' The scale of funds from the Chinese state entities is not clear. The issue has worried one LSE professor. http://www.lse.ac.uk/intranet/LSEServices/ERD/LSEChina/pdf/LSE%20and%20China%20brochure.pdf

http://www.dailymail.co.uk/news/article-1363222/The-day-LSE-sold-soul-Libya-BP-chief-makes-oil-deal-Gaddafi-drags-prestigious-university-disrepute.html

Getting in and out of the world's most secretive dictatorship is not easy. One solution is not to bother. But it is important that journalists try to shed light on dark places where freedom of thought is snuffed out. One of the great North Korea watchers, Andrei Lankov, has noted: 'No foreigner is allowed to do independent research in Korean libraries, let alone archives. Indeed, typically a foreign visitor is simply denied access to the library catalogues.'[23]

Before transmission, a few students were worried about appearing in our film. We blobbed them out. We did not mention the LSE, nor did we ever intend to. But then, of course, a very public row blew up with arguments on both sides.[24] The BBC Trust is examining complaints about our *Panorama*. For that reason, now is not the time and place to discuss these issues further.

More than six million viewers watched our *Panorama*: 'North Korea Undercover'. That's one in ten people in Britain.[25] They saw the ordinary lies the regime told us and listened to defectors – testimony the regime does not want heard. It was broadcast on 15 April, the 'holiest' day in the North Korean calendar, it being Kim Il Sung's birthday, timing which left one of our defector contributors gurgling with joy.

[23] Lankov, *From Stalin to Kim Il Sung*, pviii.
[24] http://www.dailymail.co.uk/news/article-2308876/BBC-crew-used-students-university-human-shields-film-undercover-North-Korea.html Josh Halliday: *Guardian*, 'Students say LSE has placed them at "more risk" from North Korea', 17 April 2013, http://www.guardian.co.uk/education/2013/ apr/17/north-korea-students-criticise-lse
[25] 5.4 million watched *Panorama* 'North Korea Undercover' on BBC1 and an additional 800,000 watched it on BBC iPlayer. On YouTube, the two most watched sites showing the documentary have had more than 500,000 viewers at the time of writing. The film has also been broadcast around the world by other networks. Our film, with 6.7 million viewers, may be the most watched documentary on North Korea ever.

North Korea remains the most rigidly controlled nation on earth, but some of the technological marvels of the twenty-first century are beginning to melt the ice-pack. Two million people have mobile phones, but they can only use them for internal calls. At the DMZ, one of the students I was travelling with switched on his iPhone and picked up a signal from phone masts just across the border in South Korea. He tweeted: 'At the DMZ, #JustChillin.' I switched on, and also picked up a signal. If we could do that, so could a North Korean using a smuggled Chinese mobile phone. The regime's icy grip on information is beginning to crack.

Yet the Kim dynasty remains in place almost a quarter of a century after the fall of the Berlin Wall. Perhaps the greatest mystery of this dark nation is: why haven't the people overthrown the tyranny? Barbara Demick's brilliant, harrowing study of the famine in the 1990s is called *Nothing to Envy*.[26] But a quick survey of the states that have a stake in what happens in North Korea – South Korea, China, Japan and the United States – could be summarized as 'nothing to gain'. South Korea may dislike the tyranny, but does it really want to deal with 20-odd million half-starved and miserably poor compatriots? Does China want a US ally creeping right up to its border? Does Japan want a bigger, stronger all-Korea competitor? Does the United States and the rest of the world want a terrifying transition, when the nuclear-armed tyranny falls and something different takes its place? Or is stasis the lesser evil? In 1987, President Reagan went to West Berlin and told the Soviet leader: 'Mr Gorbachev, tear down this wall.' Nothing like that bold command is being said today.

[26] Barbara Demick: *Nothing to Envy: Ordinary Lives in North Korea*, Spiegel and Grau, New York, 2009.

The threat of Armageddon cannot be lightly dismissed. Professor Brian Myers, an expert on North Korean ideology, told me: 'We may see a thermo-nuclear war. I'm sure it's not the North Koreans' plan to unleash that kind of a thing but it might come to that as a result of a disastrous miscalculation.' The counter-argument is that in the darkness of North Korea we may be missing something darker yet: that fear of change and in particular an over-hyped fear of thermo-nuclear war, a war which Kim Jong Un must know he would lose, very badly, very quickly, is obscuring the reality of a nation suffering immense misery. The tyrant's threat is masking his people's agony.

Everything here represents my own views and not those of the BBC. If you believe the press cuttings, there are times when I must seem to my colleagues a random trouble generator. I apologize to them, and to the great British public, who pay my wages, but to do difficult journalism maybe you have to be a member of the awkward squad.

But I'm a firm believer of shining light in dark places. I've written books about four states of mind-lock not essentially dissimilar to North Korea: Ceausescu's Romania, which I visited in 1985 and then in 1989, when the leader's plans for Christmas ended in a firing squad;[27] Saddam's Iraq;[28] Lukashenka's Belarus;[29] and the Church of Scientology, terrifying and creepy in 2007 and, at the time of writing in 2013, less so.[30]

[27] John Sweeney: *The Life and Evil Times of Nicolae Ceausescu*, Hutchinson, London, 1990.
[28] John Sweeney: *Trading with the Enemy*, Pan, London, 1993.
[29] John Sweeney: *Big Daddy – Lukashenka, Tyrant of Belarus*, Silvertail Books, London, 2012 (Kindle e-book).
[30] John Sweeney: *The Church of Fear: Inside The Weird World of Scientology*, Silvertail Books, London, 2013.

To understand what is going on in North Korea now, it helps that Romanian Communists, Baathist Iraqis and many Scientologists once assured me with grave solemnity of their undying loyalty to the powers that be, only for them to reveal a few years later that they had been brainwashed. Regimes fall; statues get smashed; the concrete of the mind crumbles to dust.

Outside No Animal Farm, there was a giant statue to Kim the First, surrounded by happy peasants loaded with bushels of corn. Our minders suggested we bow – the seventh time that day – and we did. Two weeks later, in South Korea, I asked a defector and the leader of a brave organization with a Monty Pythonesque name, the North Korean People's Liberation Front, if he had ever seen any graffiti. He said no at first but then he grew animated, remembering seeing one graffito in his whole time in the North. It was in a town in the north-east of the country, on the wall of a university hospital, and at six o'clock in the morning. Someone had scrawled: 'Down with Kim Jong Il'. The defector drew the ideograms in my notebook, showing how the phrase in Korean is written 'Kim Jong Il – down with' and that the name was clear and bold and the last part hurried, as if it had been dashed out. Half an hour later a crowd of about thirty had gathered, the defector said. Then the police arrived, and painted it out.

One day I shall return to North Korea. The regime is not as strong as it looks. One day the statues of the two mass-murderers will come crashing down. I will find that graffito artist. And I shall bow before him or her – and this time I shall mean it.

1

In the Land of the Plastic Toad

Of the five most creepy buildings in the world – the squat grey toad of the KGB/FSB head office in Lubyanka Square, Moscow; the alien spaceship-like Ryugyong Hotel in Pyongyang; the Church of Scientology's blue concrete angel on L Ron Hubbard Way in LA; Enver Hoxha's marble pyramid mausoleum in Tirana, Albania; and the Pyongyang Planetarium – the latter is the creepiest. A giant disco-ball of a Saturn lookalike with ferro-concrete ring, it stands proud on the plain en route between the airport's cattle-shed arrivals hall and the Big Zombie, Pyongyang itself, visible from the main road through a sickly copse.

There's something of the coelacanth about the futurology of the recent past, back then when men wore big specs and women had big hair. The Pyongyang Saturn was supposed to project just what an essential part of the future the Democratic People's Republic of Korea would be. And the present-day reality, briefly glimpsed through the windows of our coach? The planet's surface is decorated with mirror squares, so that you half expect to see John

Travolta in white suit strut his stuff beneath it. But the Bee Gees aren't big in North Korea and the mirrors have long since lost their shine. Across the Pyongyang basin a high mist or low cloud clung to the surface of the earth – nothing like as acrid as the pollution in Beijing, but gloomy nevertheless – and the effect of the great planet not shining was of a future gone to the grave.

You feel like a time-traveller, or that you are locked inside the set of a bad science fiction movie, one that goes on for 45,000 square miles. The obverse is also true for North Koreans making the opposite journey, leaving their world and travelling through the looking glass to encounter what feels like another planet. 'I felt like a frog that had just come out of its pit, from which it had contemplated the circle of sky outlined by the rim, and taken it for the whole of the world. I had passed through to the other side of the mirror,' writes the defector Hyok Kang in his book *This is Paradise!*[1]

The 'bad sci-fi' trope echoes in travellers' tales from North Korea like an over-familiar nightmare. The wonderful Italian writer Tiziano Terzani first came to North Korea in 1980. He wrote that the plane that twice a week brings the rare travellers from Beijing to Pyongyang is 'una macchina del tempo' – a time machine.[2] Bradley K. Martin, an American journalist, made the same trip one year before, and opens his book with a quote from *The Time Machine* by H. G. Wells: 'The shop, the advertisement, traffic, all that commerce which constitutes the body of our world, was gone.'[3] Christopher Hitchens, who, journalists being largely

[1] Hyok Kang: *This is Paradise!*, Abacus, London, 2007.
[2] Tiziano Terzani, *In Asia* [in Italian], Longanesi, Milan, 1999, p53.
[3] Bradley K. Martin: *Under the Loving Care of the Fatherly Leader: North Korea and the Kim Dynasty*, St Martin's Press, New York, 2004.

banned, also visited North Korea in the guise of a university lecturer, found it so extraterrestrial he called his piece: 'Visit to a Small Planet'.[4]

One dozen years on from the Hitch's galactic quest, it felt the same, that we had travelled back in time or across unknown dimensions to somewhere other than the known universe, and a place and a time spitting with hatred. An officer winding up a vast crowd of North Korean soldiers screamed on state TV: 'We will destroy the United States mercilessly.'

The reason North Korea is the most out-of-date-looking country on earth, the one whose rulers reject the modern world so utterly, is no accident. Throughout its history, Korea, especially the north, dominated by its savage mountains, has turned its back on the outside world. It used to be known as the Hermit Kingdom. Long after China reluctantly accepted foreign 'treaty ports' on the fringes of the Middle Kingdom, the Koreans held out, believing that the purity of the race must be defended at all costs.

Invaders like plains. They don't like mountains and other geographical impediments to conquering, like islands. That means that long after the old believers on the plains have been wiped off the face of the earth, the religions, languages and prejudices of the people up in the mountains linger. That's why Welsh, a language that by some yardsticks should have been at death's door from 1282 onwards, still sticks to the hilly bits to the left of England; why Gaelic still survives in the islands of the far west of Ireland and the far north of Scotland; Ladino still prospers in the higher bits of the Dolomites 2,000 years after the Romans left; why Chechen

---

[4] Christopher Hitchens: 'Visit to a Small Planet' *Vanity Fair*, January, 2001: http://www.vanityfair.com/ politics/features/2001/01/hitchens-200101

nationalism still pokes the Russian crocodile in the eye, one and a half centuries and more after Lermontov wrote his lullaby which goes something like this:

> Tum-tee-tum,
> Sleep, little baby,
> Or the Chechen
> Will come
> Tum-tee-tum
> And cut your throat . . .[5]

North Korea is as wildly mountainous as Chechnya, and as wildly hostile to any invading force. The soil is not fertile, and there are no great gold or silver mines such as made the conquistadors risk the climb into Peru. So for sensible reasons the world left Korea well alone for centuries, almost as untravelled as the dark side of the moon.

The founding myth of the Korean nation is as credible or silly as the one that they tell you about Rome. In Korea, a bear made love to a god, creating a deity called Tangun. The myth continues that Korea has been around for 5,000 years. The reality is that for big chunks of those five millennia the difference between Korea and China was not vivid. 'For much of the country's long history its northern border was fluid, and the national identities of literate Korean and Chinese mutually indistinguishable,' writes Professor Brian Myers.[6]

[5] However well ensconced the Kremlin's popsicle Ramzam Kadyrov may appear to be in Grozny, whether the tsarist goal of subjugation of Chechnya is ever, in the long term, going to succeed is open to doubt.
[6] B.R. Myers: *The Cleanest Race*, Melville House, New York, 2010, p25.

In the year 936, the Koryo dynasty was founded and China and Korea became clearly separate. In 1392, the Chosun dynasty took power, bringing with them Confucianism – and a rigidly controlled set of five castes, dividing society. At the bottom were the slaves or serfs, who continued to live miserable lives until the twentieth century. Above them were the inferior people, butchers and gravediggers and the like. Above them were the peasant farmers, merchants and tradespeople. Above them the translators, clerks and doctors and above them the ruling caste: the *yangban* or high officials of civic or military virtue, who enforced the Confucian 'Mandate of Heaven'. Elitism and social stratification is hard-wired into the Korean soul, and this truth remains so in both North and, to a lesser extent, in democratic South Korea to this day. Confucianism also demands ancestor worship and filial piety, big-time, a point made amusingly by Michael Breen when he recounts how in 2003 some bosses at Hyundai, South Korea's multi-billion-dollar mega-industrial complex, went to the company founder, Chung Ju Yung, to tell him in person that they had built the first road for tourists to travel into North Korea. At that point, Chung had been dead for two years.[7]

The ancien regime's social layer-cakery resurfaced – if it had ever truly gone away – in North Korea in 1957, under Kim Il Sung, who introduced fifty-one layers, broadly dividing society into three: the core class, the wavering class and the hostile class. The core class encompasses the regime's nabobs, ministers, secret policemen, senior army officers and top members of the Korean Workers' Party and their families, the majority of people allowed to live in Pyongyang. Our minders would be core class; and as

[7] Michael Breen: *Kim Jong Il*, p6.

foreign visitors, so, temporarily, would we. The waverers include other professionals, academics, potentially worthy citizens tainted in some way by some anti-regime toxins. The third, hostile class seems no different from the slaves of the Middle Ages: human cattle, to be driven hard and left to die, without compunction or compassion. The hostile class is held to be impure: anyone who is tainted with foreign influences, ethnic Korean families in China or Japan; anyone with a Christian background – although this encompasses the Kim dynasty itself – or anyone with ancestral wealth or 'noble' blood. Hostile-class toxins can go back three generations, so perfectly brave soldiers or brilliant athletes can suddenly lose all privileges when a grandfather who spent time in Japan or ended up a prisoner for a time in South Korea is discovered in a background check.

Family names brand an individual's identity. In the British Census for 1881, one researcher counted 400,000 separate surnames; in South Korea, more than half the population of around 50 million share five names: Kim, Lee, Park, Choi and Chong.[8] The same is true for the North, too. The reason for Korea's poverty of names is because it was only in the nineteenth century that freed serfs had to find a surname; very often they picked the name of a local ruling family. This must surely have an impact on the relationship between the mass and the individual, the caste and the single unit.

There is also a crazy geographical element to the caste system, which sees 'hostile' citizens shipped to the north-east of the country, close to the Chinese border. Time and again, you will read about

[8] Andrew Holgate: *Sunday Times*, Culture section, review of *What's in a Surname*, 25 August 2013, p31.

something dreadful happening in North and South Hamgyong provinces. This is where the famine of the 1990s hit hardest and where the regime made it hardest of all for outsiders – that is, foreigners – to monitor whether food aid was going to the people who needed it the most. This is where the most revolts and rebellions against the Kim dynasty happen – all, thus far, crushed.

One needs to look at the map of North Korea with the regime's deadly serious mind-set of racial purity in mind: Pyongyang, to the south-west of North Korea (though, of course, in the waist of the whole Korean peninsula) is the bullseye of the core class, with cities like Chongjin in North Hamgyong being on the outer limits of 'civilization'. Much of the double tragedy of the late 1990s, when immense amounts of American and South Korean food aid ended up in the hands of the regime's haves, while the have-nots perished in their millions, was because of the foolish assumption that the government of North Korea wanted to keep all of its citizens alive. On the contrary, diminishing the power and numbers of the hostile class continues to be a real but unarticulated regime goal.

Most of the inhabitants of the gulag come from the hostile class, as do many defectors. The risks of getting out seem not so bad if you are at the bottom of the heap. That means that few defectors come from the core class or have ever visited Pyongyang: the ones who do are vivid exceptions, like the Kim dynasty's top ideologist and the founder of Jucheism, Hwang Jang Yop, who defected to the South Korean embassy in Beijing in 1997. A few days later Kim Jong Il was reported on Radio Pyongyang as saying: 'Cowards, leave if you want to. We will defend the red flag of revolution to the end.' Hwang's wife committed suicide; one daughter died in suspicious circumstances, 'falling off a truck'; his other children and grandchildren were reportedly picked up and swept off to the

gulag. In North Korea, treachery is punished unto the third generation. Hwang seems to be torn in half between self-hatred, because
of the consequences of his actions for his family, and honour, that
he had to escape to tell the truth about the regime, to stop the lying.
It is a hideous dilemma that confronts every single defector.

Korea remained isolated from the outside world longer than
Timbuktu or Antarctica. In 1806 Mungo Park's fated expedition
passed Timbuktu; in 1841 Captain Ross, RN, discovered the Mount
Erebus volcano on the edge of the frozen continent. Korea's self-
enforced removal from modernity was first properly challenged in
1866 when an American gunboat, the USS *Sherman*, a side-
wheeler, chugged up the Taedong river towards Pyongyang. She
was ordered to halt by the young king's regent, but the crew
plugged on to the city, where, after a fracas, she hit a submerged
rock and was left vulnerable to Korean fire-ships. The first two
failed, but the third succeeded in setting the *Sherman* alight, and
soon everyone on board perished. This triggered a reaction in
Washington DC, newly belligerent about defending America's
standing in Asia. By the 1880s, the Koreans had been forced to sign
a free trade deal with the Americans and the end of the über-
isolationist dynasty was in sight.

But nationalist hopes of a stand-alone Korea died with the rise
and rise of Japan. The land of the rising sun's forces invaded Korea
in 1904, sneakily marching north to challenge Russian occupation
of Manchuria. The Russians fought and lost – the first significant
defeat of a Western(-ish) power to Asiatic might in modern history.
In 1910, the Japanese formally occupied the Korean peninsula,
bringing a fascist cherry to top off the Hermit Kingdom's
Confucianist – 'obey power' – cake. In 1945, the Japanese, thanks
to the Americans, left Korea for good. In the South, they were

replaced by a series of foolish and bloody pro-American dictators who eventually gave way in the 1980s to a proper democracy. In the North, the Japanese governor was replaced by a cut-throat guerrilla boss who had ended up in Stalin's embrace, Kim Il Sung – and the Hermit Kingdom's ideology of total obedience to power, isolation, racial purity and rigid social stratification is still in place today.

We rode into the city along a wide road, the surface comically bumpy, so that we bounced around inside the coach as if we were taking a cross-Channel ferry in January.

Mr Hyun and Miss Jun formally introduced themselves with a mixture of jokes and dangers, just like tour guides do in Rome or Paris. But not many tourist guides in the forty-minute 'transfer' between airport and hotel raise the possibility of thermo-nuclear war between the host country and the United States.

Mr Hyun and Miss Jun were yin and yang, gloom and sun. She seemed to be more open than Mr Hyun and certainly more sparky and feisty, and somehow she seemed to be better plugged into the movers and shakers in the DPRK. Miss Jun was always fashionably dressed and her English was more natural; Mr Hyun's accent was thicker and he wore a dark suit, white shirt, black tie, black glasses, suggesting that had he lived in the West he would have made a natural undertaker. His melancholy bent broke every now and then into a series of infectious giggles, making him oddly likeable. Both were excellent ambassadors for their country and never once said anything critical of the regime. They were messengers for a nation out of synch with the rest of the world, and that's not an easy place to be.

It would not be quite true to suggest that there was no traffic whatsoever. A few army lorries with canvas roofs, a big black Volga from

Soviet times, the odd petrol tanker; every now and then a hideously overcrowded bus chugged along; also a series of fancy-ish saloons shot by, accommodating the elite. But the ordinary traffic you must struggle through in an ordinary poor country – the tuk-tuks of Thailand or their equivalents in Bangladesh, the patched-up old bangers that should have died years ago you see on the road in Uganda – it didn't exist. Evidence of absence means something: that the law is, if you are poor, you cannot run a vehicle, still less take it on the grand road from city to airport.

My all-time favourite 'Pyongyang traffic' story happened back in 1995, and was told by Alexander Frater of the *Observer*, who had gone to North Korea as a tourist. One evening in the Koryo bar, Frater was accosted by a middle-aged Danish engineer.

'Have you heard the news?'
'What news?'
'There's been a traffic accident!'
I stared at him. This was a statistical impossibility.
'It's true!' he cried. 'An Egyptian diplomat ran into a truck!'
'Is he all right?'
'Well, the doctors are still very excited but, yes, I gather the prognosis is good.'[9]

The bumps could not be ignored. Being tossed and turned, as if inside a washing machine, suggested that the people who ruled North Korea had a soft spot for the grandiose and a weakness for detail. Why build a motorway if it makes everyone who drives along it seasick?

[9] Alexander Frater: *Observer Life Magazine*, 7 January 1996.

The big road carved through a canyon of multi-storey flats. Concrete seemed a popular construction choice; grey a popular colour. After a while, it became apparent that concrete and grey came as standard. Many of the blocks of flats boasted large slogans in red letters, but written in Korean I couldn't make out their precise meaning. They weren't selling Coca-Cola. We passed an enormous painting of Kim the First, smiling girlishly out of a red background. The Korean was later translated for me: 'The Great Leader, Kim Il Sung, will always be with us.'

It's an old trope, mocked by Shelley in his poem 'Ozymandias':

'My name is Ozymandias, King of Kings:
Look on my works, ye mighty, and despair.'
Nothing beside remains.

Never have I seen such monotonous homage to tyranny.

On we bounced, past more grey blocks, noting that the ground-floor apartments featured heavily barred windows – suggesting that the crime of burglary in the DPRK is not unknown – past a traffic policewoman in a blue uniform, standing in a painted white circle like a witch in some pagan doodah. The traffic-witch directed thin air with balletic aplomb. Onwards we went, past the Pyongyang Arc de Triomphe, deliberately a few feet taller than the real thing in Paris, before we came to a stop at our hotel, the Haebangsan. Above the hotel, in Korean, a sign proclaimed: 'Hail the light of Korea's military first-ism, General Kim Jong Un!' It sounds weird and clunky in Korean, too, just like George Orwell's Newspeak has a tin ear for lovers of the English language.

In late March the cold in North Korea still bites, with

temperatures way below freezing inside the hotel. Those last three words are not a typo. Heat is not something to be wasted if you are not a member of the charmed circle of the Kim dynasty, and the Haebangsan, in the bottom tier of upmarket tourist establishments in the capital, was not somewhere the ruling class frequented. The Kims were on show, of course, Major and Minor in black suits looking down at us from an immense painting in the lobby, set against a backdrop of a silly pink dawn, handing out 'on-the-spot guidance' to all and sundry. Above the reception desk proper was a plywood cut-out map of the world, seemingly hand-crafted by five-year-olds. The lobby itself was fronted by large windows, providing a fair chunk of natural light. As we moved to the back to take the lift, the gloom deepened. The lights either did not work or someone had decided not to switch them on. I went for a pee. The men's toilet was dank and dark, much of the floor covered in puddles of wet, cisterns gurgling incontinently. The last time I was in a hotel toilet that squalid was in the Congo, but no one there claimed that it shined a light for the rest of humanity to follow.

On the telly there was only one channel to pick. Through a very fuzzy picture, we could see Kim Jong Il doing his take on Elvis, sorry, giving 'on-the-spot guidance' or OTSG to some poor sods somewhere, nowhere, in the sticks. The voiceover was comic, a sub-hysterical woman announcer sobbing and quivering with emotion as she intoned something-something in Korean. You could tell that it wasn't critical.

Outside our hotel room, scores of ant-like builders were constructing a building, 24/7: a new joint venture with a Chinese bank – a sign of the economy opening up? Or was it just a new channel for slush money, to keep the dynasty in cognac? The construction site wasn't that noisy, because they were pretty much building the place by hand.

It crossed my mind, were the hotel rooms bugged? Breen tells a story about two Danish engineers working on a project in North Korea, and complaining in their hotel room about how boring it all was. 'If I'd known, I would have brought a pack of cards with me,' one said. The next day at work, their minder presented them with a pack of cards. The creepy bit is that they had been talking in Danish.[10]

Downstairs in the hotel bar, plastic toads of implacable creepiness sat immobile in a large smelly fish tank, empty of water and open at the top. On critical inspection one jumped, scaring the life out of us. It felt like the first real thing we had seen all day.

[10] Breen, p100.

2

Zombie Gods Seep Goo

Breakfast lay in wait in a large gilt-effect ballroom, below zero, entirely empty apart from our party and several jolly Korean waitresses who wafted in, bearing dishes of increasing weirdness. Seahorse brain, hamster droppings on catarrh, and puddles of a sinister jam-like entity jostled for our attention. OK, I'm making this up, but the cosmic good of bacon and eggs has yet to penetrate the Big Zombie. Their favourite is kimchi, cabbage steeped in brine. The food wasn't bad. But it was strange.

The magnificence of the restaurant was out of kilter with the rest of the hotel: spooky, unlit, freezing cold corridors; on the stairs, the faint scent that a small creature died in the night; the bedrooms old-fashioned, museum pieces from the 1950s. The doors didn't quite fit the frames; the carpets were ridged and rucked; the lifts clunked and snickered, and every now and then the doors would not open. It was like staying in a mega-Fawlty Towers, but with Basil, Sybil, Manuel, Polly and the Major all missing, perhaps gone away 'for a stay in the mountains' – that's North Korean slang for the gulag. The hotel's boastful grand rooms and shoddy everything else left an abiding impression that this was a society that looked great on the architect's plans but so lacked proper attention to detail as to be almost unfit for habitation.

On the steps of the hotel drive, the cold bit deep into our bones. The Korean peninsula is ten degrees further south than London, but in winter it is very much colder. The British Isles benefit from the wet, warm winds of the Atlantic beating in from the west; Korea suffers from being at the end of the Eurasian continental landmass. It felt Siberian.

There were more cars on the roads than expected, with little jam-ettes of eight or nine motors building up here and there for what passed as the Pyongyang rush-hour. In town, as on the airport highway, the cars were generally posh-ish Japanese saloons, for the elite. The absence of vehicles of the poor – two-stroke rickshaws, scooters, horse and carts – was striking. The vast majority of people moved by bus or on foot. Packs of black-clad workers moved like shoals of fish hither and yon; every third person seemed to be in army uniform.

We were calling on two dead men. On the road to the Mausoleum, Mr Hyun explained that the DPRK would be no walkover: 'Our people will beat their fists to defend our sovereignty.' No one dared get into that double entendre. He went on to explain the dos and don'ts of visiting the dead: 'The Korean people believe that our President Kim Il Sung is always with us, so when we go to the Mausoleum we don't think we are going to a mausoleum, we are going to meet him.'

The Kumsusan Palace of the Sun is a cathedral to an alien god, and son. During his life, it was home to Kim Il Sung, in death it has become his tomb. When Kim Jong Il followed him to the grave, he too ended up there. It's a vast low granite grey-on-grey building, as imposing as a battleship, with concrete patches of greyness where the windows used to be. You enter at basement level along the left side. First up is a Heath Robinson contraption to clean the soles of your shoes. You step on a wet area and then walk forwards on to a living green mat which spins tufts of plastic greenery against your soles. It's like having your feet tickled by robot ferns. No mud enters the palace.[1]

You dump your bags, wallets, cameras – anything that could record the dead – in vast cloakrooms, efficiently run, and you are then commanded to square up in lines of four. The robotization of your mind begins. Step out of line, someone hisses at you. Pretty quickly, you yourself end up helping to enforce the system that encoils you – a very small and simple edition of the mental enslavement that the regime practises against its 23 million people. We are transported along what feels like the longest Travelator on the planet. There is a second security sweep at the end, just to make sure that you're not being a naughty boy and have smuggled in a hidden camera. We hadn't.

The first thing you see when you enter the palace proper is an enormous marble statue of Kim Il Sung, belly gently swelling under a business suit, in a display of bourgeois amplitude. 'Look at me, I'm fat,' says the stone god. Kim-in-marble is attended by mega-vases flowing with flowers and guarded by dead-eyed soldiers of abstract, mathematical beauty. You are firmly guided through a series of chambers, well lit and pleasantly air-conditioned, decorated with photographs and paintings of Kim the

---

[1] Lindsay Fincher, an American tourist who went on the zombie tour in 2009, has a brilliant memory for detail, which helped trigger my reflections. See http://www.lindsayfincher.com/

First meeting Tyrants'R'Us: Stalin, Mao, Gaddafi, Ceausescu, Erich Honecker of East Germany, Gustáv Husák of former Czechoslovakia, Wojciech Jaruzelski of Poland, Todor Zhivkov of Bulgaria, János Kádár of Hungary . . . Of that crowd, only Jaruzelski – perhaps the least bad, or certainly the most tormented of the old school of dictators – is still alive.

There's a sameness about all the poses, all empty smiles and smooth bottoms, while the weeping of the tyrants' victims takes place, unheard, elsewhere. Oh, look, there's Kim One with Teodoro Obiang, the President of Equatorial Guinea, who reportedly likes eating his critics' testicles in a white wine sauce with heart-shaped croutons. Plus some nabobs you've never heard of. Step forward Moktar Ould Daddah of Mauritania. I looked him up. He was a tyrant, too.

Next you walk through a sinister grey machine, black rubber nozzles on its side blowing great gusts of air at you. It's hard to see what good this machine can do, apart from making the point that you are somehow unclean. It's decorated with antiquated 1960s dials with arrows a-flicker. I looked around for a one-eyed Donald Pleasance in a Mao suit stroking a large white pussy, but it must have been his day off.[2]

The chamber of death is so back-lit with an early morning bright pink it is like walking around inside an enormous pig's bladder. This is perhaps not quite the effect that is intended. The old dictator lies in a large glass box, a prize beetle. A blanket shrouds much of his body. His neck, once deformed by the enormous goitre, is perfect; so is the blackness of his artificial hair. The goitre should have been powerful evidence of the imperfect nature of humanity.

[2] This is a homage to a joke by P.G. Wodehouse. I can't remember which book.

Instead, it did not exist, airbrushed out of official portraits and sculptures. The writer Michael Breen met Kim Il Sung in 1994.

> One notable personal feature of Kim Il Sung was the massive grenade-sized goitre on the back of his neck . . . when we had the pre-lunch interview session with Kim . . . a guard stood on the offending side to block the photographers. I wondered whether the security folk planned this deployment using a code name for it.[3]

Breen, answering his own question, called it the Thing.

The first reference I can find to the Thing is in 1980, when Tiziano Terzani was smuggled into Pyongyang on the back of an Italian Communist Party delegation, led by Enrico Berlinguer. In a chapter on North Korea entitled 'Red Flag, Blue Blood', Terzani

[3] Breen, *Kim Jong Il*, p13.

wrote: 'The cyst on the back of his neck is bigger than a fist, but it does not seem to hinder his movements. For years, the cyst has continued to grow, but no one has dared operate. Although it seems unlikely that it is a malignant tumour, the cyst is now at the centre of endless rumours and speculation.' [4]

Professor Myers believes that North Korea's veiled ideology of racial perfection made keeping the Thing secret a necessity of state. He told me: 'Whenever you have a race theory, whenever you have an ideology that asserts that the purity of the race is important you're naturally going to have an even greater aversion to physical defects and birth defects then you would have in countries without such an ideology. This is one of the reasons why the North Korean regime was so averse to showing the growth on Kim Il Sung's neck. He could only be photographed or filmed from a certain angle so that he would look to be in perfect health to the North Korean people.'

Why couldn't he get rid of it?

'Apparently it was too big to be removed,' said Myers.

Nicolae Ceausescu's translator, Izidor Urian – of whom more later – met Kim Il Sung at least fifty times and got to know the Thing well. 'It was an accumulation of fat,' the former Romanian diplomat told me. 'Nothing more than that.' (This may not be medically correct. Goitres are normally associated with a benign tumour of the thyroid gland.) How big? He motioned to a bowl of peanuts on the table between us, bigger than my clenched fist. 'There was no official ban on photographs. But if a photograph was taken, then it would go to the censors . . . So the photographers would avoid it. He was favoured on the other side of his neck.' And, then, confidentially, Izidor leaned towards me: 'He was very afraid of doctors.'

[4] Tiziano Terzani: *In Asia* [in Italian], Longanesi, Milan, 1999, p53.

The Thing is no more, but the corpse is still with us. In his glass box, Kim's face oozes a waxiness that is monstrous. But you can't take much of this in before your robot-four shuffles towards the holy mummy, and then you bow. You shuffle to the next side, bow again, shuffle to his head, where, weirdly, you don't bow, and then to the fourth side for one last bow, and you're out. Let there be no doubt: North Korea is seized by a political religion.

The next chamber boasts a Bond-villain map of the world with snail trails of bleeping lights where Kim Il Sung went 'Choo-choo, choo-choo' on his royal train: mostly through China to Moscow, and back. The royal train carriage sits sweetly on oiled wheels, going nowhere in a hurry. It may have seemed immensely luxurious in 1953. In the twenty-first century, though, it looks trainspotterly naff. By the royal train is a royal Mercedes of roughly the same era, its radiator grille snarling, Al Capone's teeth set in chrome.

Next up is the chamber housing the glass box of God the Son, Kim Jong Il. It is the same stately gavotte around a corpse as performed for God the Father. Kim Two in death looks no less weird than when he was alive: why bow and scrape for a bad Elvis impersonator? Still, the robot conditioning kicks in, and I bow three times.

How do you embalm a stiff?[5] First, gut your corpse, extracting the offal, heart, lungs and fiddly bits. You go in through the back, leaving the front of the body as intact as possible. You never know when the dear dictator's loved ones or secret policemen want to pop by for one last kiss. Suck the blood out, pump in the

[5] Ian Vandaelle: 'Way to go: If Kim Jong Il is embalmed, here's how they'd do it', *National Post of Canada*, 29 December 2011, http://news.nationalpost.com/2011/12/29/way-to-go-if-kim-jong-il-is-embalmed-heres-how-theyd-do-it/

goo. It's a witches' brew of formaldehyde, acetous potassium, sodium chloride, glycerin and ethanol. The Russians are the masters of this sacred art, the Chinese less so. They pumped poor Mao so full of formaldehyde, he swelled up like a gigantic balloon, and then the tyrant went 'Pop!', oozing fluid from every pore. Oh dear.

You need to control the temperature and the humidity. Hence the glass boxes. Too hot, and the corpse rots. Too cold, and it freezes, then develops a kind of necrotic frostbite, and goes an unpleasant shade of green. Over about six months, the formaldehyde replaces the water in the stiff. The goo glues muscle tissue, producing that tell-tale fixity of flesh in an embalmed body. It's a whole-body Botox treatment.

The Russian boffins who keep Lenin in the pink – on permanent display in Red Square since 1924 — are rumoured to freshen him up twice a week. The goo itself starts to go funny after a year and a half, so it has to be replaced, just like you would the engine oil in your motor. The goo leaks into the suits the stiffs wear, so they have to be changed every now and then, too. Lenin has a special pump in his chest, they say, to keep the goo at just the right viscosity, more treacly than treacle.

The two Soviet heroes who first kept Lenin pickled, Boris Zbarsky and Vladimir Vorobiev, both came to a sticky end. Vorobiev died in hospital under mysterious circumstances in 1937 – the year of Stalin's Great Terror. Zbarsky was arrested by Stalin's goons in 1952, released a year later but soon died of a stroke. Zbarsky's son, Ilya, took over the family pickle factory and ran Lenin's mausoleum until 1989, when he retired.

After Ilya, the new old man on the block was Sergei Debov, interviewed by Andrew Higgins of the *Independent* in 1993, at the age of 73.[6] Debov described pickling Stalin, no easy task in 1953. 'They sent a car to collect me when he died and took me to the laboratory. My hands were shaking. He was dead but his body-guards still stood there watching everything we did to him.' Debov and his colleagues did a good job on Stalin, embalming him for all eternity. Then Khrushchev read out the secret speech about Stalin being a mass murderer, and a few years on Stalin was removed and buried in the Kremlin wall.

Debov was particularly proud of his work on Ho Chi Minh. They did the job in 1969, inside a mountain, avoiding American bombs. Two transport planes flew in from Russia with air-conditioners and other equipment to preserve the corpse: 'It was all very difficult. The war was on and there was nothing. Even dis-tilled water had to be brought in from Moscow.' Uncle Ho the waxwork still hangs out in his own mausoleum in Vietnam.

Uniting all six pickled great ones, Lenin, Ho Chi Minh, Mao, Ferdinand Marcos, Kim Il Sung and Kim Jong Il, is a sick religiosity that seeks, pharaoh-like, to continue life after death. The waxen sheen they all exude is proof of how fatuous that dream is.

The chambers leading away from Kim Jong Il's waxwork boasted similar artefacts to those in the chamber after his dad: a royal train carriage, complete with desk and, on it, an Apple Mac Book Pro. Whatever effect seeing the Apple might have on ordi-nary North Koreans, to us it smacked of repugnant hypocrisy. Only Kim the Second was allowed to use the internet. What did Kim Two watch online? An intoxicating mixture of hard-core porn, some say, and something entirely different. One story goes that the

[6] Andrew Higgins: 'End is nigh for mummified Marxists', *Independent*, 2 June 1993.

people who ran Lady Thatcher's website noted that they had a regular follower from one IP address in North Korea. Who could it have been other than Kim Jong Il?

Gifts of obeisance from various entirely predictable banana republics were offered for our inspection. But also there was a plaque of some kind from Derbyshire County Council, sent in the late 1980s, when the prospect of world revolution made Derby blush and Chesterfield's spire tilt yet more crookedly off-centre.

On the way out, two women wept openly. Was it just for show? Or, somehow harder to bear, did they really mean it? The devotion of the people to the state seems absolute. How can a nation be so in thrall to a regime that has led to the wholly unnecessary deaths of millions of its own people? Perhaps it is because they have been told a powerful fairy tale all their lives.

The fresh air seemed a gift. But even outside the house of the zombie gods, their baleful influence did not lose its hold over our minds. It was fine for us to walk in the grounds in front of the great palace. But a dozen or so workers rested on their haunches, hand-fixing paving slabs that were being repositioned and tidying up garden beds. We sensed by now that trying to photograph or film this scene of human imperfection would be unwelcome, would somehow break the power of the precious illusion. This is a land where just trying to capture the small-change moments of life places you in political conflict with the regime. Best not to bother . . . and then, yet again, the regime wins.

We got back on to the bus, crossed town and ended up at the Juche Tower, a great concrete prick jabbing at the sky, purposefully one metre taller than the Washington Monument, there to honour one of the regime's proclaimed ideologies: Jucheism. The view from the top was striking, but not quite in the way the regime would have liked. Ahead was the Taedong river, a bit wider than the Thames at Greenwich, which flows through Pyongyang, beyond that Kim Il Sung Square and the main party and regime buildings. But immediately behind was the east bank, grim grey blocks of flats, all copies of the same East German architect's design, and single bungalows, poor, mean, miserable. To be fair, the air was clean. This was the first Third World capital I've been to with no smog. The North Koreans have solved the problem of pollution. There is no industry.

If anyone is tempted to get all soppy about North Korea's green credentials, bear in mind the testimony of one defector who worked at a uranium processing factory: 'The trees next to the river died and so did all the fish.' The workers' hair fell out; blood used to seep out of the defector's mouth.[7] Health and safety does not exist in North Korea.

On, then, to an enormous plaza to inspect a vast concrete three-pronged obelisk in the centre of Pyongyang, boasting a hammer, a sickle and a lithographer's brush etched against the sky. Hammer, sickle and brush are the symbols of workers in the factory, the fields and by brain, the totems of the Korean Workers' Party. The words in concrete sang out: 'Hail the Korean Workers' Party – all the Korean People's Unifier and Leader!' No one sang back. Apart from our guides, no North Korean was present.

Remember in North Korea nothing is as it seems. The pro-claimed ideology of the nation is not the real one. The national Stalinism represented by the Three Prongs is fake. So, too, is Jucheism, neatly skewered by one authority as a 'stodgy jumble of banalities'.[8] Jucheism and Kimilsungism both serve the personality

[7] Martin, p438.
[8] Myers: *The Cleanest Race*, p46.

cult, by pretending that Kim the First was a great thinker – he was no such thing – but they are cosmetic stick-ons, like beauty spots or fake eyelashes. The real ideology of the DPRK is racial purity. That's perhaps why the regime has lasted so long, because what it believes in fits snugly with something in the North Korean psyche. To be fair, in a society so closed off from the outside world that few people know the Americans have walked on the surface of the moon, the chance of them realizing they have been told a big lie is slim. In the Democratic People's Republic of Korea, Mario Vargas Llosa's warning – 'Ideology is fiction that doesn't realize it's fiction' – will never be given air-time.

The North Korean credo is a paranoid, racially pure Nazi-esque ideology. It has much in common with fascist thought. That is the considered judgement of Professor Myers, who studied first the ideology of Communist East Germany and now spends his time soaking up the belief system of the DPRK. For example, Myers cites a hugely popular novella of the 1950s, in which two American missionaries and their son kill a Korean child by injecting germs into the blood.

> The old jackal's spade-shaped eagle-nose hung villainously over his upper lip, while the vixen's teats jutted out like the stomach of a snake that has just swallowed a demon, and the slippery wolf-cub gleamed with poison like the head of a venomous snake has just swallowed its skin. Their six sunken eyes seemed . . . like open graves constantly waiting for corpses.[9]

This stuff could have been lifted from the pages of Julius Streicher's *Der Stürmer*.

[9] Myers, p138.

When the North and the South met at the DMZ in 2006, the media were present to hear the small talk between two generals before the meeting proper started in private. The soldier from the South spoke about how quite a few farmers from his half were marrying foreigners. When the general from the North scowled at this, the southerner downplayed his remark, saying that such marriages were a mere 'drop of ink in the Han river' (the South Korean equivalent of the Thames). At which the general from the North spat out: 'Not even one drop of ink must be allowed.'[10]

Britain's former ambassador to North Korea, John Everard, questions comparisons to Stalinism in his book *Only Beautiful, Please*, arguing the regime's mainstay is 'xenophobic nationalism rather than socialism. The closest Western analogue to the DPRK is probably Nazi Germany.'[11] Pyongyang watcher Aidan Foster-Carter draws similar conclusions: 'Read North Korean propaganda in German, and the emphasis on der Führer and the triumph of the will suggest a very different (or is it?) totalitarian comparison.'[12]

Christopher Hitchens, once vilified by George Galloway MP as 'a drink-sodden former Trotskyist popinjay' – nothing much wrong with any of that – and the best writer of English prose since Orwell, observed of North Korea: 'I saw exactly one picture of Marx and one of Lenin in my whole stay, but it's been a long time since ideology had anything to do with it. Not without cunning, Fat Man [Kim Il Sung] and Little Boy [Kim Jong Il] gradually mutated the whole state belief system into a debased form of Confucianism, in which traditional ancestor worship and respect

[10] Myers, p74.
[11] Everard, p198.
[12] Aidan Foster-Carter: 'Is North Korea Stalinist?', *Asia Times* online, 5 September 2001.

for order become blended with extreme nationalism and xenophobia.'

The question that troubles many Pyongyangologists is: how has North Korea survived long after, say, the state that Stalin built was dead? The answer, perhaps, is that North Korea has outlived the Soviet Union because it was never truly Communist in the first place, but owes its stability to its roots in Korean feudalism and racism. Also, Stalinism was itself not just about command economy and the personality cult, but borrowed heavily from Russian traditionalism and xenophobia, so the Kimist jump from there to racism is not that big a leap.

'Kimism', by the way, is a term used by the Pyongyangologist Adrian Buzo as an umbrella description of the regime's ideology in his sharply written book *The Guerilla Dynasty*,[13] which he identifies as a blend of national Stalinism, xenophobia, ultra-traditionalism and criminality. Kimism was forged, says Buzo, when Kim Il Sung was a freedom-fighter-cum-robber-baron in Manchuria in the few years up to 1940, when he escaped into Stalin's Soviet Union. Buzo's insights do not conflict with Myers' judgement that the regime's ideology is far right; they effectively support it.

But why Jucheism with its talk of self-reliance? Why still bother with the pseudo-Marxism of the Korean Workers' Party, Three Prongs and all? Perhaps it's a clever trick, a decoy. There are many people in the Western world who will give an anti-capitalist regime the benefit of the doubt; hardly anyone who will stand up for a nakedly racist state. So North Korea faces both ways: putting out

[13] Adrian Buzo: *The Guerilla Dynasty: Politics and Leadership in North Korea*, I.B. Tauris, London, 1999.

the old Workers' Party rhetoric for external consumption, while telling its own people a different story of 'us against the foreigners'.

All racism is ugly, but there is something particularly abhorrent about racism even a child can sense, about a lisping tot doing elementary addition and subtraction by counting American corpses – the reason why, Breen reports, one foreign diplomat took her child out of a North Korean nursery.[14]

On the third prong, the intellectual's brush – in Western culture it would, of course, be a pen – Myers observes that the brush 'has helped keep casual foreign observers from recognizing the DPRK's intense anti-intellectualism'.[15] Western fears of minds being dumbed down by idiot TV and computer games are as naught compared with what happens in North Korea. If you belong to a nation where as a child you are taught lies about history at school, you are taught to spout banalities at university, where you cannot speak your mind, it's going to make it virtually impossible to frame the thought, Is our system as good as they say it is?

So the Korean Workers' Party's Three Prongs is a big lie in concrete, while the real belief of the system is Nazi-esque racial purity with bolted-on bits of Japanese fascism and Stalinist mind-control. None of this, of course, was mentioned by or discussed with our minders.

Our party was thirteen-strong, including nine LSE students from all corners of the world, two Russians, two Swiss, a German, a Moroccan, an African American, an Australian and one Briton, and one alumnus, Hoe-Yeong, an unflappable Singaporean. In North Korea, the students were great company, politely cynical

[14] Breen, p158.
[15] Myers, caption to Plate 9.

about the regime's nonsense, thoughtful, good fun. Two of the three BBC team had also been to LSE, my wife, Tomiko, and, going all the way back to 1977–1980, me. Tomiko – the name is Japanese, but she is British to the core – had been to North Korea with the LSE's Student Union's International Relations Club, which she ran, the year before. The odd man out was Alex Niakaris, an alumnus of the University of Wales, half Greek, half Welsh, an odd combination but then he is an odd man in many ways. He was also our shooter-producer, his fiendishly difficult job to film everything that moved without appearing to do so. He did so with great good humour.

Throughout our trip, a North Korean cameraman from the Korean International Travel Company followed us everywhere. He filmed us. He didn't know it, but we filmed him. He filmed us filming him filming us. Once Alex, being mischievous, said to me, po-faced: 'You know this place is so fascinating it would be great to make a documentary here.' I replied quick as a flash: 'We are, Alex, we are,' forgetting that this was our ultra, code yellow, secret. Alex used a Canon 5D camera, readily available in the high street. It looks life a hefty stills camera but it can shoot broadcast quality high definition video. Alex's problem was that he didn't want to look like a professional cameraman with the 5D pressed against his eye all the time, so he nursed it at chest height, unable to check the image. The result was mental torture for Alex. Wobble Vision for much of the time, but it worked. Sound was a much bigger headache. The microphone in the 5D is so-so, and normally we would have used radio mikes. Vetoing that as too risky, we busked it, hoping that we would be able to capture moments here and there. Tomiko had another stills and video camera, much smaller, and mine was the least fancy of the lot, as big as a packet of fags.

We took in loads of electronic cards but no laptops, and hoped that they would not twig our game. There being no internet or shops selling electronic stuff in North Korea, how would the cameraman know that we were filming him filming us?

At the end of the trip, we paid €40 a head for the KITC video, complete with uplifting voiceover from an excitable, no, preposterously melodramatic Korean lady. On the three prongs-in-concrete, she proclaimed: 'This monument was erected in October 1995 to mark the founding of the Workers' Party of Korea.' The Party, according to the North Koreans, can trace its origin back to the Down With Imperialism Union, founded in October 1926 by Kim Il Sung, then just fourteen years old. This is, of course, rubbish. The back history was invented years later to make Kim look good. When he was fourteen, he was still playing the church organ.

The obelisk was empty of people, of life, of movement. And that is odd. Go to Trafalgar Square in London. You may care to salute the one-eyed pirate atop his column, or not. But you will be accosted by people selling you something: maybe a life-choice or a DVD of *I, Robot* in Russian or 'All the Mongolian food you can eat for a tenner'. The same goes for any big public space in DC or New York or Paris or Berlin or even these days Beijing, though not Tiananmen Square, just in case anyone starts getting funny ideas about Chinese democracy. What was odd was that no one pounced on the evidently prosperous foreigners in the vast empty space by the KWP obelisk in Pyongyang. Clearly, there was an order not to make contact. It was the same in Ceausescu's Romania in 1985. Not a single ordinary Romanian came up to our group of journalists. Only in 1989, when I spent Christmas with the Ceausescus, as it were, did I begin to appreciate the power and terror generated by the secret police, the Securitate, before the Revolution. There was an order for any person who made contact with a foreigner to report it to the police within twenty-four hours. The police would then pass on the file to the Securitate. As a consequence, foreigners were shunned. An order very much like the Romanian one must be in place in North Korea, and it is absolutely obeyed. In eight days in North Korea, not a single ordinary individual started a conversation with us.

Our minders did not mention the regime's secret police, but they do exist. The Security Department, in Korean, Bowibu, is *the* power in the land. The world expert on the Bowibu is a former US intelligence analyst, Ken E. Gause. He reports that the Bowibu employ around 50,000 people, are based in the Amisan area of Pyongyang – there are satellite pictures[16] – and were effectively led by Kim Jong Il from the late 1980s to his death in 2011. The Bowibu are officially known as the Korean People's Army Unit 10215, which just so happened to host Kim Jong Un's second public on-site inspection since he became heir apparent in September 2010.

The Bowibu spy on everyone worth spying on: the palace's most loyal retainers, officials in the government and the Party, generals in the army, the dynasty's trickier relatives, the police, ordinary people and, of course, foreigners.

Did the Bowibu spy on us? Were our minders Bowibu or reporting to them? The answer, according to Greg Scarlatoiu, Executive Director of the Committee for Human Rights in North Korea and the publisher of Gause's report, is, 'Yes, of course.'

They spy on ordinary people through an entity called the

---

[16] Ken E. Gause: 'Coercion, Control, Surveillance and Punishment: An Examination of the North Korea Police State', Committee for Human Rights in North Korea, Washington DC, 2012, p18, p27.

Inminban, which roughly translates as 'Neighbourhood Watch'. In every single city district, town and village in the North, the local watch committee consists of between twenty and forty households – roughly around a hundred to 250 people, including children – led by busy-body snoopers who know they might get some advantage by reporting a neighbour listening to South Korean pop songs or flashing around more money than they ought to have.

The Inminbans are responsible for keeping the streets clean, polishing statues and portraits of Kims One and Two and making sure people attend the regime's self-criticism meetings. They combine being neighbourhood snoopers with the eyes and ears, at street level, of the secret police.

Leaving the concrete colossus behind, we set off for lunch, a hot-pot restaurant where you cook your own meat on a kerosene stove placed on the table. The results were OK-ish, either a bit too chewy or a bit overdone. Everywhere we ate, one got the impression that the quality and quantity of food was spectacular by North Korean standards, but pretty depressing for anyone used to eating, say, street food in China or KFC in Des Moines or fish and chips in Liverpool.

Back on the tourist bus – with one exit and one microphone in Mr Hyun's hands, it was proving a brilliant totalitarian tool – we headed south-west from the capital, towards the Yellow Sea. We visited the Kangso Mineral Water Plant, above it the proclamation: 'Hail the light of Korea's military first-ism, General Kim Jong Un!' It's possible that this was a brand new slogan. Or that they only had to change the last two characters to accommodate the change from Kim Jong Il to Kim Jong Un. Outside three bears glugged water. They were, of course, fake.

Water from a hot spring gurgled into a thick glass dead end.

There was a handsome Italian-made production line, full of brilliantly polished stainless steel vats but no sign of production at any time in the recent past. We were offered bottles of the water to taste. It had the bouquet of sulphurous muck. Being a natural diplomat, I proclaimed: 'Ah, the champagne of water!' which Mr Hyun found so funny he spat his out and bent double, giggling.

If you bottle mineral water, you should have a yard full of stacked pallets with empty bottles to be processed and packed bottles ready to be shipped off to your customers. Of that, there was no sign.

The story behind the bottling plant with no bottles starts well, with an exciting joint venture between the two Koreas, and pretty much stops with two hammer blows: the killing of a tourist and a nuclear test.[17] In 2011, the *Hankyoreh* newspaper told the melancholy tale of South Korean investor Lee Dae Sik. The 'Sunshine' or engagement policy of left-of-centre governments in Seoul had encouraged him to start up a trading business with the North. The Sunshine Policy sounds nice, but critics accuse the South and the Clinton administration of being overly credulous towards an entirely dishonest dictatorship; they satirize the 'Sunshine Policy' as the 'Moonshine Policy'.

To begin with, Lee imported Pyongyang rice vodka – soju – and sought-after agricultural products like bracken, balloon flower roots and pine mushrooms. The mood music between the two countries improved, a little, in June 2000 when Kim Jong Il hosted a visit to Pyongyang by the South Korean President Kim Dae-Jung. To the South Korean media, starved of news of the North and bored with the horror stories from defectors, Kim Jong Il came

---

[17] The *Hankyoreh* newspaper report was picked up by a website: see http://www.nkeconwatch.com/2011/06/16/losses-grow-for-south-korean-firms-invested-in-dprk/

across as witty, clever and willing to poke a little fun at himself – as it turned out, a massive misreading of a cunning psychopath. Still, the business climate improved and Lee put in serious money to build the mineral water plant. He would provide the capital – the machinery, bottles, caps and labels – and the North Korean side would provide the water from the ground and the labour. Kim told the paper that sales increased to 400,000 bottles a month.

But the political weather began to turn when President Lee Myung Bak – a big sceptic on the Sunshine Policy – won the election in the South and took power in 2008. That July, a South Korean woman tourist enjoying a walk on the beach in the Mount Kumgang tourist resort was shot dead by a trigger-happy North Korean soldier, terrified of allowing her into a restricted area.

Relations froze overnight, as the North stuck absurdly to the line that the killing was the fault of the tourist. In April 2009 the North launched a missile; in May that year a nuclear test took place, nailing the coffin lid firmly down on the Sunshine Policy. And that meant that Mr Lee, South–North entrepreneur, was screwed. 'When you apply for contact with North Korea, the [South Korean] government tells you to "please refrain from doing so". They say "please refrain", but who is going to refuse a request from the government? They are basically telling you, "Don't do it."'

One day, a fax came from North Korea, telling Lee that his contract was null and void. Three years on, when we visited the place, the most up-to-date labels we found on bottles in the plant were for 2010. Our guides neglected to tell us it had been a ghost factory for some time. Then again, how could they? We moved on from the bottling plant to the water source itself, housed in a large shed. A local guide explained the various systems they used by means of a large coloured diagram on the wall. It might have looked technically very impressive, had the power not been off. As it was, the entire technical briefing took place in the gloom. But no one said anything. It was like being there when the Emperor walked past in his 'New Clothes', naked to all and sundry. You had to pinch yourself and remember: no, this isn't a story, this is real.

Not far away was the Chongsan-ri Farm, which boasted an anti-aircraft battery on a hill but no animals and no crops. It was weird. In farms around the world, chickens cluck and ducks quack, pigs snort, dogs give you a rheumy eye, cows munch grass and sheep bleat. There were no animals of any kind.

From a nearby apartment block, propaganda loudspeakers spouted out their boring pedantic cry, but this being North Korea the tape was fucked and what you heard was a weird inhuman screeching, like pterodactyls in *Scooby Doo*. I asked Mr Hyun, was the announcement telling us that thermo-nuclear war had started? He said no. The cold was bitter. No one stirred, no one cheered. It was hard to imagine anything more hateful than having no choice but to listen to the squawking that never stops at No Animal Farm.

Outside the 'farm' was a large concrete slab, on it a giant statue-shrine in bronze to Kim Il Sung giving 'on-the-spot guidance' – OTSG – to grateful, square-jawed, heroic farm workers and their Soviet-bosomed womenfolk. At every meeting between ordinary folk and Kim Il Sung, OTSG is handed out. As Myers writes: 'Stories of Kim's "on-the-spot-guidance" are alike not only in their depiction of the hero, but in their storylines and secondary characters as well ... Both problem and solution are thus described in terms a child can grasp. Indeed, the Leader's published remarks are *always* trite: "Rainbow trout is a good fish, tasty and nutritious." '[18]

---

[18] Myers, p106.

We were asked to line up and bow in front of the Kim statue. Miss Jun stood at the edge of the front row, to lead that row's bow; Mr Hyun stood at the side of the second row to ensure the same-same. It was a Stalinist stage show, circa 1953, frozen in time, more than half a century out of date. I bowed, crossing my fingers behind my back, but that subtle gesture was not captured by the North Korean cameraman. He just filmed the moment of obeisance. Perhaps it was just an accident of timing or perhaps our guides had been sly in making us all bow seven times to the Kim dynasty – six times in the Mausoleum, and once again – on our first proper day in North Korea. After that first day, the more we saw, the less likely any of us would be to bow to the regime's gods in bronze or stone. But at the beginning of the trip we were still anxious to please, and unaware that the strange hierarchical nature of the country meant that we, as Westerners, were treated effectively as members of the elite core group – and that meant as well as being served as luxuriously as possible we were also given some allowance for, if not dissent, then at least mock-compliance.

Our tour of the farm continued. We were taken to a 'typical farm worker's house', where we posed for photographs with two tiny sweet little North Korean toddlers, and their grandma. This may have been a natural event, but it felt like something that was pre-arranged and well choreographed, the lisping tots on cue for smiles at our cameras. Two pictures of Kim Il Sung and Kim Jong Il had pride of place in the house. In North Korea, I can't remember seeing pictures of anyone else. A North Korean defector, 'Mary Lou', later told me about the care that people have to take with the portraits. She said that the wall they are hung on must be bare and clear of any other objects. Only the portraits are allowed on that wall. They have to be cleaned every morning, wiping away any dust, because you never know when the inspectors might come. And you can never put them on the floor. The inspectors test how clean the portraits are by wiping the top of the frame with a piece of white paper, looking for any dust or dirt. If they are deemed not clean enough, people are fined or punished in some way.

But even here, in this propaganda showpiece, the truth had a way of seeping out from behind the film-set. Through the window, you could clearly see someone's washing hanging higgledy-piggledy on the naked branches of a tree in the freezing sun.

Our last stop was the Ryonggang Hot Spa hotel, an old party hotel set in spacious grounds, dotted with pine trees, with a Kalashnikov-toting guard at the gate. It turned out to be an architectural tribute to 1970s Bond-villain kitsch, complete with hot tubs spouting pongy water from an off-bronze tap into an immense, badly tiled Jacuzzi-thing, as inviting as the low-tide Thames at Wapping.

Hoe-Yeong played table tennis for a bit, until the power died and his ball vanished in the gloom. Dinner kicked off in an unusual way. Our hosts spread clams on a slab of cement, soused them with petrol and then set them alight. Feeling a bit queasy, I pulled a face. Mr Hyun, attentive as ever to the need to demonstrate the very best of North Korea, picked up a clam and opened it up an inch from my mouth. I lunged forward and ate the flesh. As petrol-flambéed molluscs go, it went down my throat. Others were less enthusiastic to the point of profound nausea, so Mr Hyun carried on hand-feeding me the clams, like an infant. After three clams, I felt I was placing diplomacy against the well-being of my stomach. Mr Hyun offered me a hefty glass of soju, the local hooch. I proposed, 'Here's not to thermo-nuclear war, anytime soon' and, not wanting to seem a Milquetoast, downed it in one. The soju knocked out the taste of carbonized clam à la Esso like a punch from Muhammad Ali. Mr Hyun downed his glass, giggled infectiously and then proclaimed that I was 'Professor of Drinking'. These North Koreans, they know everything.

3

God the Waxwork Father

Alex and I got up before dawn and walked through the softening light up a steep slope at the back of the hotel, led by one of the students, 'Erica'. She had become fascinated by North Korea after watching an undercover National Geographic documentary on the country. She had gone for a walk the night before and found something she wanted us to see. From the top of a bluff on the very edge of the hotel grounds, you could peer through a bedraggled barbed-wire fence and spy a sleeping town. In the grey luminescence, just before sunrise, the town looked unutterably miserable. It wasn't just dirt-poor. Poverty stinks wherever you find it, but even in the polluted towns in the Katanga copper belt of the Congo or in the gunfire-ridden barrios of Caracas, there's some sense of energy and hope, that a few people if they graft or use their cunning can get out and end up someplace better. The crowded grey apartment blocks, like so many human hen coops, just on the other side of the fence from the core class's privilege and ease, spoke of hopelessness and helplessness, of a poverty of the human soul so deep no one in this town could possibly escape from it. The electricity was off, so the propaganda hadn't started up yet. But soon it would.

Gripping the barbed fence, I wound up my reporter's voice, nodded at the misery in concrete ahead of me and said: 'Welcome to the real North Korea.' Alex and Erica took some more footage and photographs of the town, and then we were off, hurrying back to the hotel before anyone noticed we had gone missing.

History – the study of how the past moulds the future – is too important to be left to history professors, even fake ones like me. The unholy trinity of the Kim dynasty has ruled North Korea since 1945, and the man who most stamped his bloodline on the country was Kim Il Sung. But who was the real man inside the wax?

The best book I've ever read that peers into the mind and soul of a dictator is a novel, *The Porcupine* by Julian Barnes.[1] It's set in a post-revolutionary country, clearly Bulgaria, where the old Communist tyrant is facing trial. The old brute in the novel, Stoyo Petkanov, is based on the ex-dictator Todor Zhivkov. The trick that Barnes cleverly pulls off is to make the dictator act like a real flesh-and-blood human being, not just a creature from darkness. The dictator, with his back against the wall, comes out fighting, a bruiser, contemptuous of the lickspittles, funny, amusing, hard as concrete. Barnes, who conjures with the English language like a magician plucking out a rabbit from his hat, makes you sympathize with the devil. Zhivkov's Bulgaria in 1989 was a much less dark place than Ceausescu's Romania. Back in December 1989 and January 1990, Romania was frozen, half starved and frothing with fear; Bulgaria was so much better – it had power and light and food and calm – we called it Hollywood. But the heft of *The Porcupine*

[1] Julian Barnes: *The Porcupine*, Jonathan Cape, London, 1992.

makes a simple point: you don't get to be a dictator of a country unless you've got serious qualities, of conviction, self-belief, a hardness of the soul. That goes for Kim Il Sung, too.

Kim Il Sung left Korea when he was seven years old. Apart from a brief spell back in Pyongyang when he was eleven, he spent the next twenty-three years of his life outside his own country: the simplest explanation for the taunt by his enemies that when he spoke Korean, he quacked like a duck. A dysfunctional childhood and broken education – he never completed high school – gave way to the great formative influence on his life: being in a guerrilla band in Manchuria, surviving by kidnapping, robbery and extortion. In 1940, on the run from the Japanese, he fled into the care of the only regime he ever admired: Stalin's Soviet Union, where he spent the next five years, sitting out the war. Adrian Buzo, one of the harshest critics of all Kim Il Sung's historians, writes that his broken education, guerrilla brutalism and Stalinist tutelage framed the man and his regime: anti-intellectual, deeply mistrustful of the outside world, contemptuous of morality: 'He lived in a predatory, political subculture of force which encouraged in him an outlook that accepted callousness and criminality as a daily reality.'[2]

In other words, Kim Il Sung was a Korean version of Al Capone.

Kim Il Sung's official biography is a fiction. It exaggerates and airbrushes and tells lies about history. More sympathetic Western historians than Buzo paint a softer picture, pointing out that young Kim's achievements were real enough. They say he survived an extraordinarily difficult youth – his nation under the thumb of hated occupiers, exile, loss of his father at an early age, and then

[2] Buzo, p10.

effective loss of the rest of his family – to become a hardened warrior in a cruel guerrilla war where the odds were almost impossibly stacked against him and his men. From 1935 to 1940 the Japanese Army hunted Korean Communist fighters like Kim and their Chinese Communist masters in Manchuria with a ferocity that is hard to imagine. Captured fighters were guillotined. The guerrillas repaid that ferocity in spades. Kim and his men survived by kidnapping rich Chinese farmers, extorting guns, money and food, or else ears or heads would be cut off. The Japanese police used bribery, torture and threats to play the Koreans against one another, so cleverly that the Chinese Communists, sick of a string of betrayals, turned on the Koreans, torturing, imprisoning and executing innocent men. At one point Kim Il Sung was locked up by the Chinese Communists, suspected of being a spy – a necessary introduction to how their system worked, perhaps. Hunted, paranoid, criminal, murderous, frozen, starved, Kim Il Sung was the only Korean officer of his rank in Manchuria who survived to escape to the safety of Vladivostok in the Soviet Far East in 1940, after the Japanese rolled up the resistance.

Much of the detail of Kim's war is opaque or lost in the gush of the subsequent personality cult, but it is fair to say that as a Communist resistance fighter Kim survived, and to that extent, he was successful. Buzo notes the scar tissue: 'His experience in the Manchurian guerrilla campaign seems to have rendered him extraordinarily callous and indifferent to suffering.'[3]

It is also fair to say that every single terrifying feature of North Korea's gangster dynasty he created was forged in the guerrilla war in Manchuria: the paranoia, the criminality, the murder, the

---

[3] Buzo, p237.

inurement to starvation and the cold, even the kidnapping. This is a man whose moral compass was smashed to pieces in one of the darkest and least-known wars in history. North Korea is the result.

Once Kim was gifted the pretence of power in October 1945, by a Soviet Union looking around for a Korean they could play with, he seized his opportunity with both hands. He died in July 1994, an absolute monarch, outliving the Soviet state by three years. Kim Il Sung started a civil war he almost lost, survived, prospered, killing his enemies, real and imaginary, in a series of purges, and was able to hand power on to his son. So the very first thing to say about Kim One is that he was a tough and shrewd tyrant, who outfoxed his enemies throughout his long life. 'Let them hate, so long as they fear' was the bespoke aphorism for tyrants adopted by Caligula. Kim Il Sung's philosophy of power, perhaps, can be summed up in an even crueller phrase: 'They must fear me, but they must love me, too.' No other dictator in modern history, neither Hitler, nor Stalin, nor Mao, nor Pol Pot, has demanded such slave-like devotion from his people – and got it unto the third generation.

Kim Il Sung was born Kim Song Ju on 15 April 1912, in Pyongyang.[4] His country had been annexed by the Japanese only two years before – a gross insult to Korea's national pride. Koreans had traditionally looked down on the Japanese as rustic country bumpkins. But in 1905 the Japanese had flattened the Russians in a short war, knocking the prestige of the tsar and marking the first victory of an Asian military might against a Western power in the modern age. The rise of Japan, and

---

[4] Dae-Sook Suh's *Kim Il Sung: The North Korean Leader*, Columbia University Press, New York, 1998, and Martin's *Under the Loving Care of the Fatherly Leader* are the authorities on young Kim Il Sung; Breen's *Kim Jong Il* has the better jokes.

Kim's part in his country's struggle against it, scarred his life. Kim's father and mother were both Christians; his maternal grandfather had been a Presbyterian missionary, a fact readily admitted by the official biographers. That would seem to be an odd admission for a Communist ruler, but an understanding of Christianity's role in the making of Korean independence makes it less so. Around the turn of the twentieth century, Confucianism was the official religion of Korea, but its grip on people's faith was weak, especially in the North. One layer beneath the surface was an ancient shamanism or paganism, which still has its sway amongst the poor today, away from the Kim dynasty's propaganda. Christian missionaries, especially Protestants, arriving from the 1880s onwards, when the Korean government signed a treaty with the Americans, were extremely successful in Pyongyang, which became known as Korea's Jerusalem.[5] There was a political, patriotic component to Christianity's popularity. Confucianism was, in essence, Chinese; Buddhism Japanese; Christianity a third force which somehow chimed with Koreanness. Come the Japanese takeover of the whole of the Korean peninsula in 1910, the men from the land of the rising sun turned out to be an effective recruiting sergeant for Jesus. Christianity was somehow considered to be un-Japanese. Today, South Korea is one of the most Christian nations in the whole of Asia, with around one in four of the population holding to the faith. In the North, despite decades of repression, Christians continue to oppose the regime with a heroism that is breathtaking.

Kim Il Sung was to adopt another faith from the West – Marxism-Leninism – and his belief in that soon blotted out the old

[5] Martin, p15.

religion. His autobiography states: 'I, too, was interested in Church.' But after a while: 'I became tired of the tedious religious ceremony and the monotonous preaching of the minister, so I seldom went.'[6] Other accounts suggest that he deliberately downplayed his old devotion. For example, they say that both Kim Il Sung's father and he himself played the church organ.[7]

Mischief-makers might add that the Presbyterians' stress on the Elect of God does not sound so very different from the 'core class' of the Korean Workers' Party.

Kim's father had been a peasant farmer who became a backstreet doctor, treating people with traditional herbal medicines. When Kim was seven, the family upped sticks and shifted across the border into north-eastern China. Kim described his family's move into exile as being 'like fallen leaves to the desolate wilderness of Manchuria'.[8] The relocation had a lasting legacy for the young Kim. He started school and became fluent in Mandarin – which stood him in good stead when keeping the trust of the Chinese Communists was a matter of life and death. The downside was his Korean started to suffer. To make up for weakness in his mother tongue, shortly before his eleventh birthday, his father packed him off to Pyongyang, a journey of 250 miles, so that he could brush up on his Korean while staying with his maternal grandparents. Two years later he was back in Manchuria. Shortly afterwards, his father, never a well man, died at the age of thirty-two. Kim continued his education in Chinese, and learnt his Marxism from a teacher, Shang Yue, at the age of fifteen. Shang became a famous

---

[6] Martin, p16.
[7] Martin, p59.
[8] Kim Il Sung: *With the Century*, vol. 1, Foreign Language Publishing House, Pyongyang, 1992, p62.

historian, who later recalled his star pupil being 'diligent' and asking the right sort of questions. One young Korean friend, who later became a pathologist in Nebraska, admired the young Kim greatly: he was not interested in trivia but 'very enthusiastic on political and social problems . . . Imposing . . . a charmingly handsome man . . . a future leader, he had able leadership already in those days.' He stood out, 'like a crane in a flock of pheasants'.[9]

The rest of his youth is a murky story. Kim's activity as a young Communist was discovered by the Chinese police, and he was gaoled in the autumn of 1929, aged seventeen, in the city of Jilin. Kim was banged up in a cell in the cold, sunless side of the gaol, which in winter was wallpapered with frost. The police tortured him, breaking fingers, says the official version. Breen writes cynically that this allegation of torture is 'unconvincingly written up'; I agree. There is no detail. After some friends bought him out, he left his family and joined the guerrillas. First, you had to adopt a nom de guerre. To begin with, they called him 'Star of Korea' but dropped that in favour of 'Be The Sun' or Il Sung. (So in English, his name would be Kim Be The Sun.)

The narrative now gets clogged with propaganda. Suh, who is always fair to young Kim, points out the Japanese military issued several reports on Kim and produced maps detailing the whereabouts of Kim's troops.[10] Korean newspapers – then, of course, under Japanese censorship – regularly reported on Kim's banditry. Guerrilla wars are never fought according to Queensberry Rules. The crueller the government forces, the crueller the guerrillas become – in part to survive. If the Japanese tortured and killed

[9] Martin, p26.
[10] Suh, p345.

captured guerrillas, so did Kim Il Sung and his men against people they suspected of being in league with the Japanese. Some South Korean anti-Communists have asserted that Kim stole the real Kim Il Sung's name, leaving the poor guerrilla leader a kind of 'Man in the Iron Mask'. Suh states bluntly: 'Kim is not a fake.'[11]

The start of 1935 saw a breakdown in relations between the Chinese Communists and their Korean brothers. Koreans were tortured into confessing they were secretly working for the Japanese. They weren't, of course, but hundreds were executed. Kim survived this baptism of paranoia well, perhaps because his Chinese was so fluent, and his manner so steely self-confident. In 1937, Kim led a brief raid across the border into Japanese-occupied Korea at Pochonbo. Not a great battle, but enough to make a name for himself with the Japanese enemy, his Chinese Communist allies, and, observing development from not so far away, officers of the Red Army. Kim dynasty propaganda later airbrushes out the involvement of the Chinese – and, providing a rear base and supplies, the Soviets – and asserts that he was the effective leader of a stand-alone Korean Communist military operation in Manchuria. Lankov notes grimly: 'This version has nothing to do with reality. No Korean People's Revolutionary Army ever existed.'[12]

Officially, Kim Il Sung and his merry men fought like tigers against the Japanese from within Korea. In February 1942, the guerrilla band was holed up on the slopes of the sacred Mount Baekdu, on the Chinese/Korean border, when Kim's heavily pregnant wife, Kim Jong Suk, gave birth to a son, Kim Jong Il. The magical birth was heralded by signs in the heavens: a swallow, a double rainbow across the sky over the mountain and a new star in the firmament.

[11] Suh, p52.
[12] Lankov: *From Stalin to Kim Il Sung*, p52.

The official story is rubbish. By 1940, the Korean resistance in Manchuria was pretty much broken. In December 1940, Kim and his gang fled across the Amur river to the safety of the Soviet Union.[13] There, they camped out the rest of the war in the garrison town of Khabarovsk. Buzo writes that Kim Il Sung's exposure to Stalinism happened at a pivotal time in his life, that it was his only positive experience of the outside world. Stalin's portrait hung in every railway station, for example. Kim Il Sung liked what he saw, and he wanted it for himself.

Buzo makes a subtle point about Stalinism, that, as well as being about a command economy, the drive for heavy industry and the personality cult, it 'embodied the traditionalism of old Russia', borrowing enlightenment, if that is the right word, from the likes of Ivan the Terrible.[14] Kim's version was never just Stalinism, pure and simple, but a blend of that and ultra-traditionalism. The Israeli sociologist Shmuel Eisenstadt defined key elements of that as: 'legitimation of the ruler in religious terms; the political role of the population embedded in their societal roles; limitation on the access of members of peripheral groups to the political centre', and limitation of innovation.[15]

Buzo, who sticks the boot into Kim Il Sung the hardest, defines the regime's ideology as Kimism: a blend of Korean ultra-traditionalism, Stalinism and the criminality learnt when he was a guerrilla. That seems to be a fair assessment, and not so far from Myers' sense of the regime's ideology in the twenty-first century as being a xenophobic racism.

It was in Khabarovsk in 1941, according to reliable Soviet and

[13] Lankov, p55.
[14] Buzo, p45.
[15] Shmuel Eisenstadt, *Daedalus*, vol. 102, no.1, pp1–28.

Korean sources, that Kim Il Sung and his wife, Kim Jong Suk, had a baby boy, known in Russian as Yura and in Korean as Jong Il. Kim Jong Suk, known in Russian as Vera, was described as being an attractive and smart peasant woman, with noticeably darker skin than other Koreans – a feature she passed on to her son, Kim Jong Il.

The power that eventually broke Japanese imperialism was neither Korean, Chinese nor Soviet. The American dropping of atomic bombs on Nagasaki and Hiroshima ended the second world war, but came so fast that it caught the great powers unawares. Military facts on the ground and negotiations between Stalin, Truman and Churchill at Potsdam had divided up Europe into Western- and Eastern-controlled halves, but the division of Korea happened on the hoof. Two American colonels in the War Department – one of them Dean Rusk, subsequently a secretary of state under JFK and LBJ – studied a map, drew a line along the 38th parallel, and took over the South. They appointed an aged nationalist, Syngman Rhee, to run things south of the border. The Republic of Korea – ROK – the state Syngman Rhee created, was, to begin with, not much different from Franco's Spain: neo-fascist and profoundly undemocratic, where enemies got tortured or murdered. But in 1987 civilian rule replaced the military there and from then on it has gone from strength to strength.

For Koreans, the division was brutal, uncalled for and undeserved. The schizophrenia between the South and the North had no Korean origin, but was a consequence of the new Cold War game. In time in Korea, the war would blow hot. What many Koreans feel is so unfair about their divided country is that Nazi Germany was broken into two because of Hitler's folly. The Koreans had been the victims of fascist aggression by Japan, but they, too, suffered division, which is continuing into the twenty-first century, two decades after the fall of the Berlin Wall.

But who was to be the face of the North? In 1945, Mao and the People's Revolutionary Army were still fighting the Kuomintang, the inept, corrupt Chinese conservatives; the Communists who were calling all the shots were based in Moscow, not Beijing. To begin with, the Soviets ran North Korea pretty much as the Japanese had, as a colony, to be looted, the women raped, ordinary civilians walking along the road 'bumped' out of the way by drivers in their jeeps.[16] For the first three years, the supreme ruler of North Korea, according to Lankov, was General Terentii Fomich Shtykov, a political commissar who, in 1938, had presided over a committee investigating 'counter-revolutionary crimes'. In plain English, he was one of Stalin's most trusted mass-murderers.[17] But Stalin's men knew that naked Soviet power could not last for long.

They needed a front man, someone they could use, but not so strong that they could not control him. To be the leader of the other, northern Korea, the Soviets looked around and could find no one who was perfect. The Korean Communists who had survived the Japanese occupation in Seoul and Pyongyang were discounted as being unreliable. The obvious candidate was Cho Man Sik, Korea's version of Mahatma Gandhi, who had preached non-violent resistance against the Japanese, but now that they were gone wanted independence immediately. The more the Soviets studied Cho, the less suitable he became. And then they remembered Kim Il Sung, tucked away in their back pocket.

---

[16] Breen, p20.
[17] Lankov, *From Stalin to Kim Il Sung*, p2.

Kim surrounded himself with his old comrades, two hundred former guerrillas who had been with him in Manchuria. But, of course, they had never been the only Koreans to fight the Japanese. Brave Communists had faced torture and death inside Korea; others had fought the Japanese in Manchuria, alongside the Chinese or the Soviets. All of these factions had their leaders, who waited for Kim to make a mistake.

Kim Il Sung did not win power by popular assent. Far from it. He was not well known inside Korea, and overtook other Communist claimants to the throne. But Kim's Soviet backers already had plenty of experience at suppressing dissent. In North Korea, they rolled up opponents, gagged free speech, strangled free political parties at birth, rigged elections – and anyone who disagreed was entertained by the secret police. The job of suppression was markedly easier than in eastern Europe, because there had been no tradition whatsoever of free speech, parliamentary democracy or free newspapers. North Korea slipped from colonial occupation to authoritarian dictatorship relatively smoothly. Despotism was some way off yet.

The Soviets presented their new man to the people of Pyongyang at a mass rally in October 1945. Photographs in which Kim was seen to be sporting a Soviet sash were later airbrushed by North Korean propaganda, so as to remove the taint of him being a Soviet puppet – but that's exactly what he was. Kim read out his prepared speech in his halting, thick-tongued Korean; some thought that this young man could not possibly be the famous guerrilla leader Kim Il Sung, and the myth of the Man in the Iron Mask had begun. Kim was a young-looking thirty-three-year-old in a blue suit that was too tight for him. Cho's personal secretary, clearly a hostile witness, said he sported 'a haircut like a

Chinese waiter'[18] and made little impact on the crowd, speaking in a 'monotonous, plain and duck-like voice'.[19] Another witness to the events in that year said that Kim reminded him of a 'fat delivery boy'.[20] Some people in the 300,000 crowd started to whistle and yell abuse. It wasn't a perfect reception, but if you've got the secret police on your side, that doesn't matter.

Cho, Korea's Mahatma Gandhi, was leaned on to support the Soviet fiction of 'trusteeship' – a shadow policy he recognized and rejected as effective colonization. Elbowed out of power, Cho was humiliated, then arrested by Soviet police and held in the Koryo Hotel for a time while they hoped he would become more accommodating to Soviet policy. He was accused of 'secret co-operation with the Japanese police' – but no evidence was put forward. This seems like a black lie. He did not bend, so his hotel room was downgraded to a prison cell and then he vanished. It's most likely that in October 1950, when the civil war was going badly, with United Nations troops pushing north, and Pyongyang was evacuated, Cho was shot in the traditional Stalinist fashion, with 9 grams of lead to the back of the head.[21]

[18] Martin, p53.
[19] Buzo, p251.
[20] Andrei Lankov: *The Real North Korea*, Oxford University Press, Oxford, 2013, p4.
[21] Lankov, *From Stalin to Kim Il Sung*, p24.

4

'No photos, no photos'

After breakfast we left the hot spa hotel and headed to the West Sea Barrage, celebrated in the following poem:

> O shine for all centuries to come;
> Great monument of the 80s built
> By our design, our technique, our strength;
> The great creation made in our own way.
> Only a great leader
> A great party can conceive the idea.
> Only a great people can build you
> West Sea Barrage, the world's greatest.
> Rise high to symbolize the power of self-reliant Korea
> And tell and retell the everlasting achievement
> Of our Great Leader
> Forever and ever and ever.

Shoot the poet. The West Sea Barrage is an aquatic Stalinist folly. It cost $4 billion, larger in scale but no different in kind than my hotel door not fitting its frame. The dream was that by build-ing a barrage five miles across the Taedong estuary where it flowed into the West or Yellow Sea, they would make more arable land, conserve more fresh water for irrigation and have a road and rail bridge to boot. On the day we visited, halfway across the thin thread of concrete rippling across the surface of the sea, our coach came to a stop. An ancient lorry slowly reversed, then tipped its cargo of enormous rocks into the waters. Mother Nature is gobbling up the barrage, and the dream is in danger of falling back into the sea. Behold, Kim Il Sung was no less silly than King Canute, when he commanded the sea to obey him . . .

At a morose visitor centre, adorned with the usual what-nottery of photographs and tributes to Kims One and Two, we were invited to sit down and watch a movie. It turned out to be a comic masterpiece. The film opens with footage in black and white, the pictures juddery, of a long shot from a crane, of worker-ants beavering away on the causeway; flags rippling in the breeze; two big lorries dumping rocks into the sea. A commander with a chunky walkie-talkie gives orders to two flunkies, who shiver in the cold; rocks slide into the sea with an almighty splash. The film switches to colour and three red bulldozers moving like synchron-ized swimmers in too-perfect unison shove soil into the great splashes, all to a rousing-ish soundtrack of plinkety-plonk music. The finale is a cheesy colour snap of Bad Elvis grinning at the camera, in the foreground cherry blossom; in the background the estuary sliced in two by the ribbon of concrete. The film, especially the early sequences, looked so ancient I assumed the dam had been built in the 1950s, and only when writing this book did I realize that it was started in 1981 and completed five years later.

I tried to ask some boring questions about the barrage, but got nowhere and gave up. As ever in North Korea, it's virtually impossible to get at the facts, but there are concerns that, far from adding to arable land, the dammed river has backed up upstream, losing land. As at the Three Prongs, the Mausoleum and No Animal Farm, by osmosis one sensed our hosts would have appreciated a more positive response from us; I felt like a truculent spotty Herbert teenager in a sulk. Yet the dam was falling apart, and it was hard to see any real benefit it had made for ordinary people. The force of the regime's propaganda was beginning to have entirely the opposite effect on us: the louder the taped soundtrack of praise for the regime, the more hollow the reality.

Along the road out of the barrage, we saw our very first disabled North Korean. He was a young man on crutches, who looked as though he might have fallen off a motorbike. The lack of disabled people in a poor nation is one of those peculiar absences that make one feel uneasy about North Korea. All societies have disabled people, poor ones especially so. If they have vanished off the face of the earth, somebody powerful has made that happen.

Our next destination was the Daean Heavy Machine Complex, a vast industrial eyesore with an enormous smokestack dominating the surrounding area. Roadworks meant we could not take the direct route to the plant, so our coach was forced to make a long detour into the local town, cross a river, and then go back to the complex. This turned out to be bad news for our minders, because on the long way round we ended up seeing all sorts of things they did not want us to see. No smoke emerged from the chimney of the complex. It was hard to be definitive from the moving coach, but it looked as though the main building was a ruin, empty sockets where there should have been windows and walls.

Although out of the capital, we were in the Pyongyang corridor, very much the richest area of the country. Some analysts say that North Korean heavy industry is now working at only one fifth of its previous capacity in the 1980s. From what we saw with our own eyes in this complex, it was five fifths dead. Up in the north-eastern city of Chongjin, previously known as the City of Iron, one reporter described the industrial zone as a 'forest of scrap metal'.[1]

Our coach slowed to a crawl, picking its way along a heavily rutted road, running parallel with a river. The more we saw, the worse it got. Out in the sticks, away from the capital and the tourist-friendly roads, there was real poverty on view: raw and mean and not to be photographed. Underneath a lengthy banner proclaiming: 'Everyone must strive towards making a better life for the people and to build a strong and prosperous nation', a woman dragged an immense bundle of clothes behind her on a tiny trolley, a boy walking by her side. Out our cameras came; Mr Hyun hit the mike: 'Please, do not take photographs.' A woman, squatting by the side of the road, in front of her a small white placard. Was she selling something? Begging? 'No photos, no photos,' commanded Mr Hyun.

In the river, a woman was washing her clothes. You see this all the time in Africa, but there the temperature is warm; it was freezing cold here, and in late March lumps of ice were still to be found in places away from the sun. For a woman to do her daily washing in a freezing river tells you things: that there is no regular supply of running water at her home; no washing machine; no cheap launderette. Further on, on the bank of the riverbed, two women were

[1] Philippe Pons: 'Incursion en Corée du Nord', *Le Monde*, 4 December 2006.

scavenging for something in the mud. 'No photos, no photos,' said Mr Hyun.

Now that we were seeing more of the real North Korea, I felt more irritated that our every movement was choreographed by our minders.

They took us to the Heavy Machine Complex showroom, yet another grandiloquent chunk of concrete hymning public good while ordinary people lived in squalor. At the back of the room was an enormous diptych of Kims Major and Minor standing on a mountain top with wispy clouds caressing their feet, the backdrop dark pink – an exact copy of the portrait of the two Kims in our hotel. Occupying most of the space was a model of the complex, complete with tiny trains and a proud chimney. 'We make heavy electrical power machines,' the local guide, sporting a vivid orange traditional Korean dress, said.

And then the lights went out. In the electricity generating machine factory, no electricity.

She carried on in the gloom while we tittered our disbelief: 'This is embarrassing,' I boomed. Their film of our trip features the complex model in Stygian gloom: clearly the cameraman wasn't shooting in the brief moments before the power outage.

The tragicomedy of North Korean power supply is that there isn't enough home-grown energy in the country to maintain full power; the country does not trade enough to make good the energy deficit through imports; and the demands of the palace are so warped they deprive the rest of the economy of the energy it needs to thrive. That last element was beautifully explained by Hwang Jang Yop, the highest-level defector ever. Hwang, who fled in 1997, recalled a revealing moment at the Party's Central Committee meeting. After a series of blackouts in Pyongyang – Hwang isn't clear but most likely back in the 1980s – Kim Il Sung asked the Minister of Electric Power to explain why he had been inconvenienced by brown-outs or decreases in electricity supply when watching movies. The minister stood up to reply: 'Currently, there is not enough electric power to meet the requirements of the factories. Because of the heavy load in transmission to the factories, the voltage of electricity supplied to Pyongyang tends to drop.' Kim One replied: 'Then why can't you adjust the power supply transmitted to factories and allocate more to Pyongyang?' The minister explained: 'That would stop operations in a lot of factories.' Kim cut him off and ordered: 'I don't care if all the factories in the country stop production. Just send enough electricity to Pyongyang.'[2]

On our visit, the only place where warmth and light seemed guaranteed was the Mausoleum – an absurd distortion of priorities which would never happen in a functioning democracy. The brown-outs and power cuts always led to a muffled cheer or sardonic grins on our trip: proof positive that the regime's propaganda was dross. But it speaks a deeper truth about the abject failure of a command economy to deliver economic satisfaction to the greatest number.

Hwang set out the fabulous bureaucratic merry-go-round under Kim Jong Il when rival bits of the state wanted their lights on and there wasn't enough power to go around. The defector wrote that in 1996, North Korea produced 2 million kilowatts of electricity, only a fifth of what was required. Back then, there were 15,000 factories needing 10 million KW. Of the 2 million KW available,

[2] Hwang Jang Yop: 'The Problems of Human Rights in North Korea', http://www.dailynk.com/english/keys/2002/8/04.php

0.8 million was needed for vital facilities where the power supply could not be cut. Wastage through faulty and ancient wiring burnt up 0.2 million KW en route, leaving only 1 million KW. This dire shortage of electricity meant that the key government agencies – one would assume the secret police, the army and the Party – went directly to Kim Jong Il, without going through the cabinet or the National Planning Committee, to ask for priority in power supply. Their requests were sanctioned by Kim Jong Il and his word was law. The agencies took Kim Two's orders to the Ministry of Electric Power and demanded that they be given top priority in electricity supply. The ministry could not meet Kim Jong Il's orders. Instead, it went back to the Dear Leader, telling him that there was nothing the ministry could do. 'Kim Jong Il,' wrote Hwang, 'handed the appeal to the secretaries in the Party central committee and gave them the task of resolving the problem through discussions.'[3]

Not for nothing does former British ambassador John Everard compare the North Korean regime to Kafka as performed by Dad's Army.

We asked for a tour of the Heavy Machine Complex. In the unlit gloom, Miss Jun heroically translated for the local guide: 'Now the Korea peninsula situation is getting worse and worse, on the verge of civil war. So now they're producing military things, so they can't show the whole factory.' This may have been true. Most defectors say that all the military factories are in the mountains. To us, it seemed a pitiful excuse, like telling the schoolteacher: 'I'm sorry, sir, but the dog ate my Juche homework.'

[3] Hwang Jang Yop, 'Problems of Human Rights', http://www.dailynk.com/english/keys/2002/8/04.php

What kind of industrial complex is it that has no smoke, no power and no noise? In the early 1980s I worked on the *Sheffield Telegraph*, before the high-volume steel industry died, and many a night I went to sleep listening to the rhythmic banging from the steel mills. The Daean complex was silent. No sound of any work being done.

In the blackout, the male toilets were impenetrable, so we pissed outside. The manufacture of urine was the only product of the Daean Heavy Machine Complex that day. Our route back to Pyongyang took us through the poor area of Daean town again. An ox pulled a meagre cart, old people moved hither and yon, seemingly without purpose, a man pulled a hand-cart, his breath ballooning out as the temperature dropped below freezing. The poverty of wealth and soul was grinding, and grindingly obvious. Mr Hyun and Miss Jun were even more on their guard. 'No photos, no photos,' they cried out, as joylessly as the scene in *Monty Python and the Holy Grail* when they call out: 'Bring out your dead.'

John Everard suffered from this censor complex so much he called his book *Only Beautiful, Please*. He recalls that the security forces did not follow him and his staff everywhere, because North Koreans policed them well enough.

> The moment the foreigner did anything upsetting a crowd formed and the security forces appeared quickly. The most common trigger for this was illicit photography. Koreans are very conscious of their country's image and any attempt to photograph any aspect of their country that was less than flattering of their country angered them. A Korean People's Army officer, proud of his English, once explained the rule to me as 'Only beautiful, please.'[4]

[4] Everard, p131.

Is this a display of patriotism? Or is this regime brainwashing at work, so deep in people's minds that even foreigners must conform at the national lie factory?

At a bridge over a river, we had to stop because our coach was too high to pass underneath a pole stretched across the road for some reason. Our driver got out to have a row with whoever was manning the checkpoint. A lorry full of hay overtook, but riding on top of the load was a man, who would surely come a cropper. As the lorry got up to the pole he stood up and nimbly jumped over it, and landed back safely on the hay, and the lorry sped on, into the dusk.

It was as nimbly executed as the Buster Keaton stunt when the front of a house falls on top of him and he emerges, unscathed, through a window. A light, silly moment, but also proof that these people, under another system, might be bright and fun and full of life. But of that, in the Daean Heavy Machine Complex, we saw no sign.

5

Jimmy the Gold-Smuggler

Alejandro Cao de Benós's website sings the praises of the 'Juche-oriented socialist state which embodies the idea and leadership of Comrade Kim Il Sung, the founder of the Republic and the father of socialist Korea' on one page, and the joys of doing capitalist business in North Korea on another.[1] The Hermit Kingdom, says Cao de Benós, will become the most important trading hub in North-East Asia in the next few years, boasting the lowest labour costs in Asia and workers who show the utmost loyalty: 'As opposed to other Asian countries, workers will not abandon their positions for higher salaries once they are trained.' That might be, perhaps, because they and their families could be sent to the gulag for three generations if they do. On and on Cao de Benós goes: 'Lowest taxes scheme in Asia ... A government with solid security and very stable political system, without corruption ... Transparent legal work.'

[1] Alejandro Cao de Benós's website is available here: http://www.korea-dpr.com/business.html

None of that is true.

In the Big Zombie we endured a surreal and surreally boring meeting with three North Koreans who were selling the idea of business opportunities in the country. A PowerPoint presentation followed, with Venn diagrams sporting gnomically entitled spheres such as 'Economic Investment' and 'Joint Venture Committee'. Business gibberish had arrived in Pyongyang, big-time. I didn't want to bring attention to myself, because the entrepreneurs had email and, therefore, either in Pyongyang or more likely in Beijing, access to the internet. They were clearly in the elite of the core class, especially licensed by the regime to come and go at will. Remember, there are only two flights between Beijing and Pyongyang a week, so this licence covers just a few thousand people. All of them will have family in North Korea; all of them know that if they defect, their family will suffer, horribly.

But I couldn't quite forget the sight of the poor North Korean woman doing her washing in the freezing river, so I put up my hand and asked: 'Why would anyone invest in a country if its leader is threatening thermo-nuclear war against the United States?'

Silence followed.

After a long pause, someone mumbled something about not being involved in politics – a statement that doesn't quite wash inside the world's most totalitarian regime – and the meeting droned on.

Leaving aside the threat of Armageddon, North Korea ought to be a smashing investment opportunity for the more icy-hearted capitalist. In 2007 a worker's monthly wage in the comparatively wealthy region around Pyongyang was estimated at around £40

($60, €50), before tax.[2] If you can get away with paying your work-force £1.50 a day, then why isn't everyone piling in?

The downside – apart from the government being as crazy as a box of frogs – is that everything else doesn't work or costs an arm and a leg. The power supply is a joke. We experienced at least one power cut every day we were in North Korea, some days more than one. The railway system is largely electrified, so delays of several days come as standard. As far as shipping goes, the West Sea Barrage restricts ships to 50,000 tonnage – pitifully small in today's world – and the locks can only handle one ship a day. Worse, the docks are comically old-fashioned and controlled by the military, who charge extortionate rates. For example, one container shipped from the South Korean port of Incheon to Nampo costs $US1,000, almost as much as a journey to Europe. The round trip takes twenty-four hours for a journey of only 60 miles.[3] That means business investors have to fork out enormous sums on simple logistics, so the vast majority don't bother.

Despite all this, I did meet one North Korean entrepreneur, but not in North Korea.

Meet Jimmy the Gold-Smuggler. He's a tiny chap, only 5 foot 2 inches tall, but he carries with him his own personal high voltage charge. Jimmy – not his real name – is lithe and vivid and, as the North Korean regime found out to their cost, as hard to control as an electric eel. He was the runt of the litter, far smaller than his two brothers who ended up in the army. When he was

---

[2] Stanislas Roussin and César Ducruet: 'The Nampo-Pyongyang corridor: A strategic area for European investment in DPRK', Seoul National University, 2007.

[3] Ahn Mi-Young: 'Slow boat to North Korea', *Cargo News Asia*, 7 May 2001, http://cargonewsasia.com/timesnet/data/cna/docs/cna6106.html

little, his big brothers would save his bacon when he got into a scrap. His family were ordinary folk, his father a factory worker off sick because of bronchitis, his mother working on a farm, but they were doing better than most because the two oldest sons were in the army. They were not rebels, but regime conformists, who did their best to stay alive while doing pretty much exactly what they were told. Jimmy was the black sheep.

The family lived in the forgotten far north-east corner of Korea in the town of Saebyol in North Hamgyong province, only an hour's walk from China. The border is formed by the Tumen river running down from its source, the sacred Mount Baekdu – where regime legend has it that Kim Jong Il was born – to the East Sea or Sea of Japan. Up in the hills, the Tumen divides China and North Korea and then close to the sea forms the border between North Korea and Russia for its last 11 miles. The Russian name of the river is Tumannaya, which means foggy. In the dead of winter, the surface of the river freezes over, making it so easy to cross all you have to do is run. In the late autumn and early spring, the ice is weak, and great care must be taken because the current is strong and drowning a serious possibility.

Jimmy had a friend, let's call him Mark, a smuggler who was making a small fortune bringing in second-hand clothes from China. Around 1997, when the famine was at its height, Mark told Jimmy that North Korea was much poorer than China. The famine had shattered much of Jimmy's belief in the system. He'd seen dead babies, dead old people, dead middle-aged people lying slumped in the street, at railway stations or just by the doorstep of their homes. Never many bodies in one place, he said, just one or two.

At fifteen, Jimmy got the itch to travel and one moonless night in late November, around two o'clock in the morning, when the guards were, he hoped, asleep, he found himself face-down, crawling across ice not even as thick as your finger, the only sounds the creaking of the ice as it took his weight and the barking of dogs from China. The Tumen here, far away from the sea, was around 100 metres across, and most of the surface was hard ice. But the middle section, around 10 metres across, was perilously thin. Jimmy described a trick the smugglers used: they took two sticks, maybe 5 feet long each, and crawled forward, one in each hand, using them to spread their weight and get some traction on the ice. One stick at a time, Jimmy crawled on. To be fair, at 5 foot 2 and not an ounce of fat on him, he would stand a far better chance at crossing thin ice than you or I.

He made it. On the other side, Jimmy gorged himself with five or six bowls of white rice at one sitting. Everything Mark had told him about China turned out to be true: the food was abundant, you could eat meat and white rice every day, luxuries you only had on feast days back home, the electricity worked, you could watch whatever you wanted on telly, you could go to karaoke bars and party all night long.

Jimmy returned with 40 kilos of second-hand clothes on his back – the bag he used was the same size as he was. They smuggled second-hand 'sports clothes', T-shirts, trousers – they were not allowed to wear jeans in North Korea then – into the North. Jimmy reckoned that, if the average wage was 500 won a month, he made around 2,000 won, worth roughly £200 ($170), around four months' pay in one run across the border. He could have been shot by the border guards or captured and then executed, but he loved the buzz.

He did his best to keep his family in the dark about what he was up to. But the regime's spell over him was entirely broken. Jimmy was determined to go back, and did so, again and again. Each trip, his profits grew. And then, trouble. He was on the Chinese side of the river, working his way from village to village, trying to keep away from the Chinese border guards and the police until he could get to the town where he could get hold of more second-hand clothes, when he was caught. He spent a week in a police cell in China. They fed him properly, three times a day, and then he was sent back to North Korea. He was only sixteen, and categorized as a simple 'border-crosser', not a political defector, and after a roughish time, they let him go.

His family were angry with him, and they beat him up a little, but that didn't dent his conviction that there was something profoundly wrong about North Korea. Pretty soon he was on his way back into China. Not long after, Jimmy realized that smuggling second-hand clothes from China to North Korea was never going to make him a rich man. Instead, he switched to smuggling a commodity out of North Korea, where there were no real markets, into China. That commodity was gold. Jimmy explained that in the north of North Korea there was plenty of gold. Miners would sell you nuggets for a fraction of the price he could obtain in China; if you looked in the right place, you could find some yourself, just lying in streams or on the surface of the earth. His trade built up, he got to know 'fences' on the Chinese side who would give him a good price for his gold. He also realized that with gold – far less bulky than second-hand clothes – he could swim across the river when it wasn't frozen, tripling his potential profits. Boats were never an option. They would be spotted by the border guards and destroyed. The more often he crossed the border, the richer he became. His biggest shipment had been 900 grams of raw gold nuggets worth around 150,000 won (£15,000, $17,000) and every-thing worked brilliantly. And then he got too greedy.

Inside North Korea, someone betrayed him, and he was trapped by the police and caught with his biggest cache of gold yet: 3 kilos, worth 500,000 won (£50,000, $65,000). Had he been eighteen when he was arrested with 3 kilos of North Korean gold, he would have been executed, he said, but because he was a minor he just got fifteen years in prison, hard labour.

He ended up in Prison Camp 12, also known as the Chongori Re-Education Centre. His camp was for common criminals, not part of the political gulag. But conditions sound grim. Everyone who enters the camp is greeted by a big black metal gate, and when it opens up a big sign behind it says, 'Escape is suicide!'

Jimmy admitted he had a hard time, but back then, around the turn of the millennium, Prison Camp 12 was not one of those nightmare camps you hear about where guards kill people for fun. People, he said, just died from malnutrition. He was hungry for a whole year. They gave the prisoners three thimbles of corn a day or some salty soup, sometimes with bits of cabbage. The food was so bad that even a pig would have turned his nose up. If anyone managed to catch a rat, they were the luckiest person alive because it was at least meat. Some people ate grass, others bits of corn in cowshit.

His mother got him out after a year, bribing the doctors and the guards, claiming he had tuberculosis. It cost his mum around £400, a king's ransom in North Korea. The authorities are nervous of anyone with TB. With a prison population on the edge of starvation, dozens can die with one outbreak, and that can be bad for production targets. Corruption has grown more common, by all accounts, since the famine. Money can only buy so much: if someone is in serious trouble with the Bowibu, then no amount of money can save them.

Since Jimmy was banged up inside Prison Camp 12 – around the year 2000 – conditions have reportedly got far worse. It's become the main prison camp for would-be 'border-crossers', people who jump the border to make money, not necessarily to defect for good. But since the famine, when everything went to pot, crossing the border has been treated more severely. The One Free Korea website reports hard labour is much heavier at Prison Camp 12 than at other ordinary re-education centres, and torture and beatings are routine. The website says that anybody who has crossed the border is automatically sentenced to up to three years of forced labour at Prison Camp 12, under instructions that they are to be punished as traitors. This marks a change from Jimmy's period of captivity, when 'simple defectors' – not gold-smugglers – got a few months in prison and then were freed.

One defector who had a hair's-breadth escape from Prison Camp 12 said: 'Chongori is a living hell. Yodok [the notorious Camp 15] is a much better place.' If the physical beatings don't finish them off, inmates of Prison Camp 12 are doomed to die of malnutrition.[4]

The website's information squares with the general clamp-down against defectors running to China, which has taken place in the last five years. Similarly, numbers of successful defections to South Korea have fallen by half. It fits that the authorities are not just stepping up border patrols, but making life far tougher on those who try to defect.

Another inmate of Prison Camp 12, Lee Jun Ha, wrote a diary

[4] http://freekorea.us/camps/12-2/#sthash.lZfwljB1.dpuf

of his experience, published by the Daily NK website.⁵ It's a haunt-ing read, and it backs up details of Jimmy's story. Lee recalled that, when he entered the camp, he saw a large metal entrance gate: 'To the right, written in large black letters were two frightening warn-ings: "Those caught trying to escape will be shot!" and "Escape is suicide!"'

Lee continued: 'Off to the left I saw a group of inmates with sanitation tags on their arms haphazardly loading logs on to a big truck labelled "Independence #82". Or I thought they were logs, anyway. As I looked closer I realized they were corpses. My heart rose into my throat and I went stiff. Only one thought came to me, "I'm a dead man."'

Jimmy's 'sick letter' trick only worked for a while, though. After a spell, the authorities want you back in prison. To deal with that problem, Jimmy went on the run, and while on the run it made sense to get back to the only job he knew well: smuggling gold to China. He got caught three times, and he managed to escape three times.

The first time, he was fingered by someone in China. The military caught him but it was too late at night to take him to a proper cell, so one of the soldiers handcuffed him to the post of a bunk bed and then crashed out, fast asleep. Using the skills he learnt as a key-cutter in Prison Camp 12, Jimmy unpicked the lock of the handcuffs and was out of the barracks before you could say 'Kim Jong Il'. The second time he got nicked was in North Korea. He was locked in an office with iron bars over the windows, while

⁵ Lee Jun Ha's Prison Tales: 'The Humiliation and the Sadness', Daily NK website, 16 September 2009, http://www.dailynk.com/english/read.php?cataId=nk02800&num=5031

the authorities went looking for further evidence against him. While they were away, he used a poker from the fireplace stove to jemmy open the bars of the windows and – remember he is the smallest fully grown man I've ever met – wriggled out through the gap to freedom. The third time was the most unlucky. He got caught close to his home town, and that made everything more difficult. Elsewhere in North Korea he could grease palms, but in his home area the authorities knew he had previous. Execution or an eternity in Prison Camp 12 were the only options. He'd been locked in a room. There was no way out. Or so he thought, at first. He studied the doorframe and noticed there was a significant gap between it and the door. Through that gap he realized that the door was not properly locked but held on a latch. He searched the room and found a length of wire – and he was out.

The risks of continuing the smuggling lark were just too great. By this time he'd met and fallen in love with a woman who had become his wife, let's call her Grace. She was reluctant to leave, being, he explained, much more brainwashed than he was, but she didn't want to split with him, so the two of them dared to try and make it across to China, one last time.

It was March 2003, and the once-frozen river had thawed since the winter, although chunks of ice as big as boulders still flowed downstream. Grace was very scared, so to reduce her distress he swam across the river carrying her on his shoulders. It was an extraordinary feat, because the river at that crossing point was 120 metres wide, the water freezing and he is such a tiny man. Once on the Chinese bank, he collapsed and passed out for an hour.

Although Jimmy had known what life was like outside the North, for Grace it was a great shock, and after a few days she wanted to go back, even though she could see life was better in

China. He won the argument, knowing that to go back would mean certain death. Jimmy had saved up a lot of money and he had plenty of contacts in China, so within twenty days he and Grace managed to get to Vietnam, where they waited three months for an opportunity to be sent to South Korea, and then spent another three months in an immigration centre. Once there, the terror of being caught and sent back was gone, and Grace settled into her new life well.

After working a couple of years in South Korea, he was the victim of a confidence trickster and lost a lot of his money. It broke his confidence because he didn't know that conmen would take advantage of people like him. Upset and at a loss, a relative suggested that he and Grace come to Britain.

The Gold-Smuggler turned Harry Houdini of North Korea now makes his living as a fishmonger in New Malden, in south-west London, just off the A3.

Jimmy's thrived in Britain, and is making so much money that he can afford to send back £1,000 every six months or so. He wires the money to a broker in China, who takes a cut. The cash, most commonly in Chinese yuan, is smuggled across the river to another broker on the North Korean side. The smuggling is often done by border guards, the brokers their relatives or friends. The brokers, Chinese and North Korean, together take a slice of around 30 per cent, so Jimmy's mum ends up with £700 – not bad for the black sheep of the family. They live so close to the border that she has a Chinese phone. She rings once, and he phones her back. They talk on the phone to make sure that the money has come, that they haven't been cheated, and chat about simple, family things. They last spoke two months before we met. Kwon, my translator, had his computer out and together we looked at his old home town on

Google Earth. The sight of it made him homesick. He'd go back tomorrow, if they would let him do so in peace. Which, of course, they won't. When he sees North Koreans weeping over Kim Jong Un on the television, he thinks they are stupid and naive. I asked him whether he thought the tears of joy were genuine. He said yes, because they have only ever lived inside the North Korean bubble. On Kim Three, Jimmy said that he hoped he dies, either the West knock him down or someone inside the North overthrows him, the quicker, the better. And at that, rebellious as ever, he broke into a grin.

6

Pyongyang Zoo

In 1991, Osijek in old Yugoslavia – new Croatia – was full of blood. One day photographer Paul Jenks and I walked in the back door of the town's hospital, because the Serbs were raining down artillery shells on the main entrance, and found ourselves in the morgue. No power, not much light. Flies gorged themselves on the blood of twenty dead men, their ribcages zipped wide open for post-mortem, like so many blood-pink human butterfly wings.

Sick of the killing, we went to the zoo, empty of people but still full of animals. The front line was the wild goat enclosure. Paul and I convinced Rose, an impossibly sexy zookeeper-cum-warrior, to feed the animals. I still have Paul's picture of Rose feeding a giraffe a biscuit, her Kalashnikov on her shoulder. The war between Serbs and Croats stopped, but a few days later Paul was shot dead in strange circumstances.[1] Three years on, I returned to

---

[1] *Dying For The Truth*, Hardcash Films, 1994, tells the story of Eduardo Rozsa Flores, the man who most likely ordered the killing of Paul Jenks. Flores was himself gunned down in Bolivia in 2009.

Osijek, to investigate who had killed Paul, and I went back to the zoo. It was snowing, and the zoo looked entirely empty. Then, hopping into vision, came a crowd of wallabies. It was a magical moment. Since then, in times of war or places ruled by fear, I go to the zoo.

Baghdad Zoo in Saddam's time was one of the most melancholy places I've ever been to: the animals mangy, the creatures' loss of liberty no different from the humans'. There was even a photo-graph of Saddam in the aquarium, so the guppy could pay homage to the big man with the moustache. But even there in Baghdad Zoo under Saddam, I didn't have a minder who followed me around from cage to cage. At Pyongyang Zoo we had three: Mr Hyun, Miss Jun and a new local guide, who spoke a smattering of English and greeted us at the entrance.

Zoos, I know, are not good because they restrict animal freedom. But in many parts of the world, free-moving, free-living animals get shot for their ivory, their skin or their meat, or because they are in the wrong place, and I fear that my grandchildren's generation will only know the great animals through trips to the zoo, or places like them. And there is the fascinating anthropology of the zoo: looking at them looking at us. My addiction to zoos is partly because they remind me of the time when my children were little and every moment with a five-year-old staring at a gorilla picking its bottom is full of low comedy; partly because, brilliant as David Attenborough's natural history documentaries are, you can't smell an elephant on the telly; and partly because zoos are No Man's Land, where people can think about what makes us human and them animal, and what combines all of us living creatures, where politics stops.

But not, of course, in Pyongyang.

Somewhere around were a brace of chimps presented by General Suharto of Indonesia, and a warthog, a gift from Robert Mugabe. Hitchens tells the story of a friend who goes to Pyongyang Zoo and finds the animals half starved, stunted. He inspects a parrot, who looks at him with a beady eye.[2] He looks back, morose. And after a short interval the parrot opens its beak and says: 'Long live the Great Leader Kim Il Sung.'

Our tour started with homage to Kims, Major and Minor. The local guide, dressed in hunting pink, told us how the zoo had been built thanks to the wise and inspired guidance of Kim Il Sung and Kim Jong Il. After a while you zone out. The praise to the Great Leader and the Dear Leader slides over the surface of the mind like those darker globules of vinegar slide among the olive oil in fancy restaurants. Something like this must happen inside the minds of the North Koreans too. You listen to it, but your thoughts are elsewhere.

The aquarium came first: dimly lit pools of green, mouths opening and closing behind thick walls of glass. Sturgeon, big mothers gulping at not very much, then Siamese sharks, who are not proper sharks but fish, box jaws, big fins, nasty teeth, piggy-eyed, and some of the ugliest creatures I've ever seen. The tour cameraman has a nice shot of Alex filming them. I was keen, no, impatient to get to the elephants.[3]

Marching along we saw a bunch of soldiers digging a great hole in the earth by hand, their earthworks planted with nine red and blue Korean flags. Coming the other way were two old men

[2] Hitchens on North Korea: at 6.00 in http://www.youtube.com/watch?v=P8-Vr_r36Fg

[3] I like 'nature's great masterpiece', as John Donne described the elephant, so much I've written a novel about them called *Elephant Moon*.

carrying immense bundles on their backs – fodder for the elephants? Chickens for the lions? Anywhere else in the world, zoo staff would move supplies around on little electric trucks. In North Korea, the trucks have human axles.

Miss Jun wanted to slow me down: 'Professah! Professah! Not so fast.' I liked her, but the lack of freedom to go for a walk on your own, the inability to escape made my teeth grind. One felt infantilized.

The big cats lived in a terrace of iron cages. A lion trotted up and down his scruffy patch of concrete morosely, but he was trumped by a magnificent white Siberian tiger, lean and mean in a cage constructed of criss-crossed wire that didn't look that strong.

'I've never seen one before. In this respect,' I told Miss Jun, 'North Korea is superior to Britain.'

'DPRK,' whispered Miss Jun. The regime hates being reminded that it is one of two geographical halves, and both Miss Jun and Mr Hyun would always correct us if we used the phrase 'North Korea'.

Alex was filming us. 'Could we feed one of the students, maybe Alex, to the tiger?' I suggested. 'Alex, I think it would be a useful sacrifice.'

Tyger, tyger, burning bright, smacked his chops and looked like he fancied a bit of Welsh rarebit el Greco. The snack unforthcoming, Tyger washed his whiskers with a great paw, and rolled his back against a spot of concrete warmed in the sun. As we were about to move on, Alex's camera caught a plaque, saying in Korean, then English: 'The animals presented by the Dear Leader Kim Jong Il, on September 22, Juche 99 (2010), Korean Tiger *Panthera Tigris Altaica*.'

Juche 99 is a result of the regime's decision to create a new calendar, with Juche Year Zero starting on 15 April, Anno Domini 1912 – the date on which Kim Il Sung was born. The Juche revolution is so powerful it can turn back time. Or so they would like to have us believe. In Juche Time, 2013 is Year 101. What is striking about every single attempt by an authoritarian state to reset the clock is not success, but failure. The French Revolutionaries did it, renaming 22 September 1793 as the beginning of Year II. The months got new start dates and lovely new poetic names, so that late October, often foggy, became Brumaire – the foggy one – and the next month Frimaire, because it is frosty in late November. Napoleon scrapped the whole thing because it was silly and didn't work. Pol Pot in Cambodia reset his totalitarian clock to Year Zero in 1974. That experiment in blood and time lasted but four years.

The Juche Year Zero, although backdated to 1912, actually commenced operation in 1997 after a governmental decree. On our trip, for all practical purposes, it was never used and very rarely alluded to. Some of the regime's propaganda which used the Western calendar before 1997 has been cast in bronze or stone or even chiselled into high peaks up in the mountains. Take, for example, the dates on the Arc de Triomphe lookalike in down-town Pyongyang. On one leg of the arch is written '1925', 'the year in which Kim Il Sung set out on the road to national liberation', and on the other '1945', commemorating the year of liberation from the Japanese. Surely, these dates should be converted to Juche Time? But would people, especially foreigners, guess the significance of '13' and '32'? Or would worshippers of the Douglas Adams cult believe that '32' was a typo for '42' – the answer to life, the universe and everything?

The cost of airbrushing these dates to the new calendar must be so astronomical no one has bothered. So Juche Time lingers on, an embarrassing experiment in time travel, but not one that bites very hard on ordinary or even official life. Just how long will Juche Time last? Either not a second longer than the regime, or nuclear Armageddon, whichever happens first.

Our tour continued. It turned out that the big cats had a big back garden at the rear of their terrace of cages, and we could look down on them from on top of an elevated concrete walkway. A lion and a tiger were mixed up in the same paddock, but seemed to be getting along nicely. Well, they weren't eating each other. The zoo was turning out to be far more impressive – or, to be exact, far less pitiful – than, say, the Heavy Machine Complex. Perhaps that's because the zoo animals and the children who come to gaze at them are core class; the factory workers not.

The elephant house seemed top notch, the elephants living behind a wall of glass, presumably to keep the heat in during the bitterly cold Korean winters. But the light was natural and beginning to die as dusk approached, so we could only make out some grey myths in the gloom and, closer to us, the unmistakable grassy cannonballs of elephant poo.

At this point it emerged that our local guide in hunting pink had met the new leader, Kim Jong Un. I pronounced it Kim Jong Oon, but Miss Jun corrected me – the Un rhymes with Bun. The zoo guide's face lit up at the very mention of his name. When? On 26 May 2012, a date forever great in her memory. 'It was the happiest moment of her life,' translated Miss Jun. The guide had also met Kim Jong Il, in 2008. Which was her favourite, I asked, a question which caused Miss Jun to gasp. You could see the unease on their faces begin to grow. The local guide replied: 'If you have a daughter and a beautiful wife, which do you love the most?'

I replied: 'I am sorry for my foolish question,' and Miss Jun buckled, laughing with relief. On the other side of the glass, a young Asian elephant tucked into some juicy grass, oblivious to the human follies going on behind him.

The zoo was hardly busy, but there were a good number of schoolchildren around, most of them in fancy-ish Chinese-made puffa jackets. Pyongyang is the home of the elite, who number some 200,000, maybe more. Part of the solidity of the regime is that they know their lives of relative privilege will be over if the dynasty falls. It's different in, say, China, where there is no nation state of 'South China' that will take over the whole shooting match if the Communist Party falls from power. The very success of South Korea means that it is harder for those who have a stake in the regime to welcome change. Change means takeover by South Korea; change means the end of privilege, and perhaps the end of life. So the calculation by members of the outer circle of the elite in Pyongyang is different to that of their counterparts in Baghdad under Saddam or Tripoli under Gaddafi. After Saddam or Gaddafi, the big players would, with a bit of luck, still be big players. If Kim Jong Un falls, then Pyongyang's privileged will end up in a new whole Korea, run by the South, ignorant, backward, poor and utterly discredited. And the consequence of that lack of hope means, thus far, no rebellion.

The snakehouse was the tackiest show in the zoo. In sepulchral light, the snake keeper, an old lady of indeterminate age, dressed shabbily, walked into a large glass box and picked up an enormous Burmese python, caressed it, then shoved its head a few feet from ours, though we were on the other side of the glass. Snakewoman had looked after the snake for thirty years, but last year she also met Kim Jong Un. As the great snake slithered and coiled in front of us, its forked tongue flashing in and out, I asked: 'What did she think of Kim Jong Un?' The coinciding of the question about the young deity with the snake freak show was too much, and the conversational temperature between Miss Jun and me dropped 20 degrees. I changed the subject, fast – 'Is she not afraid of that snake?' – and we moved on to look at the creatures that creepeth upon the face of the earth. As ever, they were ditchwater dull. Lizards flicked their tongues; insects did their insecty thing, the usual.

The plaque outside the snakehouse-cum-aquarium said: 'To the Dear Leader, Comrade Kim Jong Il, by Mr Jonas Wahlstrom, Director of the Skansen Aquarium, Sweden.' I wondered to myself how many creatures in the zoo had perished in the bleak winters during the famine when North Korea could no longer heat or feed or provide power and light to its people. Quite a few, I would imagine. The story goes that even in the Central Committee office in Pyongyang – the dead centre of power for the Korean Workers' Party – the water in the fish tank froze to ice, entombing the goldfish therein.

On we walked around the zoo. No litter underfoot, because there were no kiosks flogging ice cream or sandwiches or coffees. It was forbiddingly tidy. On the way out, our guide opened a door and we were given a special treat. The white tiger was munching his way through a chicken, every bone going down with a sinister crunch.

Our last stop of the day was a bookshop in town. There were countless books by Kim Il Sung and Kim Jong Il; in short, nothing worth buying.

7

The Scariest Place on Earth

Day Four: It's good morning Pyongyang, until we switch on the TV news. A newsreader in Barbara Cartland pink shrieks something in Korean. It doesn't sound like there's been a royal wedding, Kim dynasty style. Her delivery is extraordinary, comic-opera aggressive, to my ear profoundly, almost mockingly, silly. It's only when we get back to London and get the tapes translated that we realize what she's saying. It's not good news:

'The military leadership is announcing from this moment that mainland America, Hawaii, and US military bases in the Pacific rim, South Korea and the surrounding area are being targeted. Our troops and long-range rockets are being prepared for war.'

That very morning we were going into the DMZ, which President Bill Clinton once called 'the scariest place on earth'. The DMZ is certainly the most badly named place on earth, because it bristles with soldiery, landmines, barbed wire and machine-gun nests. From further back, the North Koreans have chemical and nuclear weapons targeted at Seoul, ready to rain down a 'sea of fire'; the South Koreans rely on the American nuclear umbrella.

In the old days, the North Koreans could just have hit Seoul very hard – a tragedy for South Korea, but a local disaster, not a planet-wide one. What is different now in the second decade of the twenty-first century is that North Korea has got serious missiles and nuclear bombs. Some missiles fizzle out and go pop shortly after launch, to the embarrassment of the dynasty and the relief of the rest of the world; but they have succeeded in lobbing a missile over Japan, which fell into the sea on the far side of the island nation. This is very bad news.

North Korean propaganda has put out a graphic of deadly missile fire raining down on Washington DC, Texas, Los Angeles and Hawaii. The voiceover spouts: 'If we compare it to body parts, the Washington missile is to take out the eyes and ears that monitor the world in one strike.'

We didn't see masses of military traffic on the road down to the DMZ; a few lorries and jeeps, that was all. The land is barren, denuded of trees, because they were chopped down for firewood or even, during the famine, for bark to eat. It's the least green countryside I've ever seen outside of the Sahara. Big puddles walled by low cliffs of mud lined the road; in the summer they would be rice paddies; further off, dead fields stretched away to the horizon. It was late March, and there wasn't that much agricultural work being done, but what we could see from our coach was being carried out by hand. Every now and then we would see an ox pulling a plough. Tractors were a rarity. By the side of the road, peasants carried enormous, ballooning bags of firewood or other goods on their back. It was like driving through a film-set for the Middle Ages.

Modernity did intrude, though. On high escarpments we could make out the black fingers of anti-aircraft guns poking at the sky. Every five miles or so, and especially where the highway was channelled between high rocks either side, two twin concrete pillars faced each other, as high as a two-storey house, their bases conspicuously thinner than the bulk of the block. They were tank traps, so constructed that just a small fag packet of TNT would bring the concrete pillars crashing down, blocking the road. The road south to the DMZ is, of course, also the obvious route any invading force would take north. The twin pillars reminded me a little of the Two Kings in the *Lord of the Rings* film trilogy, warning travellers to turn back, before it was too late. We pressed on.

The coach slowed to a stop at a checkpoint. Generally, our coach would whizz through any official stop point, while ordinary folk had to go through the hoops, but today things seemed a little edgier. The checkpoints weren't much: a concrete booth at the side of the road, a chain across the tarmac; in one case, just a line of small rocks. Mr Hyun called out: 'No photos, no photos.' The soldiers at the checkpoints seemed jumpy, and that edginess communicated itself to Mr Hyun. As the coach accelerated away, one of the students at the back took a sneak shot of the soldiers. At the next checkpoint, trouble. The soldiers at the last checkpoint had radioed ahead to the next one, and when we turned up Mr Hyun got an earful. He went straight to Alex – not the culprit – grabbed him by the cuff and dragged him off the coach, and demanded he delete everything he had filmed.

Alex fiddled with his camera, selecting the 'stills' memory, and deleted a couple of boring shots of the countryside. Mr Hyun came back on to the bus, breathed a bit more fire, and then we were on our way again. To me, it felt like Mr Hyun was acting out a role, but then it wasn't my collar that was felt.

The start of the DMZ proper was marked by an electrified fence, and past that a small lip in the road. To left and right we could see a concrete wall, not much higher than a man, and beyond that a depression or a waterless moat affair, making the job of the invader that bit tougher – if, of course, the invader was foolish enough to come through the front door, exactly as the defender expected. Edged around the moat was a decoration of barbed wire, the old-fashioned kind that you rarely see in the West, apart from at remote Welsh hill farms.

We passed two ox-carts while Mr Hyun announced that we were now approaching 'the DMZee' – he instantly corrected his American pronunciation into the Queen's English, 'the DMZed' but we noticed all right. The coach slowed underneath a concrete block suspended above the road, another tank trap, and parked outside a building with the feel of a bad motorway service station from the 1960s. Inside was a lecture room, complete with photographs of the Kims, Major and Minor, and a map of the DMZ. Our host was the colonel in charge of the DMZ that day, a jolly chap in a too-large hat who didn't seem to have a care in the world. If thermo-nuclear war was about to happen, this guy would most likely be dead in the first five minutes.

On foot now, we walked to the southernmost tip of North Korea. Just before we got there, we passed a shrine to Kim Il Sung, on which the Great Leader's wisdom was scrawled in giant Korean ideograms on a fat slab of marble. It clearly says: '1994.7.7.' Did the Great Leader get the wrong date? No, Juche Time didn't come in until three years later. But no one had bothered to retrospectively correct the general's old-fashioned use of the Western calendar.

Miss Jun addressed us urgently: 'This area is a battlefront, be careful all the time. Don't use your camera.'

This was, of course, rubbish. The DMZ was far quieter than, say, Hyde Park, although it was the only place I heard birdsong in our whole stay in North Korea. 'Landmines are great for bio-diversity,' a lunatic collecting butterflies for London's Natural History Museum in the middle of a minefield in Angola once told me.[1] I suspected the birds were South Korean, peering in at the misery of the North.

Bang on the DMZ crossing point – where no one crosses – you look down on three blue huts. On the other side, you can see the South Korean base, a fancy pagoda affair dripping with CCTV cameras. They filmed us. We filmed them, etc., etc. Not a soul was to be seen on the other side. Normally, South Korean guards strut their stuff, while North Koreans do likewise. Occasionally, American troops join the face-off. Today, no one was in sight, apart from a small coachload of students and a fake history professor. What the American and South Korean military made of our posturing in front of their cameras, who knows? The North Korean colonel happily posed for pictures with all of us: 'Thermo-nuclear cheese!'

No better opportunity to find out what the prospects were of us being so much burnt toast. 'At the moment,' I asked the North Korean colonel, 'this is a war of words. Do you think there will be a shooting war?'

The colonel replied: 'There is no shooting so you can't say this is

---

[1] We were making a documentary about landmines in the same minefield – an activity no less lunatic than lepidopterology.

a war. I don't know if war will break out. Whether there is a war depends on the Americans.'

There was something about my grey beard which the colonel liked. Leastways, as the coach took us away from the very front line to a small museum where the original Armistice agreement is kept, he came and sat next to me. I was keen for Alex to shoot this cosy scene: proof, if proof were needed, that despite the official propaganda the North Korean officer in charge of the DMZ that day could not have been more relaxed. But Alex was so spooked by Mr Hyun back at the checkpoint that he didn't take the snaps.

In the museum proper, the colonel picked my brains about the prospect of war. I tried to think of a diplomatic formula for telling him 'I don't think all-out war is that likely because your regime is full of shit'. What I actually said was: 'In Britain, we're less afraid because we're further away.' For some reason, Miss Jun translated that as: 'He wants to leave now because he is afraid war might break out,' to which the colonel slapped me affectionately on the back and, laughing, said: 'Don't worry about it.'

The new leader's photograph was hanging in pride of place in the Armistice museum: Kim Jong Un gripping a pair of binoculars with black gloves, scowling at the unseen enemy, while elderly North Korean generals in Sovietische hats too big for them looked on nervously. Of all the fingers on nuclear triggers, Obama's, Putin's, Cameron's, the leaders of China, France, Israel, Pakistan, India and North Korea, Kim Jong Un's are the most immature. In a society like North Korea, moulded by Confucianism, which venerates the wisdom of the old, and where the last two leaders were in office until they were very old men, Kim Jong Un's youth is a negative.

Journalism, or at least the glamorous end of journalism, is about breaking news, best intoned in a basso profundo with a ticker running along the bottom of the television screen reinforcing the message. But perhaps the more interesting bit of the job is – so long as your evidence is strong – telling power and money: what you say is not true. Kim Jong Un had been screaming thermo-nuclear threats at the outside world through the loudhailer of the North Korean propaganda machine. When *Panorama* broadcast the colonel's 'Don't worry about it', that may have pricked Fat Boy Kim's balloon.

Perhaps Kim Jong Un was talking up the threat to make himself look good in the eyes, not of his people – they don't matter to him – but his generals. 'Behold, I am a man the West should be afraid of.' But only a fool plays around with the idea of making nuclear war a reality. And that is not good for the peace of the world.

After we left Pyongyang, we flew to London, and then after a few days flew almost all the way back, this time to South Korea. There, I met Professor Myers, whose life's work is to study the mind-set of the North Korean regime. Did he think war likely? Myers said that the regime didn't want war but it might happen by miscalculation. I asked him to talk me through a possible pathway to such an event.

'It would be very easy actually. All it needs is for the North Koreans to launch another attack along the lines of the ones that they launched in 2010.'

In that year, the North Koreans shelled an island in disputed waters in the Yellow Sea, not far from the crumbling barrage we visited, killing two South Korean farmers and two soldiers. A South Korean frigate in international waters but not far from the disputed islands sank – and the only credible explanation for the sinking was that a North Korean torpedo was responsible. Forty-six South Korean sailors were killed.

Myers continued: 'If they were to sink another South Korean ship or attack one of those islands in the Yellow Sea again the South Korean administration this time would probably respond with more force than it did in 2010. Now, being a "military-first" state, North Korea cannot simply let even a small military defeat ride. If that defeat becomes known to the North Korean public as a whole ... the regime has to fight back, it has to raise the ante and come out of it with some kind of victory. So I do see that kind of a situation escalating quite quickly into war.'

In trying to calibrate the likelihood of a war, and of that war becoming nuclear, one should never forget the stance of the South. From its formation in 1945 by the Americans to the late 1980s, it endured a series of deeply unpleasant dictatorships, with a thin and unconvincing gloss of elections and a muzzled free press. From the Seoul Olympics in 1988 onwards, democracy in South Korea has flourished, as has the economy, which, at number eleven in the league table of the world's richest nations, puts into shade the miserable ruin up north. The South puts up with its neighbour from hell with great patience. The question is: has that patience got a limit? The darker war games in the Pentagon look at the following scenario: that North Korea kills a number of South Koreans in an attack that Seoul believes must be responded to; that the South's response triggers the North to launch an artillery strike on Seoul, including using its chemical arsenal; and that forces the Americans' hand, requiring them to launch their tactical nuclear weapons to push back, at which point the North Koreans push the big red button for full-scale thermo-nuclear war.

But not everyone who knows the North intimately believes the regime's martial posturing is for real. The North Korean People's Liberation Front works out of the top floor of a ramshackle house in a run-down part of Seoul, but its members are North Korean defectors with military experience, and their best contacts are in the North Korean military too. When I met Jang Se Yul of the NKPLF he told me that he had spoken to a military source in the North just three days before. What did your source say? I asked.

'There will be no war,' said Jang.

Why was your source so certain that there will be no war?

Jang made an important distinction: 'We should separate the army into two different groups: the senior officers and the ordinary soldiers. The senior officers don't want a war but the soldiers have been brainwashed. They are in a state of conflict. The senior officers are aware that this whole thing is a political show but the soldiers consider real war a possibility. The officers are used to this kind of situation.'

How strong is the internal position of Kim Jong Un?

'The regime's opposition who can actually act are very rare but there are quite a few supporters. The opposition who can act? Maybe five people, maybe two.'

He wasn't specific, nor I suppose could he be.

'But their supporters,' he continued, 'are a much bigger number, generally the wealthy. You'd think the poor would support the opposition, but surprisingly most of the opposition comes from the upper-middle class. The reason behind this is that they have more information.'

How do they know the truth?

'There are many routes for information about the outside world. Forced labour' – North Koreans who work abroad, some in logging camps in Russia, often under miserable conditions for little money but far, far better than they know in the North – 'traders, people who have to go abroad on diplomatic missions, anyone who goes to China. If an ordinary person gets to see or hear one piece of information about the outside world, then the rich in Pyongyang get to see or hear a great deal. And the restrictions on information for these people are less rigid compared to those for "normal people".'

Exile warps minds. A group of defectors who are desperate to see the end of the regime may well overegg their opposition pudding. But at the time of writing, all the regime's talk of thermo-nuclear war has come to naught, and the North Korean People's Liberation Front's analysis has proved, thus far, right.

Telling porkies about one's readiness to stage nuclear war wasn't the only big lie hanging in the air at the DMZ. Three million people died in the Korean civil war. Who started it matters. I asked the colonel whether it might have been the North. He said something-something in Korean.

'That's not true,' translated Miss Jun.

'It's not true?'

'That's not true,' she repeated.

Telling lies about history matters, too. Towards the end of his long life, Stalin grew increasingly dejected: 'I am finished. I trust no one, not even myself.' But in 1950, Stalin trusted Kim Il Sung's optimism that war against the South would be swift. Kim had pressed Stalin repeatedly to be allowed to make war against the South, convinced that it would crumble under pressure. The Soviet Commissar Shtykov met Kim on 30 January 1950 and told him the good news that Stalin, after a lot of hesitation, was now in favour of war. Shtykov's cable to Stalin reads: 'Kim Il Sung received my report with great satisfaction.' In April, Kim went to Moscow. As a Soviet memo at the time records:

> The attack will be swift and the war will be won in three days: the guerrilla movement in the South has grown stronger and a major uprising is expected.[2]

The three-day war ended up lasting three years. It was a terrible mistake, one that millions – but neither Kim nor Stalin – paid for with their blood.

At first, things went brilliantly for the North Koreans. Diplomats in the British embassy in Seoul, only 40 miles from the border, listened to the sound of battle on the streets outside, and waited for the knock on the door. The ambassador was Vyvyan Holt, a brilliant linguist and a good and sweet man, almost too innocent for the cruelties of the Cold War chess game; one of his aides, the double agent George Blake. The British capitulated to the North Koreans, who treated them with a rapidly decreasing degree of civility.

Kim's soldiers swept the whole of the peninsula, apart from one fraction of land around Busan (formerly called Pusan), a port in the south-east. Then the Americans struck, twice. Diplomatically, they secured United Nations backing for the defence of South Korea, meaning that soon Australian, Belgian, British, Canadian, Colombian, Dutch, Ethiopian, French, Greek, Luxembourg, New Zealand, Filipino, South African, Thai and Turkish troops were on their way.

Militarily, General MacArthur staged a brilliant amphibian

---

[2] Lankov, *The Real North Korea*, p10.

invasion at Incheon, and punched his way through to Seoul and then further and further north, almost all the way to the Chinese border. The Korean People's Army all but collapsed, a broken force. Pyongyang was evacuated, Kim's prisoners shot in a mass killing.

But as the United Nations forces neared the Yalu river and the Chinese border, Mao felt threatened. The Chairman struck back, sending hundreds of thousands of Chinese troops into the North. The human wave attacks by the Chinese overcame the United Nations forces, especially the British Gloucestershire regiment, who were dreadfully mauled. The Chinese elbowed the North Korean army aside and pushed down to the 38th parallel. By the summer of 1951, the front line was pretty much where the border between the two halves of Korea had been at the start. Everyone was in favour of a ceasefire, apart from Stalin, who kept the war going for two more years. When Stalin died in March 1953, his successors in the Kremlin soon gave the go-ahead for peace talks, and a ceasefire agreement took effect from July 1953.

The Korean civil war was a disaster for humanity. Atrocities occurred on both sides, as happens in every war. The United Nations forces, led by the Americans, used their firepower to bomb the North, the Soviets and the Chinese to the negotiating table, dropping more explosives on North Korea than they had on Nazi Germany. The effect was to flatten the North. Only three buildings survived intact in Pyongyang. Hundreds of thousands of civilians died in the bombing.

The detailed history of the war has been told brilliantly else-where.[3] Werner Bischof, a Swiss photographer for the Magnum

[3] Max Hastings: *The Korean War*, Simon and Schuster, New York, 1987.

agency, took some incredibly powerful images of refugees on the run from the war.[4] A second series of photographs has recently been unearthed in the old, Communist-era archives of the Hungarian Foreign Office by an academic sleuth, Balazs Szalontai.[5] One picture of Pyongyang looks like Hiroshima or Nagasaki after the atomic bombs. One can make out a kerbstone, a few spindly trees here and there, the skeletons of three buildings. The rest, as far as the eye can see, is rubble. A second picture shows three child corpses huddled, as if in sleep, in the foreground; a few feet away a man and a woman, lost in grief.

The suffering of ordinary people was hideous. Maria Balog, a Hungarian diplomat working for the Soviet satellite, reported on 7 February 1951 from Pyongyang:

Korea has become a pile of ruins. There are no houses or buildings left. Cities and villages have been blown up, or destroyed by bombing, or burned down. The population lives in dug-outs in the ground. The people are literally without clothes or shoes . . . There is no food. They eat the frozen cabbage roots unearthed from under the snow. Cholera . . . typhus . . . infections, meningitis . . . They are not prepared against these epidemics; there is no medicine; and there are not enough medical personnel. There is no soap. Here, for instance, women wash their clothes without soap, in the river because there is no firewood.[6]

[4] Werner Bischof: 'An Era Defined by Exile', *Time*, http://lightbox.time.com/2013/07/25/an-era-defined-by-exile-korean-war-photos-by-werner-bischof/
[5] Chris Springer, Balazs Szalontai: *North Korea Caught In Time: Images of War and Reconstruction*, Garnet, Reading, 2010.
[6] Springer, Szalontai, pxii.

More than sixty years on, I saw with my own eyes that women still wash clothes in the freezing rivers of North Korea.

Blake, originally a Dutch citizen who became a British spy and then turned double agent for the Communists during the Korean war, cited the bombing campaign as the thing that turned his mind against the West:

> In Holland, during the war, when I heard at night the heavy drone of hundreds of RAF planes overhead on their way to Germany, the sound had been like a song to me. Now, when I saw the enormous grey hulks of the American bombers sweeping low to drop their deadly load over the small, defenceless Korean villages huddled against the mountainside; when I saw the villagers, mostly women and children and old people – for the men were all at the front – being machine-gunned as they fled to seek shelter in the fields, I felt nothing but shame and anger.[7]

But one cannot condemn the American bombing on its own, while ignoring the cause of the war. The RAF bombing of Germany during the second world war which so heartened Blake was morally no different than the Allied bombing of Korea which so sickened him. Innocent men, women and children were killed by the RAF. But no one in the RAF had wanted to drop bombs over Germany until Hitler invaded Poland and started the second world war. Equally, the American bombing of North Korea was in response to a war started by Kim Il Sung.

The terrible destruction caused by the bombing created a cruel reaction. The North Koreans and the Chinese were especially hard

---

[7] George Blake: *No Other Choice*, Jonathan Cape, London, 1990, p141.

on captured American and British airmen, some of whom were tortured, some shot, and some brainwashed and returned to the West with broken minds. The rules of war were pretty much abandoned.

Our coach moved on to Kaesong, a weathervane city just north of the DMZ. Before the Korean war it had been in the South; in 1953, the border was redrawn so the North could have it. It's now home to an industrial zone where Northern workers, mainly women, work in factories owned by the South. Kim Jong Un closed the zone, which stands on the northern side of the border, in the spring of 2013, when his nuclear sabre-rattling was at its fiercest. By the autumn, talks about reopening the zone were progressing. People in Kaesong looked the most prosperous of all in North Korea. They cannot have been happy that the Young Leader had cut off their opportunity to make money, but were in no position to protest about it. If there ever is an uprising, Kaesong might be the place where the first spark ignites.

After lunch off cripplingly low tables in a fake inn, the bus disgorged us outside an enormous statue to Kim Il Sung, high up on a hill. Here, Kim the First is cast in bronze, wearing a Mao jacket underneath an open long-length coat, standing on a white plinth which rests on the summit of a long series of steps. Below them is a preposterously wide road leading downhill away from the statue, so Kim Il Sung dominates the landscape for as far as the eye can see. By this stage in the tour, we were done with bowing, but our minders didn't even suggest it. There was something revolting about this statue, a bronze god demanding adoration, and something revolting, too, about the mind-set of the people who require him to be adored.

Yet even here, there was evidence that the power of the Kim cult might one day turn to dust. Two million North Koreans now have mobile phones, using a heavily circumscribed Egyptian mobile phone system, Orascom. The system is the opposite of 4G – you can't surf the internet because there is no internet and you can't make a call outside of North Korea because the system blocks all international calls. So the digital revolution that has rocked the world is locked out of North Korea. Or is it?

The youngest student of all, 'Dylan', an African American and quite the coolest and most fashionable of our whole party, and also the sleepiest, powered up his iPhone on the hill by the Kim statue, and got a signal from mobile masts in the South, just a few miles away. Dylan tweeted: 'At the DMZ, #JustChillin'. Soon, the whole party were on their phones, texting away. The thing is, if we can do that, so can an enterprising North Korean with a Chinese phone.

Working out what is happening on the outside may no longer seem unimaginable, and that spells trouble for the regime. The ice-wall blocking out the world of information is beginning to crack, not just for the elite, but for ordinary people too.

Gaddafi's Libya back in the late 1990s was another state where information about anything was lost in fog. It seemed astonishing that such a bonkers regime had been able to stay in power, by that time, for three decades. I was also surprised to see so many satellite dishes on people's houses. Clearly, Gaddafi was losing his grip in the information war. It took a long time, but fourteen years later it was the tyrant's turn to face a horrible death: first a grenade blast, then being stabbed in the anus with a bayonet, all of it caught on a mobile phone, news that was no doubt received in Pyongyang with a degree of unease.

8

Facing the Final Curtain

Kim Il Sung faced the first great threat to his grip on power in 1951, when it was clear that he'd made a terrible mistake in assuming that the South would fold, and the Americans and the West in general would let that happen. Even while the civil war was at its height, and American bombs were raining down on North Korea, he cracked down on enemies of the state, real or imagined, and they were sacked, imprisoned, shot or simply disappeared.

Two years later, the moment the shooting war stopped in the summer of 1953, there was another purge. This time, Pyongyang staged its first major show trial. There were a dozen defendants, the most prominent Yi Sung Yop, the former secretary of the Central Committee and one of the very, very few guerrillas who, unlike Kim, had enjoyed a full education. The prosecution charged that an American diplomat called Harold Noble in Seoul told Yi through a hapless go-between to create anti-Communist insurgents in the North, prior to the American invasion at Incheon. 'At this point,' writes Lankov, 'any notion of plausibility seems to have deserted the script writers of the show trial; it is too improbable that the Americans would have trusted their agent with such highly classified information.'[1] But the script writers had made an even bigger error, by attaching a date and a place for Noble's order to Yi's man – court papers showed that it happened on 26 June 1950, when the American was supposedly in Seoul. On that date Noble was on holiday, in Japan.[2]

All of the accused spoke their lines well. One defendant kept on repeating: 'I am a running dog of American imperialism.' When it came to the turn of the defence lawyers, they stated that all the accusations against their clients had been proven. Yi told the court: 'Had I two lives, to take them both would have been too little.'[3] Yim Hwa, a writer who had tried to kill himself, apologized to the court, and demanded to be executed. Lankov summarizes: 'The trial which had started as farce ended as black comedy.' Ten got death sentences; two, long spells in prison.

Why beg the regime for execution if you face certain death? Offstage, out of sight of blind justice, they torture your loved ones in front of you, and threaten to torture them some more, or execute them, unless you stay on script.

But the regime may have been sensitive to the mocking publicity it got in the international press for the script-writing errors; from then on, it became more fashionable for people just to disappear. Kim did all this when his stock was low, and his particular blend of national Stalinism was out of favour. For Stalin's death in March 1953 had cast a cold wind against those leaders of Soviet satellites who were seen to be too dictatorial, too enamoured by their own

[1] Lankov, *From Stalin to Kim Il Sung*, p95.
[2] Suh, *Kim Il Sung*, p133.
[3] Lankov, *From Stalin to Kim Il Sung*, p97.

personality cults. In eastern Europe, the new mood of de-Stalinization saw some leaders toppled from their plinths. In the Kremlin, Nikita Khrushchev ruled the roost. The new breed of Soviets saw Kim Il Sung as yesterday's man. Many Soviet and Chinese archives remain locked up, but the fall of the Berlin Wall has meant that the documents of Communist ambassadors from satellite countries are now readily available. Szalontai has unearthed a fascinating insight by Soviet Counsellor A.M. Petrov, reported by Hungarian diplomat Laszlo Keresztes, from 1955:

> It is a serious error that Comrade Kim Il Sung is surrounded by bootlickers and careerists ... Whatever is said by the leader, they [other high-ups in the Korean Workers' Party] accept it without any dispute. Thus the mistakes are not revealed openly, only in private and belatedly ... The personality cult has not changed at all, and it is a primary and decisive factor in every mistake.[4]

So by the time of his tenth anniversary in power, Kim Il Sung's Soviet mentors were bemoaning both the extreme nature of his personality cult and the fact that it was not changing. Szalontai's detective work is a great piece of historical research because it challenges an excessively sentimental nostalgia that shrouds our view of the first Kim, indulged by many North Korean defectors and consequently some Western analysts, who write with syrupy regard for the 'Great Leader'. The nostalgists argue that Kim Il Sung was, whatever else you say about him, dedicated to the cause, and that it was his son, Kim Jong Il, who built up the personality

[4] Balazs Szalontai: *Kim Il Sung in the Khrushchev Era: Soviet–DPRK Relations and the Roots of North Korean Despotism, 1953–1964*, Stanford University Press, Stanford, 2005, p73.

cult from the 1970s onwards. At the time the Soviet Counsellor wrote that memo about Kim Il Sung's personality cult, Kim Jong Il was nine years old.

The Soviet memo signals, too, a fundamental change in the relationship between Moscow and Pyongyang. In 1945, Kim was little more than the Kremlin's puppet on a string. While Stalin was alive, Kim, more or less, did the bidding of the Vozhd. From the death of Stalin onwards, Kim Il Sung increasingly became the master of his destiny. And something of a show-off.

Enver Hoxha, the one leader of a Communist nation possibly even more peculiar and vain than Kim Il Sung, visited Pyongyang in September 1956. The guerrilla leader-turned-dictator littered Albania with concrete pillboxes, wrecked its economy, locked the country up from the outside world and was, according to the Tirana rumour mill, a closet homosexual who had his lovers murdered after sex. Reporting for the *Observer* in 1991, after Hoxha was dead but before the Albanian revolution when they knocked over his statue in Skanderbeg Square, I put the gay sex murderer point to President Ramiz Alia, his successor. Alia was Hoxha's lickspittle, a smooth-fleshed nonentity who inherited the tyrant's machine of repression, but could not control it. The interview had been extraordinarily boring and halfway through I decided to follow an *Observer* tradition of being rude to princes, remembering the example of the late Patrick Donovan, who had once interviewed the King of Greece. (At the end of the interview, the king asked to inspect Donovan's notebook. On it was only one thing, a doodle of a large black cat.) I asked the president the following: was it true that Hoxha was a homosexual who had the secret police murder his lovers after he had finished with them? Alia had replied: 'No, he was a family man,' and closed the interview.

In 1997 I met the deputy prisons director, Bedri Choku, who had been in the worst prison in Hoxha's gulag, Spac. When I told Bedri this he shook his head: 'No,' he said, 'that's wrong. With me in Spac in 1969 was one of Enver's lovers, a man of about sixty. He was very discreet about it, but if you were a friend he could trust, he would talk about it. They had sexual relations. Enver did not have him killed, because he had saved Enver's life during the war. He sent him to Spac instead.'[5]

Dictators, they're so fucking weird.

Enver wrote up his trip to the DPRK as follows: 'On September 7, 1956, we arrived in Pyongyang. They put on a splendid welcome, with people, with gongs, with flowers, and with portraits of Kim Il Sung everywhere. You had to look hard to find some portrait of Lenin, tucked away in some obscure corner. The revisionist wasp had begun to implant its poisonous sting there, too.'[6] Later, Hoxha, who had a sharp tongue, was even more dismissive: 'Kim Il Sung is a pseudo-Marxist, vacillant, megalomaniac, revisionist.'

Kim Il Sung never quite made it to Albania.

The Great Leader was in a strong position, but that does not mean he was totally secure. Earlier that summer of 1956, Kim had gone to Moscow on his armoured train to discuss Khrushchev's new policy of stepping away from full-throated Stalinism. While the cat was away, the mice plotted. Choe Chang Ik was his greatest danger, the leader of the Yanan group, Koreans who had spent time in China and were mentored by the Chinese Communist Party. He and his supporters were alarmed about the personality cult and angered by the forced collectivization of agriculture – the

[5] John Sweeney: 'Travels in Absurdia', *Observer*, 16 March 1997.
[6] Enver Hoxha, *The Khrushchevists*, Tirana, 1980, edition in English.

so-called co-operative movement. One complained: 'Tax gathering was accompanied by beatings, murders and arrests. The Party's activities are based on violence, not persuasion. The co-operative movement is based on violence.'[7] The moment Kim came back, he smelt trouble. Kim felt something was amiss, it was reported, when on his return at Pyongyang airport he saw Choe turn pale.[8] All his life Kim Il Sung hated flying and preferred to go by train. It seems on this one occasion he made an exception. Perhaps he was tipped off about the plot, and overcame his fear of flying to hurry home before the plotters became too powerful.

The conspirators planned to topple Caesar at the Party plenum by getting delegates to criticize him openly, but the nerve of the 'August plotters' broke, and their dagger missed its target. Two or three attacking speeches were made, but they fell on deaf ears. Kim Il Sung's secret police were on to them, and very soon the plot crumbled. He was not so strong that he could have Choe killed immediately; instead, the regime's public enemy number one was made the manager of a pig farm.[9] Lankov points out that this ploy was a direct steal from Stalin's playbook: humiliating demotion first, then torture, then the firing squad. That's what happened to Bukharin; all we know for certain was that Choe was purged and died in 1957, probably not of old age.

By the Workers' Party plenum in 1958, Kim Il Sung had wiped out all possible heads of internal opposition: first, Communists from South Korea, then Soviet Communists, then those who had close links to the Chinese. Left standing at the end of the game were a small handful of guerrillas who had been with Kim in

[7] Lankov, *From Stalin to Kim Il Sung*, p182.
[8] Suh, p150.
[9] Lankov, *From Stalin to Kim Il Sung*, p175.

Manchuria, and a larger mass of slavishly loyal robots, who did his bidding. What is remarkable is that Kim managed to play off the Soviet Union and the Chinese against each other, tilting to one side, then the other, but always looking after number one. He played this game deftly, probing Soviet and Chinese Korean clients and friends when the moment was right, exiling some, demoting others, executing opponents when he could get away with it.

The vendetta against enemies of Kim was dressed up in the regime's ideology. One old comrade, Yu Song Chol, had been Kim's interpreter in the Soviet Union, and had twice snubbed the guerrilla boss, along the lines of: 'I'm your interpreter, not your servant.' In 1958, he returned from studying in the Soviet Union to Pyongyang where he was placed in the care of the Thought Examination Committee. It's hard to imagine a more Orwellian title. The attack on his mind was so painful he begged to be killed, but eventually they let him escape back to the Soviet Union in what Martin rightly describes as an outcome 'at the lower end of the horror curve'.[10]

From 1958 onwards, Kim Il Sung was safe to repudiate the Soviet Union's new policy of demonizing Stalin as once he had been worshipped. The moment in 1961 when Stalin's waxwork was taken out of its glass box and buried in a grave – albeit in the Kremlin walls – was a breaking point. While Stalin's personality cult became a thing of disgrace across the Soviet empire, in Pyongyang the cult of Kim grew like Topsy. As far as the DPRK was concerned: 'Stalin is dead. Long live the Korean Stalin!'

Veneration for the leader; the ordinary people of North Korea could go hang. The regime continued to treat its people as if their

[10] Martin, pp109–110.

standard of living – even their ability to stay alive – was a matter of no importance. The Russians, in particular, were sceptical of Kim's relentless pressure to get on with heavy industry while bleeding agriculture dry. After the end of the Korean war, the economy in the North was all but dead. The leadership sent out their subordinates to bring in more food, in some cases half of a peasant's crop. The regime forbade private grain trade and forced villagers into collective farms. The result was not overnight economic success but famine. Szalontai uses his Hungarian sources to tell the story of 1955: people on the move from the always under-nourished north-east, many starving to death along the way. The victims were not just peasants in the sticks but also residents of Pyongyang, reduced to eating grass. No one knows how many people died in the North in 1955; nobody counted. But the evidence of famine is real and casts a big shadow on the claims that the North was economically more successful than the South until the late 1970s. People in a thriving economy do not eat grass.

Peter Valyi was a Hungarian government delegate, who was shocked by the poverty and disease he found in post-war North Korea:

> The people had no place to live, so they build small wooden huts for themselves. One part of the city is composed entirely of such [dwellings] ... The flats are unhealthy. Tuberculosis is spreading ... Another disease is intestinal worms, which is terribly widespread, for there is no animal breeding; human excrement is practically the only thing they use for manure ...[11]

[11] Springer, Szalontai: *North Korea Caught In Time*, pxxi.

To counter the lack of food, the dynasty came up with sillier and sillier solutions: in 1959, Kim Il Sung urged that everybody grow rabbits; in 1999, his son's 'on-the-spot guidance' was for people to breed ostriches. The simplest solution of all – a free market, effectively regulated – was not to be considered.

As ever is the case with North Korea, the regime survived by getting out the begging bowl. The Chinese and the Soviets injected the country with masses of food aid; other Soviet satellites like Poland, Czechoslovakia and Romania helped out with doctors and materiel. By 1957, the famine was over. Szalontai's Hungarian diplomats note the rebuilding of Pyongyang, but even as late as 1977 they warn: 'Shops are empty. People are hungry.'[12]

After our spell by the Kim Il Sung statue sending text messages by piggy-backing off the South Korean mobile phone system, we went to the Koryo Museum, which has been made a World Heritage Site by UNESCO. Hoe-Yeong, a man of high culture, found this exhibition of North Korean antiquities no different than the rest of the dodgy nonsense we'd been shown: 'Some of the most fake-looking ancient artifacts I've ever seen anywhere in the world.' To be fair, it is acknowledged in guidebooks that many of the exhibits are copies, the originals held in another museum in Pyongyang, also open to visitors.

That night we ended up in Daedonggang Diplomatic Club restaurant and karaoke bar. As we poured over the menus, the power failed, and I had to mull beef stroganoff versus chicken kiev by a thin prick of torchlight. It was like camping at the Drones Club. While we ate, some of our party went on a trawl of Westerners who might have gobbets of information. They met one

[12] Springer, Szalontai, pxxv.

man, working for an international NGO, who didn't want to talk. He was giving out medical aid but he did let on that, in two years in Pyongyang, he had been allowed out of the capital to monitor how his aid was being distributed just four times.

The karaoke bar was no less dire than any other karaoke bar in the world. Many of the songs were in Chinese, and for the second time that day Dylan pulled a blinder. Looking at one particularly impossible-to-decipher set of Chinese ideograms, he said: 'I know that song!', stood up and rattled it out in what to my ears sounded perfect Chinese. As well as studying International Relations at the LSE, Dylan had been learning Chinese at school in the States. He sounded pitch-perfect.

Having been to the place that may yet end the earth, the theme from *Titanic* was the only song for me. (There is a certain poignancy to my choice which eluded me at the time of karaoke song selection. The date the great ship sank with so many lives lost was 15 April 1912 and also Kim Il Sung's birthday: twin disasters that day, some say.) I sang dreadfully. The German and Swiss women plumped for 'Barbie Girl', perhaps the most Swiftian satire on the emptiness of Western materialism ever written. I did Ken's lines, so deep-voiced it hurt my larynx. We looked at Mr Hyun. He did not let the honour of the People's Republic down. His song of choice? 'My Way'.

Mr Hyun had a powerful baritone. When he stopped, we gave him a standing ovation. Christopher Hitchens noted that Frank Sinatra's 'My Way' was a big hit in the karaoke bar during his trip back in 2000: 'There's a special plangency to the line about facing the final curtain.' Regrets? Forget about it. On the way home on the coach, Miss Jun had a lullaby for us – the nation's reunification song. And so ended the most surreal day of my entire life.

9

Cruel Christs of Pus

To the soundtrack of the Beatles' hit song 'All You Need Is Love', in 1967 the Western world rocked to 'The Summer of Love'. At roughly the same time a train from Chairman Mao's China was shunted across the Yalu river over the Friendship Bridge into North Korea, carrying ethnic Korean passengers wearing placards around their necks: 'Look, this will be also your fate, you tiny revisionists!'[1]

The passengers were long dead.

The corpse train spread the contagion of Mao's Cultural Revolution to North Korea. Kim Il Sung, the father of the half-nation, was denounced by Mao's Red Guards as a 'fat counter-revolutionary pig'.[2] Kim did not challenge his massive neighbour to the north directly. Rather, he created his own version

[1] Bernd Schaefer: *North Korean 'Adventurism' and China's Long Shadow, 1966–1972*, Cold War International History Project, Woodrow Wilson International Center, Washington DC, 2004, p10.
[2] Suh, p52.

of Mao's murderous paranoia, purging North Korea of all 'unclean', 'impure' or foreign elements. The logic was simple: the purer the nation, the safer Kim's grip on power.

But the purge didn't just kill current enemies. It looked backwards in time for potential treason, too. In dictatorships like North Korea, history can kill. The old Soviet joke understood the danger from the past: 'Trouble is you never know what's going to happen yesterday.'[3] The crocodile's tail of yesterday's history becoming today's treason was probably no more lethal than in North Korea at the time of the Summer of Love.

That wasn't good news for two lifelong Communists who had come to North Korea to help the struggle continue by translating the works of Kim Il Sung. Ali Lameda was a Venezuelan poet living in exile in East Berlin in 1965 when he first made contact with the North Koreans. The notion that beguiled Ali was that North Korea was socialism's shining city on a hill, one of the vanguards of world revolution. He arrived in Pyongyang in the middle of 1966, taking charge of the Spanish section of the Department of Foreign Publications. There, he met the Grand Old Man himself, Kim Il Sung, and also Park Hun Chol, a senior government minister.

Ali translated Kim's works and regime propaganda, already in English, into Spanish. His colleague was Jacques Sedillot, a Frenchman, also known as Manuel Cedillo, more than sixty years old, who had fought for the Left in Spain and Algeria. He translated the regime's English into French. Ali described him: 'A magnificent man, truly internationalist, honest and courageous.' The two became firm friends.

[3] E. Crankshaw: *Cult of the Individual*, Belfast, 1975, p6.

The Venezuelan was treated handsomely, boasting a special apartment at the Pyongyang International Hotel and a car and driver. His German girlfriend, Elvira Tanzer, came with him to Pyongyang: 'I went because I was so in love with him,' she later said. But the curious anomie of North Korea set in, like dismal drizzle. Ali noted that his driver was changed weekly, so he could never establish a friendly relationship with any of them. Ali explained: 'We felt stifled ... [an] overwhelming feeling of isolation ... However much my sympathy lay with the great work of national construction of the Korean people, I could never communicate.'[4]

Ali wrote to his friends and family abroad, sharing his sense of frustration at this enforced isolation. Innocently expecting his private correspondence to remain private, he condemned North Korea's abject poverty and suggested that this was not the Communism he had dreamed of.

The work was deeply frustrating. Ali and Jacques set about translating the regime's fairy tale. But the fables of Kim Il Sung, the child prodigy, were blackly farcical. Things came to a head when Jacques was dispatched to France to recruit more translators. Instead of carrying out his instructions to the letter, Jacques, who had after all been a colonel in the Republican Army against Franco's Fascists, undertook an opinion poll, asking around 250 people what they thought of North Korean propaganda. Ali summarized Jacques' report: 'Propaganda which says that, at 14, Kim Il Sung was the leader of the Communist Party, had launched a revolution and directed an army – a child leading a Communist

[4] Ali Lameda: *A Personal Account of the Experience of a Prisoner of Conscience in the Democratic People's Republic of Korea*, Amnesty International, London, 1979.

Party revolution in a country without a Communist Party, beating the Japanese army, and so on, it seems very hard to believe.'

Jacques' report also touched on Kim Il Sung directly, reflecting an opinion from a French source who made an unflattering comparison between the modesty of the Nicaraguan revolutionary hero Augusto César Sandino and the Great Leader. Ali's reaction was sensible: 'When he showed it to me, I told him what a good report it was, a first-class piece of work, but, as regards Kim Il Sung, he should, I suggested, obliterate that.' The Frenchman stuck to his guns, arguing that the Koreans should change their propaganda.

Michael Harrold, a somewhat eccentric British sub-editor who spent seven years in Pyongyang from 1987, bemoaned the absurd quality of the propaganda he had to deal with: 'I got one across my desk today – "The Yankee soldiers took out their bayonets and sliced through the women's breasts like bean curd!"'[5]

The precise trigger for the disaster that befell Ali and Jacques is not quite clear. Izidor Urian, Ceausescu's translator, told me that he had met Ali. The former Romanian diplomat explained that on a tour of the Museum of Korean History, Ali had walked past statues of past Korean emperors, about which his guides said 'absolutely nothing'. When they came to a statue of Kim Il Sung, Ali asked: 'And which emperor is this?' 'This,' said Izidor, 'was the starting point of his tragedy.'

Ali wrote that in September 1967 the two translators went to a banquet thrown for employees of the Department of Foreign Publications. Ali made veiled jokes tilting at Kim Il Sung. Jacques, a quieter man, was probably more discreet but the Koreans knew

[5] Breen, p104.

about his report questioning the vanity and absurdity of the propaganda. Three days later, there was knock at Ali's door. Two police officers and seven plainclothes men from 'Public Security', the Bowibu, told Ali that he was an enemy of the Korean people – no formal charges were mentioned – and led him away. His girlfriend, Elvira, was left alone, forbidden to leave the city. That same night, Jacques was also arrested. He was accused of being a French imperialist spy, the blackest possible insult for a lifelong Communist and veteran of the civil wars in Spain and Algeria. Ali wrote of the charge against his friend: 'It was grotesque for it to be said that he was a spy, an "agent of French imperialism".' Later, their boss, the Korean director of the Translation Department, was also picked up.

Ali found himself in a damp, cold cell 7 feet long by 3 wide in the Interior Ministry prison, and the long, endless nightmare began. He was interrogated for twelve hours at a stretch, the formula remaining the same.

Confess, they said.

'Confess what?'

You know what there is to confess. Talk.

'But if it is you who are accusing me, you tell me.'

The sounds of the prison were bleak beyond the saying of it. People coughing up blood, random howls, screams. 'You can soon learn to distinguish whether a man is crying from fear, or pain or from madness.'

He was not routinely tortured like the others. On one occasion, a guard, furious that he had not showed sufficient deference, gave him a beating, kicking him with his boots and hitting him on the soles of his bare feet. To persuade him to confess, they used hunger as a weapon. Better to be beaten, Ali wrote, as it is possible to grind one's teeth and withstand physical pain; to be continuously starving is worse. When they did feed him, the meal was a hunk of dirty bread, weighing about 250 grams, and a bowl of water with a few chunks of vegetable in it. The metal dishes the food was served on were always filthy, the same ones the prisoners had been using for years, never washed. No change of clothes. To his knowledge, the only medicines used to treat prisoners were terramycin, an anti-bacterial drug, and cooking oil.

'Young prison guards newly assigned to the camp often expressed their amazement at such conditions,' wrote Ali. 'I was not tortured, if by this one means the systematic infliction of pain but, if terrible hunger and continual nastiness come under this definition, then I was.'

When Ali was released one year later, he had lost 22 kilos (50lb, or more than 4 stone). He was covered in sores, seeping blood. After two months under house arrest, they told him that he would be free to leave the country, but that Elvira had to go first. He was allowed to see her off at the airport and returned to pack his bags. They were playing with him.

At five o'clock in the evening, the police returned, more brutal than before. He asked why they were arresting him for a second time. 'You know why,' they told him. Ali concluded they had installed a microphone in their apartment and had recorded his conversations with Elvira. 'What did they expect me to say to her, when I returned from a year's detention in such a bad physical condition?'

His literary work had been confiscated on the orders of the Party Central Committee; it was described as 'bourgeois filth'. His second arrest, Ali wrote, 'after believing I was at last to be released, was one of the worst moments I was forced to endure.' Then came his trial. It was a joke, but not a funny one. He asked for a lawyer of his choice and that the tribunal should be held in the open, but such demands were dismissed as 'bourgeois'. Ali was provided with a so-called 'defence counsel'. The only people present apart from the judges were two uniformed policemen and a young interpreter. The trial lasted for one day, from nine o'clock in the morning till five in the afternoon. He was suffering from fever and was given nothing to eat all day. Like his interrogators, the judges demanded that he confess his guilt. The tribunal did not make any specific accusations – there were no formal charges – but the accused had to accuse himself before the tribunal.

'Thus,' wrote Ali, 'there was no necessity for the tribunal to produce any evidence. I had no right to defend myself, I could only admit guilt.'

Ali did not oblige, but insisted that he had committed no crimes, that he had only come to Korea as a servant of the government. When he tried to ask questions, he was abruptly interrupted and told that he had no right to defend himself.

The prosecutor informed him that he had been in Korea to sabotage, spy and introduce infiltrators, that he was working for the CIA.

Ali said that was absurd.

The prosecutor read from the Penal Code, which emphasized the gravity of his crime and demanded the maximum penalty for the crimes he had committed: death. Ali's defence counsel chipped in, making a lengthy eulogy to Kim Il Sung, and asked for twenty years for his client. The tribunal retired for five minutes and came back, granting Ali's defence brief his wish: two decades with forced labour. Ali was handcuffed to the bars of a Black Maria for three hours. The temperature outside was way below freezing. Opposite him in the van, sitting on a seat, was a guard who spent the journey loading and unloading his gun.

Outside, the howling of wolves.

The mountain country of North Korea in winter is beyond cold. Temperatures regularly drop below −20 degrees Celsius. Ali was dumped in a filthy cell, where he slept on the bare floor, with no blanket or mattress. He stayed there, constantly handcuffed, fearing his wrists would break with the strain.

After three weeks, he was taken to the main camp around ten o'clock at night, and placed in a cell which had no heating apart from for five minutes at night when a pipe burbled with hot water. The windows were iced up. His feet froze, and stayed frozen for six weeks. His toes became hideously swollen, all his toenails fell out and he could only hobble because of the sores and ulcers on his feet.

His main source of information was the prison screws, who let drop that he had been put in a punishment cell, which should not really have happened, but since he was a foreigner, and it was the first time a foreigner had ever been held at the camp, there was no isolation cell in which to hold him. As a foreigner, he was not to be allowed to come into contact with the other prisoners.

The prison regime was always the same: the prisoner must sit cross-legged, perfectly still, for sixteen hours, from six o'clock in the morning until ten at night. He must be rock steady, immobile, looking straight ahead towards the bars of his cell. The bars were iron rods that ran from ceiling down to the floor. Between the cells was a corridor along which the guards patrolled. The prisoners had to stay awake all day. The official explanation was that a prisoner should be constantly examining his conscience. A prisoner must not stretch his legs. If he did so, he was beaten. Ali found this last rule unbearable. He lost all feeling in his left leg, and he feared that he would end up paralysed.

The cold, the filth, the hunger and the loneliness were beyond words. Barefoot, afflicted by lice, diarrhoea and fevers, knowing nothing of what was happening outside the bars that imprisoned him, Ali found himself living a Kafka story. To survive, he wrote poetry inside his head and recalled Oscar Wilde's *The Ballad of Reading Gaol*.

> I never saw sad men who looked
> With such a wistful eye
> Upon that little tent of blue
> We prisoners called the sky.

Worst of all, Ali feared that no one in the outside world had any idea where he was. It was a 1960s version of the oubliette, the medieval torture by which prisoners were dropped into a hole and forgotten.

Once, he came across a French prisoner, a man who said that he was a French journalist who lived at 2, Rue d'Alembert, Paris, that his name was 'Pierre . . .' but the stranger had spoken too much, and the guard smashed his rifle butt into him, so the surname remains unknown.[6] In Paris, I knocked on the door of the building. No one knew of a Pierre who vanished forty years ago.

From chatting to the screws and snatched conversations with other prisoners, Ali started to work out how many camps there were. He concluded that the gulag contained some 150,000 souls spread around some twenty camps.

[6] Juan Paez Avila: *Ali: El Viajero Enlutado*, Ala de Cuervo, Caracas, 2003, p25.

Ali is long dead, but I managed to track down his nephew, Carlos David, an artist who lives in Paris. Sitting in his tiny flat in Alfortville, decorated with a 1973 poster in Spanish, 'Free The Poet Ali Lameda', Carlos told me how word somehow got back to Venezuela that Ali was locked up in North Korea. Elvira is the most likely source, but I have so far failed to trace her. Carlos's father, Carlos Diaz Sosa, Ali's brother-in-law, was a Venezuelan journalist turned diplomat. He used his contacts in Communist embassies to put the word out. For years, they heard nothing. Every entreaty was met with no response. They had no idea whether Ali was still alive. Then in 1973, North Korea started the long road towards becoming a member of the United Nations, and its Foreign Minister, looking around for votes, asked the Venezuelan legation in New York for their vote. The Venezuelans asked: What about Ali Lameda? The Foreign Minister asked: 'Is that a rock on the railway track?' The Venezuelans nodded. The Foreign Minister said he had no idea of the case, but would report back. Eventually, word came back from Pyongyang that Ali Lameda was alive, and then pressure from Caracas grew. Carlos Diaz Sosa asked the Cubans to intercede but, it seems, Castro did not lift a finger, thanks to a doctrinal dispute between the Cuban and Venezuelan Communist Parties. Every time the Venezuelans threw a diplomatic reception and heard that the North Koreans would be attending, in capitals like Warsaw and Prague, Carlos Diaz Sosa flew in from London, where he was based, and presented the North Koreans with letters for Kim Il Sung and the imprisoned poet.

The Romanians, the North Koreans' closest allies in the Soviet bloc, brokered the deal. Seven years after his first arrest, on 27 September 1974, Ali was allowed to leave North Korea. On arrival in Bucharest, the poet had to sign a letter swearing that the dire state of his health and the torture scars on his body were the result of captivity in a Venezuelan prison. The regime was trying to cover its tracks. Ali was in a terrible state. Thin, half mad, he had a tumour on his back and paralysis in his left leg that resulted from being forced to squat cross-legged for years. But the regime fattened him up before releasing him. In Berlin, Ali underwent surgery on the tumour and the frozen nerves in his leg. In late December 1974, he ended up in London, where his Venezuelan family were living in Finchley. Carlos David, then fourteen, had to give up his bed for his uncle: 'The grown-ups stayed up all night for three nights, talking, talking, talking. It was as if my uncle had come back from the dead.' Which, in a way, he had.

His poem, 'Pieta', recalled from memory because to write it down would have been the death of him, told the truth:

> Life, in the abstract, in its great coach – how nice;
> But amidst vomit and outrage the real thing triumphs,
> It flows, sewage and decay . . .
> I suffer moons, hungers, cruel Christs of pus . . .
> I give in bone the explanation of this, my misfortune.

Ali died on 30 November 1995. His friend Jacques Sedillot never made it out of North Korea, dying some time in 1976. Ali's report for Amnesty in 1979 is a line in the sand, the first account by a Westerner, and a Communist to boot, of the true nature of the regime.

From that year on, no one could have any doubt that the North Korea gulag was a serious contender to be the worst place on earth; that Kim Il Sung's regime had nothing whatsoever to do with

Above left: Kim Il Sung, the *über*-effeminate God-the-Mother, smiles down on the nation. Note the absence of the goitre on the side of his neck, airbrushed out of official photographs.

Above right: Kim the Second doing his Bad Elvis impression.

Below: Following his father's death in 2011, Fat Boy Kim arrived on the scene, eager to impress.

Big Brother is always watching.

Above: Construction Pyongyang-style. Opposite our hotel an army of workers build a new bank, almost entirely by hand.

Below left: North Korea's Arc de Triomphe straddles the main road into town. It's a few feet taller than the real thing in Paris. Note Pyongyang's un-traffic.

Below right: Hammer, sickle and brush, the totems of the Korean Workers' Party. The words in concrete sang out: 'Hail the Korean Workers' Party – all the Korean People's Unifier and Leader!' No one sang back.

The architecture of oppression: the Pyongyang Planetarium (**right**) and the spaceship-like Ryugyong Hotel (**below**), quite possibly the two creepiest buildings in the world.

Above and below: The regime's pomp and ceremony may look impressive but such peacocking distracts from much darker truths.

Above: When we visited there was little sign of life. Were the locals instructed to avoid us? I don't know. But the bleak empty streets (**above right**) told their own story.

A young boy at No Animal Farm eyes us foreigners with suspicion.

When Tomiko visited in 2012, her group came across this creepy, silent crowd in Kim Il Sung Square. A haunting vision if ever there was one.

Above: Long-distance haulage, North Korean-style.

Right and below: Pyongyang's elite make use of the Metro, descending into darkness.

Above: Kim Jong Un is cheered into office, keen to impress the old guard.

Right and below: Kim 3 began testing long-range rockets, then threatened thermo-nuclear war. Was the power play a bluff or a step closer to Armageddon?

Above: The author at the DMZ with the colonel in charge. On the day of our visit, North Korea was threatening war against the United States, but the place was almost deserted.

Below: As I came to learn, the regime is fond of fences. They might keep the people in, but, as we discovered at the DMZ, they're not so effective against mobile-phone traffic.

Above: A rare glimpse of life in the North Korean gulag.

Right: A satellite image of a camp in Haengyong – one of many such camps.

Bottom: The author outside an apartment block in Pyongyang. The bars on the windows suggest crime is common. Are the people so desperate that even life in the prison camps is not deterrent enough?

Above: We managed to catch a glimpse of this lady from our tour bus. The sign in front of her suggests she is begging.

Below: After creeping out of our hotel at dawn, we came across this sleepy North Korean town on the other side of a barbed-wire fence. Eerie doesn't even begin to describe it.

Private James Joseph Dresnok, the American who went to North Korea and stayed.

Above: The Romanian artist Doina Bumbea (**left**), and Venezuelan poet Ali Lameda (**right**), were both victims of the North Korean regime. We'll probably never know how many people have been lost in North Korea's darkness.

Below: A satellite image shows just what a black hole the nation is.

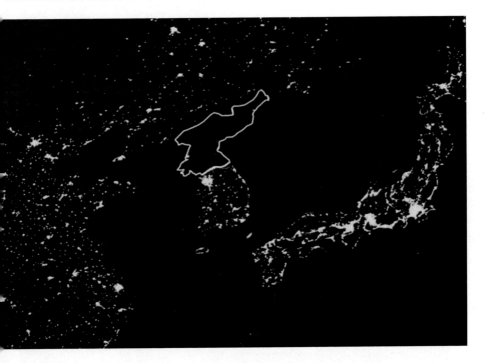

Above and right: Over the border in South Korea protests against the regime are common.

Below: Many North Koreans now have access to mobile phones, threatening the state's control over the flow of information to its citizens. As more and more people are able to speak to relatives in the South, China and the rest of the world, the regime's grip on information is beginning to crack.

advancing the brotherhood of man; and that it used hunger as a weapon to ensure that its people obeyed.

Alejandro Cao de Benós of the Korean Friendship Association dismisses criticism of the North Korea gulag: 'These are re-education camps. With 23 million people, sometimes you may have a few criminals. We believe not in punishment but in rehabilitation. It's a kind of psychological therapy.'[7]

After reading Ali Lameda's report for Amnesty and his poem, that is a sentence I would never utter.

[7] Hume, 'His dear leader: Meet North Korea's secret weapon – an IT consultant from Spain': *Independent*, 21 January 2012.

10

Pissing on Marble

In December 1969 two Italian Communists set off to Pyongyang, on the first ever delegation of the PCI – the Italian Communist Party – to North Korea. The two men were both heroes of the Italian Left. Emanuele Macaluso is a Sicilian leftist senator who has spent his life challenging the morbid power of the Mafia in his home island and throughout Italy. His friend Antonello Trombadori was then a famous artist, who during the second world war had been locked up by Mussolini and then the Nazis before escaping. If Communism ever had a human face, Macaluso and Trombadori were it. The artist died in 1993, but Macaluso is still with us: a brilliant little gnome of a man, eighty-nine, whose impassive shrugs suggest a pint-sized version of Marlon Brando's Godfather.

Their trip to North Korea took place at the height of the rift between the Soviet Union and China. That spring the Chinese People's Liberation Army had attacked a Soviet position on a disputed island in a river of the far west of China, leaving fifty-nine dead, including a senior colonel. The Chinese also managed to capture a then-secret T-62 tank. Both sides had tested nuclear bombs, and the Communist world stood on the brink of a terrible internecine war. The shooting died down, but the ideological conflict continued. As the two great Communist powers clashed, smaller Communist parties tried to reach out to one another, to find common ground. Both the Italian and the North Korean parties were keen to show the Soviet Union and China that they could entertain independent relations between friendly socialist parties without the interference of either big brother.

Logistically, however, they were stumped. The Italians had to fly to North Korea via Moscow, and the Russians were not keen on the PCI doing its own thing. So for three days they lay stranded at Moscow airport, the excuse being the weather. On the fourth day, the North Koreans, who had been growing increasingly impatient, made Kim Il Sung's very own jet available to the Italians. As they embarked, Trombadori could not help but notice the similarities with the Pope's personal plane, which he had recently travelled on as a journalist: comfortable large beds, elegant rooms for conversation, and excellent food. The Catholic Church and the North Koreans had different ideologies, but, as it turned out, the same taste in executive air travel.

The North Koreans held the Italians in high esteem. At the very least, the visit of the PCI delegation to Pyongyang meant that Kim Il Sung could claim to have friendly relations with the largest Communist Party in western Europe. Both Macaluso and Trombadori were thus received almost as if they were heads of state. Despite their familiarity with Soviet satellites, they soon realized that North Korea was a world unto itself. Macaluso had walked around Krakow visiting the churches. In Budapest, he'd enjoyed some of the admittedly meagre nightlife. None of this was possible in Pyongyang.

The Italians were escorted everywhere by an official of the Korean Workers' Party. When they were taken shopping in one of the main squares of the city, they were amazed to see that everyone else had already been made to leave. No soldiers, no workers, no civilians walked across the square. The PCI delegation was shown the house where Kim Il Sung was born, the cradle where he'd slept and the desk where he'd studied. Macaluso, a Sicilian, no stranger to religiosity, said: 'They showed us a shrine containing pool cues that had been used by the Great Leader as if they were a saint's relics, all whilst he was still alive.'

The visiting Italians found the food ghastly. Macaluso recalled how even the most privileged North Koreans still kept all their vegetables and other food in brine because of the lack of fridges. He didn't comment on this habit, just pulled a very miserable face.

Kim Il Sung, to the two Italians, was no saint. He was far more approachable than the cult of personality would have suggested, smart and sly and also, it seemed, more than a little paranoid. He told them about the attempts on his life that had been organized by Khrushchev. To the Soviets, Kim implied, for the North Korean leader to exercise independent relations with China was to be guilty of treachery.

Macaluso pointed out the contradiction between North Korea's claim to political independence and its support for the Soviet invasion of Czechoslovakia, crushing the Prague Spring in 1968. After the translator had spoken Macaluso's words, Kim Il Sung remained silent. The other officials in the room looked in disbelief at the Italian Communist. Several months later Macaluso received a publication in French from the North Koreans, which amended their position on the Prague Spring and the Czech demands for 'socialism with a human face', signalling opposition to Soviet force majeure.

The relationship between the Italians and the North Koreans, however, was not without tension. In Italy, the PCI had to compete at free elections with other parties who took human liberty as standard. The PCI delegation tried to discuss cultural and personal freedoms with the North Koreans, with very little success. The East Germans would listen to the Italians talk about liberty and counter-attack, pouring acid scorn on the PCI's ideas. The North Koreans simply ignored them. Macaluso said their attempt to get Pyongyang to engage on political freedom was 'like pissing on marble'.

Buzo analyses the marmoreal nature of the regime in his book *The Guerilla Dynasty*: 'A particular facet of Kim's personality which compounded the stultifying effect of ideology was his pervasive mistrust. The purges, the elaborate, multiple overlapping security agencies, the continuing high levels of repression ... Kim clearly perceived the threat to his system posed by interaction with even other socialist countries.'[1]

No wonder the Italians found getting across their far more human version of Communism to their host hard work. Buzo asks why North Korea declined into economic backwardness in the 1970s:

The major part of the answer lies simply in the extent to which Kim Il Sung lost touch with reality. Physical isolation, paranoia, an overbearing, browbeating personal manner, the corrupting effects

[1] Buzo, pp242–3.

of power without accountability, the cumulative effect over decades of daily exposure to extravagant flattery, growing megalomania . . . all combined to give Kim the illusion of control over events and deprive him of any real capacity for self-reflection and self-correction.[2]

Kim Il Sung had become a delusional illusionist.

[2] Buzo, p245.

11

'Would the Dear Leader not be offended by such a gift?'

The Kim Jong Il Museum of Gifts is housed in a fancy palace in the countryside about half an hour or so out of the Big Zombie. Outside the entrance doors, which would have let in a troop of Indian elephants, stood what felt like half the Korean People's Army, but the crowd was only around 5,000-strong. They were in town for the big parade the following day, a parade we only got to hear about after the fact. Still, the massed ranks of Korean squaddies helped conjure up the awe and veneration constantly urged on us by our minders for the Leaders, Doris Day and Midget's Turd. Thing is, by Day Five, we were becoming inured to their blandishments. Worse than that, some of our party were up for devilry.

The Kim Jong Il Museum of Gifts can be easily confused with the International Friendship Exhibition, which is a bigger effort, mostly dedicated to gifts to Kim One, housed in a colossal pagoda in the mountains three hours' drive from Pyongyang. Both museums are the Kim dynasty's version of an attic, where you bung all those useless gifts various aunts have given you over the years. Or the drinks cupboard where you dump the sticky yellow booze you quite liked on holiday but tastes horrid back home in Blighty. The idea of venerating that kind of junk is frankly absurd.

This being the Democratic People's Republic of Korea, we were asked to do exactly that. First, we had to put white nylon over-socks around our shoes, lest we muddy the marble. Then we had to dump our bags and stuff, especially cameras, in a large cloakroom. I was excited by this tour because I collect tyrant kitsch. At home, up in our attic, we have a moth-eaten Saddam Hussein carpet – I put it up there after they hanged him; at the bottom of a pile of books at my desk is a copy of *Omagiu – Homage* – which I borrowed from the Romanian Communist Party Central Committee building on Christmas Day, 1989; in the Frontline Club, inside a glass case, is Udai Hussein's snorkel mask, which fell into my hands.[1]

When it was my turn to dump my stuff at the cloakroom, I somehow forgot to hand over my BlackBerry, complete with naff quality camera-phone. A few moments later, Mr Hyun kindly invited a Korean security woman with a hand-held metal scanner – playing the role of Franz Beckenbauer in the 1972 World Cup – to give me the sweep-over. Beep-beep went her machine, and Mr Hyun escorted me back to the cloakroom to hand over my phone. I felt like a naughty boy.

They wiped us all clean. But, somehow, Erica managed to smuggle her iPhone in. We hadn't asked her to, but she had managed to get her iPhone in.

Our tour commenced with the obligatory local guide, a

---

[1] The Frontline Club is a drinking den in London for old war reporters; unofficial motto: 'All the women have a past; all the men have no future.'

gimlet-eyed lady with a frozen moue on her mush. First off, there was Kim Il Sung, sitting on a big marble throne, ready and willing to accept posthumous presents, and then we started processing through engine sheds of junk, tat from all four corners of the globe. There were vases, naff oil paintings, military paraphernalia and what-nottery. On and on it went. Without cameras, it was hard to recall it all, and one is left a bit like a contestant on Bruce Forsyth's *Generation Game*, having to remember the objects briefly revealed on the conveyor belt: a cuddly toy, a fondue set, roller skates. Stand-out nonsense included a mug advertising the Abba musical *Mamma Mia!* a *Mamma Mia!* badge and a Twin Towers fridge magnet. As Kenny Everett's transvestite character Cupid Stunt used to exclaim: 'It's all in the best possible taste.' We started to titter; our local guide became more and more cross.

The Hitch visited the bigger museum in the mountains. He, too, had found it hard to keep a straight face, confronted with a bear's head from Ceausescu, a chess set from Gaddafi, a crocodile-skin suitcase from Castro, an old gramophone from Zhou Enlai, an armoured train from Chairman Mao and a VHS copy of *Space Jam*, donor unknown. The most famous objet d'art in the Kim Il Sung Gift Museum is a stuffed crocodile, stood on its legs bearing a tray in its claws holding six goblets, for all the world like a waiter. It was a gift from the people of Nicaragua.

'I began to get the giggles,' wrote Hitchens, 'imagining that Kim Il Sung had thousands and thousands of dotty aunts and batty uncles, and had solemnly resolved to keep every one of their rubbishy birth-day and Christmas presents in case they ever came to call.'[2]

² Christopher Hitchens: 'Visit to a Small Planet', *Vanity Fair*, January 2001, http://www.vanityfair.com/ politics/features/2001/01/hitchens-200101

At our museum, the soldiers trooped in behind us, some grinning, some staring but not impolitely. They, of course, are the target audience for all this: that foreigners so admire the Kim dynasty they wish to celebrate or at least appease its majesty, like the Tributes in *The Hunger Games*. Of the truth, that this is probably the most mocked regime on the planet, they have no idea.

In the halls housing tributes to Kim Jong Il, we came across a painting of Bad Elvis astride a white Siberian tiger. This was probably the worst example of tyrant kitsch I have seen with my own eyes in my entire life, and I'm something of an expert. Kim Two appeared to be wearing Elvis's white-rhinestone cowboy suit with matching shades. To big up Midget Turd, the artist had drawn the tiger's back curiously short. Rather than riding a majestic big cat, it looked as though Kim was on the back of a pale tabby cat: the effect was irresistibly comic.

Jais, the student from Morocco, pointed to Elvis-on-tabby and asked, deadpan: 'Would the Dear Leader not be offended by such a gift?' Stony-faced, Mr Hyun asked Jais exactly what he meant. The local guide seemed apoplectic. I moved away, trying to suppress hysterical giggles. It was like getting the funnies inside a courtroom: the worse it is, the funnier it gets. Tomiko explained that Jais was from Morocco and that in his country all cats, including tigers, were considered vermin. Mr Hyun looked unconvinced. In semi-disgrace, we were asked to leave.

12

The Man Who Went to North Korea and Came Back Mad

In 1971, the Romanian dictator Nicolae Ceausescu went to North Korea. He liked Pyongyang so much he returned in 1978, and the film of this second trip is on YouTube. It's an unforgettable five minutes of two tyrants just having fun.[1]

The video opens with Ceausescu in a black suit and tie and Kim Il Sung in a light grey Mao suit. The two big men are standing up in an open-top limousine, driving through the streets of the Big Zombie in an immense motorcade led by twenty police motorcycle outriders. Thousands line the streets, crying 'Hosannah!' or some such in Korean, but the actual soundtrack of the video is supplied by a living-dead choir, roaring out a weird soundwave, ebbing and flowing rhythmically. A pod of ladies in white Korean traditional dresses holding pink doodahs in each hand whirr, rotate and clap in perfect synchronicity, as if each one is a music-box

[1] http://www.youtube.com/watch?v=qd3H9X-Yl2k

149

mannequin; balloons are released; a footbridge painted with rainbow colours arcs across the motorway, on it more ladies in white doing their stuff. The limousine passes two portraits, one of the Romanian, the other of the North Korean. Ceausescu is centre-frame, passing the camera, waving manically; Kim Il Sung is more restrained. He's been to this kind of party before. He doesn't quite yawn, but he accepts the mass adulation like the Fonz might. The motorcade swings into Kim Il Sung Square, and then the fun begins.

Maybe a hundred thousand people crowd the square, maybe more. Closest to the motorcade, more ladies dance, waving things that look like paper flower bouquets, creating the impression of so much multicoloured seaweed floating this way and that in the tide. Half a dozen black-suited security men trot along beside the limousine as it passes a maypole, then yet more ladies, this time North Korean versions of Mary Poppins, waving their brollies aloft. The two great men enter a vast stadium, clapping Mao-style, lightly on their hands, while the masses roar their adoration. Then they sit down at two vast wooden desks, as big as a lifeboat on a Channel ferry, and feel the love. The masses oblige.

Opposite the stage, a sign at least 100 feet wide, created by a vast throng of people holding up flash cards, proclaims: 'Traiasca Tovarasul Nicolae Ceausescu Conducator Iubit Si Stimat Al Poporului Roman!' which means: 'Long live Comrade Nicolae Ceausescu Esteemed and Beloved Leader of the Romanian People!' The show continues, with the flash-card crowd building Kim Il Sung, against a background of heavy industry, using a walkie-talkie pointing to a giant tractor and lorry. A real biplane puffs out show smoke at an extraordinarily slow speed; fireworks make white puffy clouds against a perfect blue sky; the twosome shake hands aloft, Kim Il Sung jolly and delighted, Ceausescu a bit peevish.

A few video frames back from the end, you can make out, sat between the two dictators, a small Romanian diplomat in a black suit, grinning at the fun; thirty-five years later that man sits in front of me in his small flat, not far from the centre of Bucharest: living history.

Izidor Urian – small, wiry, sprite, instantly likeable, his English extraordinarily precise for a man in his eighties – first went to North Korea, by train, in 1954. Back then, the journey from Bucharest to Pyongyang lasted fourteen days.

With Izidor now was his wife, Emilia, who clucked around her husband, a loving hen, occasionally putting her head to one side and smiling as a detail of something that happened four, five decades ago eluded him. Their flat was no palace, being on the seventh floor of a typically nondescript block in a not conspicuously fashionable area of the Romanian capital. But, within, the walls were decorated with pictures of Korea and framed ideograms, the calligraphy dark strokes against the white of the artist's paper.

Why North Korea? 'God decided.' In the early 1950s the Communist lords of Romania were looking for bright working-class boys to become the new diplomatic corps, and Izidor, who fitted that bill, was picked for Pyongyang. He became so fluent in Korean that, in the 1990s while serving as ambassador of Romania to South Korea, he won the first prize in a translation competition for foreigners. But, boy, did he suffer for his art.

To begin, I asked Izidor about that trip to Pyongyang in 1978. 'It was extremely difficult for me,' he said, ruefully. He had been working on the Asian desk for the Romanian Ministry of Foreign Affairs but at a few days' notice he was ordered to fly out to Pyongyang. Ceausescu arrived, the visit started but the leader hadn't brought an official note-taker. 'My job was to translate, but I also had to make notes at the same time. I scribbled notes, then at night I stayed up to two or three in the morning, transcribing my scribble into formal memos. After three or four days of this I was so exhausted I could barely function. Once, during the visit, Ceausescu and Elena' – his ghastly wife, a barely educated numb-skull the Romanian propaganda machine had magicked into a doctor of chemistry – 'had left Pyongyang and we were going on a train to a mountain residence of Kim Il Sung for a short break from talks. We were in a special carriage. I told them that I was so exhausted I could neither see nor hear. It was Elena who was nastiest: "Why can't you take notes, write every word down?" I replied that I had been translating all day and writing up the notes all night. I hadn't eaten in two days. "Why not?" asked Elena. "I can't eat and translate at the same time. When you leave, I have to leave too, so I don't get to eat," I replied. Elena barked back the Korean translator had no problem. "That's because there are three of them, and they work in rotation." Elena put on her nastiest face and said: "It's not your place to complain."'

Ceausescu, who everyone says was a kinder man than Elena when it came to handling servants, intervened and Izidor finally got some rest. At the end of the North Korean trip, Izidor was booked on a flight back to Bucharest, but Ceausescu interrupted, saying that that was a waste of money, and told Izidor to come on the Romanian presidential jet with the rest of party to Hanoi. On leaving Hanoi, it turned out the runway was too short, the jet too heavy, so they dumped Izidor on the tarmac. He had three dollars on him. One week later, he managed to hitch a flight to Pakistan in a cargo plane. On that flight, no food and drink, only cold. At Karachi, he spent the last of his money on two bottles of 7-Up, which was his only food and drink for the seventeen-hour flight back to eastern Europe. The translator shook his head: 'That's why I shall never forget that visit.'

He recalled Pyongyang in 1954, immediately after the Korean war: 'It really was as it says in the Bible, "Not one stone upon another." No buildings, no electricity, no running water, no heating. Our embassy was a small villa, a little away from the city. It had no glass windows, only scraps of cardboard. Later, they built an apartment building for us. There was no heating. In winter, it was extremely cold. Eventually, they brought me a very large duvet and I sewed up the bottom of it, making a sleeping bag.'

How did he find Kim Il Sung? 'Like a god.'

The Great Leader was charming to Izidor, very friendly, had a ready laugh: 'He wanted everybody to know that he was looking after the ordinary people. That was true but there was some acting, too.' The Romanian seemed to have the mind-set of many North Koreans of the older generation, happy to give Kim the First the benefit of the doubt, but more critical of Kims Two and Three.

Izidor recalled translating for Ceausescu in Korea, and there was no chair, so he was obliged to stand. 'Kim noticed, and said, "Why are you standing? Grab yourself a chair."' On Kim Il Sung's last trip to Europe in 1985, Izidor accompanied him on the train journey from Bucharest – remember, he hated flying – to the eastern border. As dawn came up, Kim sent word to Izidor to join him for breakfast, a sumptuous affair. Nothing much was said during the meal, but Izidor remembered the generosity of the god-king. Izidor recounted one of the fables told in North Korea, how Kim was being driven through the countryside when he passed a woman whose tractor had broken down. Kim ordered his chauffeur to stop and then tow the broken tractor to the nearest town. 'The common people believe this story. My commentary: it's not impossible that this story is true.'

What was the difference between Kim Il Sung and Kim Jong Il? 'As far as foreign relations were concerned, Kim Il Sung was an excellent player; he juggled between China and Russia. Kim Jong Il had nothing of his father's ability to play foreign interests against each other. That is why Kim Jong Il only ever visited China and Russia, no other countries. Kim Il Sung tried to save and maintain the Communist system, using political means on an international scale. Kim Jong Il did not use politics, but did his best to provide security for the country by force. The consequence was long-range rockets and three nuclear tests.'

Izidor did four spells in the Hermit Kingdom: from 1954 to 1960, from 1962 to 1965, from 1968 to 1973 and the last tour from 1979 to 1983. He became aware of a great change in the mood in North Korea when he returned in 1968. Before that date, foreigners from fellow Communist countries like him had been free to travel around the whole country; afterwards, Izidor and his fellow diplomats were locked inside Pyongyang, and had to apply for official permission to move around the country, permission that was granted extremely rarely. The diplomatic lockdown reflected a deeper paranoia.

The two great moments of Izidor's career under Ceausescu were the two presidential visits to Pyongyang, in 1971 and 1978. In the great scheme of things, relations between two minor Communist powers on either side of the world were not so very important, but the pay-off for both Ceausescu and Kim Il Sung was that they could display their independence to Moscow and Beijing.

However, many Romanians mark the 1971 trip to Pyongyang as the knife-slash in time when Ceausescu lost his reason, and sent his country galloping off in the wrong direction, towards a national Stalinism. Sergiu Celac was Ceausescu's English translator until he got the sack in 1978. I met him in 1990. Celac noticed the dramatic change in Ceausescu on his return from North Korea: 'Up to 1971, by Marxist standards, he was able to generate new ideas within the limits of the system. After his visit to North Korea in 1971, something of crucial importance must have happened to his mind. What he saw in North Korea was an image of "real socialism" – that is, total regimentation. Of course, everything in Romania was fundamentally wrong from the beginning. But the practical approaches until 1971 were mitigated by a degree of realism and independent thinking, which had not yet become militant and destructive nationalism. I think that all his life he believed in what he considered to be the generous idea of socialism and Communism. But in 1971 he apparently discovered the use of pyramidical organization inherent in one-party rule, and the crucial importance of the top of the pyramid. He hated and despised Stalin who had enjoyed just such a position, but Ceausescu hated Stalin because he saw him as a leader of an evil empire. The evil was its imperial character, not its ideology. Hence Ceausescu was blind to his own messianic bent. So 1971 was the moment of rupture for him and the date of the misfortunes he brought with him.'

If so, then Ceausescu's Romania was the only successful export of Kimist ideology.

How much was Izidor aware of the dark side of the DPRK? He took a deep breath, and paused for a time. A diplomat since he was nineteen years old, and someone who served a Communist dictatorship of increasing repression for most of his career, and for eighteen years lived and worked in the worst tyranny on earth, Izidor knows that words can be as heavy as lead.

He looked down at the white tablecloth in front of him: 'If some-one disappeared, you couldn't find them.' He told me the tragedy of Georgeta Mircioiu, a Romanian woman who married a North Korean. She fell pregnant, but went home to have the baby some time in the early 1960s. She returned to North Korea for a time, but her baby fell sick and she went home once more. She was never allowed back to North Korea. They said her husband 'had left for the mountains', the code phrase for the gulag. The time-frame is roughly the same as the 1967 purge that did for Ali Lameda and Jacques Sedillot, when any suspect foreigner or North Korean connected to a foreigner entered the shadows. To begin with, Georgeta was able to send and receive letters from her man; then the letters stopped. For many years, maybe fifteen, maybe twenty, said Izidor, she never gave up, she insisted that he was alive, she pressed the Red Cross. 'Nothing . . .'

Suddenly, she received a hint that he was alive, after all that time. 'Her hope was relit. Then,' said Izidor with immense melan-choly, 'she got a death certificate.'

He also told me about the tragedy of Doina Bumbea, a beautiful Romanian artist who vanished off the face of the earth in 1978. (See Chapter 17: 'The American Who Went to North Korea and Stayed'.)

How long does Izidor think the regime will last? 'Thirty, forty, fifty years . . .'

I said my goodbyes to Izidor and Emilia and returned to the city centre. At the heart of Bucharest is the square in front of the old Central Committee building, where Ceausescu made his last, stumbling speech before his helicopter took him away. On Christmas Eve night, 1989, the square was littered with tanks and armoured cars, residue of the battle that day. The old Royal Palace was a pockmarked ruin; every building had its bullet acne, and some had been blasted into rubble. Here and there flames still licked at windows; roofs glowed a dull red. Despite the gunfire, people seethed around, shouting, singing snatches of songs. Small bonfires illuminated their faces, some black with dirt, others the colour of whey, all exhausted. Shards of glass and spent bullet cases crackled underfoot.

The songs died and the crowd flattened when an army gunner started blasting away pointlessly from a window inside the Central Committee building. There was no answering fire. The sniper he was furiously exterminating existed only inside his head. A student came up to me: 'You must understand what a mind-fuck Ceausescu has been for us.'

On Christmas morning I went looting in the Central Committee building itself. The windows had been shot to pieces; the floor was peppered with spent bullets, broken glass, fallen masonry. In one room was a stack of photograph albums, including one picture of a man in a Mao suit and Ceausescu. I ripped it out of the album and stuffed it in my coat. The man in the Mao suit, I now realize, was Kim Il Sung.[2]

After the shooting of the Ceausescus, the palace bodyguard in Pyongyang was increased from 4,000 men to 70,000.[3]

[2] Sweeney: *The Life and Evil Times of Nicolae Ceausescu*, p8.
[3] Martin, p547.

13

The Washing of Brains

'It was a bright cold day in April, and the clocks were striking thirteen' is the opening sentence of the novel that prefigured the horrors of North Korea, George Orwell's *1984*. But even the Old Etonian seer would have been surprised, I expect, by the weird hollowness of the life of the mind, North Korean-style.

The Pyongyang University of Foreign Languages is no ordinary college. As always, we had a local guide who showed us that the foreign language institute had been created under the wise guidance of Kim . . . blah-blah-blah. The KITC video has a jaunty middle-of-the-road jazz number playing as our party wanders around the university. The video shows a great slab on a wall where Kim Jong Il's giant ideogram hangs – dated '2009.12.17', showing that only twelve years after Juche Time was established, it had been abandoned by the regime propaganda functionaries. They show us pictures of Kim Il Sung and Kim Jong Il, empty corridors, emptier classrooms, a huge room where students might sit at the desks, listening to tapes whirring away of 'The cat in the hat . . .' or whatever, entirely vacant. Something is missing. This is a university with no students.

Where are the students? They are at a meeting, said Miss Jun. All of them? Yes, she said. This may well have been entirely true. It's apparently quite common for the regime to demand 100 per cent presence of all students at a rally or even the rehearsal of a rally, and nothing takes precedence over obeisance to the state. 'Sorry, I've got an essay to write . . .' is not a functioning excuse in the DPRK.

They showed us an intranet computer terminal which was linked to a library catalogue, of sorts. On the KITC video, you can clearly hear me ask for a book by 'George Orwell . . . *Animal Farm*?' To my intense disappointment, they had Orwell's great satire on Stalinism. Or, correction, the book showed up on the electronic menu. I never saw a hard copy of it. The computer may have been lying. But it's entirely possible that they do have *Animal Farm* in a North Korean university, but only because its true nature – to my mind, the greatest satire ever written – has somehow escaped the clod-ears of the regime's censors. If so, raise a glass to Orwell's memory. In fact, do that anyway.

The tour of empty spaces continued. In the corner of one room was a stack of simple learn-to-read magazines, heavily thumbed. Knowing North Korea, one wondered whether any of the fancy computer terminals and voice-booths actually worked, or whether the foreign language students had to learn most of their English the old-fashioned way. As there were no students around, we could hardly ask them.

One reason for the absence of students may have been because the Pyongyang University of Foreign Languages is a spy school. Its most famous alumnus is, according to US Congressional testimony,

Kim Hyun Hee.[1] Her claim to fame – and that of her school-cum-university – is mass murder. The victims were 115 innocent people, mostly South Koreans, the passengers and crew of Korean Air Flight 858, which blew up mid-air on 29 November 1987. Kim and her fellow agent had planted the bomb, then got off at its first stop-over at Abu Dhabi. The two agents were tracked down to Bahrain; Kim's partner dutifully killed himself by smoking a cyanide-laced cigarette but Kim failed to puff hard enough on her suicide smoke. She was arrested and detained. In her memoir, *The Tears of My Soul*, she records what happened next: 'I was thrown onto a bed and handcuffed to the frame. A moment later a middle-aged Caucasian couple entered the room. Both had blond hair and blue eyes, and they looked at me curiously, but without malice.' They were a British couple, Ian Henderson, the Chief of Police in Bahrain, and his wife, Maria. Kim recalls Maria telling her: 'It's going to be all right, dear ... Don't worry about a thing.'[2]

And so Kim Hyun Hee's de-brainwashing commenced. The story is as grim as anyone could possibly imagine: a beautiful, gifted young woman, fluent in Japanese, good at English, trained to commit mass murder by the North Korean state. Hand-picked because of her talent at the foreign languages university, she was sent to a secret terrorist-training base in the mountains, and was then shipped halfway around the world to blow up her fellow Koreans. Kim Jong Il's logic was that such an outrage would

---

[1] Yoichi Shimada, Professor of International Politics, Fukui Prefectural University, House Committee on International Relations: Subcommittee on Asia and the Pacific, Subcommittee on Africa, Global Human Rights and International Operations, 27 April 2006.
[2] Kim Hyun Hee: *The Tears of My Soul*, William Morrow, New York, 1993, p122.

frighten foreigners from coming to the 1988 Seoul Olympics. Far from it; such was the world's disgust at the bomb that all talk of boycotting the games by the Communist world – in 1988, at the very fag-end of its existence – stopped. Kim Hyun Hee was sentenced to death, but subsequently pardoned and served a relatively short time behind bars. She emerged from prison a chastened woman, and her book is a convincing account of someone who was effectively a victim of mental enslavement, a killing machine with no real idea of what she was doing to her fellow human beings when she planted the bomb.

At a press conference in 1990, she expressed deep remorse: 'Being a culprit I do have a sense of agony with which I must fight. In that sense I must still be a prisoner or a captive – of a sense of guilt.' She now lives in a safe house somewhere in South Korea, constantly guarded, for fear of revenge from her victims' families, or, perhaps, more likely, from the North Korean regime, which has reportedly branded her a traitor.

In the twenty-first century, the Spy School/University of Foreign Languages has been keeping up the good work, with some of its students selling North Korean arms and nuclear materials on the international black market, according to an anonymous defector in 2010. *Chosun Ilbo*, the South Korean newspaper, reported that international sanctions against North Korea had made it difficult to export weapons in the ordinary way. The defector, who was under police protection and did not want his identity to be revealed, fearing reprisal attacks against family members still in the North, said that the black operation is run by 'traders' from the 'Surveillance Division of the People's Armed Forces' – one of the DPRK's myriad spy agencies – fluent in English and Chinese after studying at Pyongyang University of Foreign Languages.

The scam works like this: North Korea sends containers across the Yalu river to China, one third or half filled with weapons, missile components or technical equipment for higher-grade nuclear enrichment. The client, more often than not, is the research centre of Iran's Revolutionary Guard. As you may imagine, this trade is very black indeed. The 'traders' use their language skills in English and Chinese to broker deals with bent shipping agents in ports outside North Korea – presumably in China. The shipping agents or 'forwarders' fill up the rest of the container with innocent machine parts or whatever, own the paperwork, and all trace of the true origin of the black goods has vanished. The defector explained that these 'laundered' containers are relaundered in Hong Kong, Singapore or other ports. 'The containers are mixed with other cargo in those transit points. They are searched, but not thoroughly,' the defector added. 'Even if customs or other officials roll their sleeves up and search for weapons, how can they possibly find the arms among the mountains of other containers headed to other countries?'[3]

None of this was mentioned on our guided tour.

Off we went across town, to the Grand People's Study House, a giant pagoda affair right next to Kim Il Sung Square. In our world, you might call the Study House the national library, but a clue to the real theme of the place was soon evident: an enormous marble statue of Kim Il Sung in a Mao suit, sitting down in an armchair, hewn out of rock, a newspaper in his hand. Behind him are mountain peaks, pink-tipped at dawn, with a sugar coating of snow. After a while you learn to date the propaganda from the

[3] 'How North Korea goes about exporting arms', Chosun Ilbo, English language version, 10 March 2010, http://english.chosun.com/site/data/html_dir/2010/03/10/2010031000953.html

clothes the Kims wear. Kim Il Sung sports Soviet Commissar chic in the 1940s and early 1950s, shifting to Mao suits in the 1960s as the rupture with the de-Stalinizing Soviet Union was at its height. Mao suits may have become a tad unfashionable during the Cultural Revolution when the Red Guards were taunting Kim Il Sung as 'a fat revisionist', but were back in fashion for most of the 1970s. However, the end of Maoism and China's slide – or ascent – to free market economics means that by the start of the 1980s Kim Il Sung throws away his Mao clobber and starts wearing a proper suit. When Kim Jong Il pops up in the propaganda statuary a few years later, he's down and dirty in the Mao suit, while his father looks more the conventional statesman in the classic CEO business suit. So I would place this statue of Kim Il Sung in Maoist garb no later than the 1980s, and perhaps a decade earlier.

They told us that the Grand People's Study House was home to 30 million books. There were stacks of books around, but nothing approaching a fraction of that number. Down a corridor, Kims Major and Minor smiled down from the wall underneath a flickering fluorescent light. The walkway opened up into a chasm, lit by a dim-watted chandelier but the temperature was freezing. I wore my coat throughout. We were taken to a strange place, like the area in an Argos store where you sit and wait, and wait and wait, for the goods you've ordered. You file a request on an intranet computer. I asked for Solzhenitsyn. Nope. Did they, by any chance, have a copy of George Orwell's *1984*? No joy. Instead, a miniature metal sleigh shot out from a mouse-hole kind of orifice in a wall bearing three books. One couldn't help wondering whether there really were 30 million books in there, or just one man sitting behind a wall with three books, who gave the sleigh a push every time Western visitors popped into the Grand Study House.

The three books that whizzed down the ramp were: *The Adventures of Huckleberry Finn*, something so boring I can't recall and *Discovering Food and Nutrition*, which is funny because North Korea's stand-out event in the last twenty years, apart from three nuclear tests, is famine.

They showed us a reading room, full of ordinary North Koreans toiling over books. Were they for real? Or just for show? No one looked up as our chattering party of thirteen foreign weirdos, half of us filming everything that moved, and Alex continually filming me, wandered in and made our on-the-spot inspection. And that is extremely peculiar.

While investigating Scientology in 2007, our *Panorama* crew were given a tour of the Church complex on L Ron Hubbard Way in Los Angeles. I darted through the front door a split second in front of our minders, Tom Cruise lookalike Tommy Davis and Mike Rinder, who has since got out. What I saw was a whole room full of people, poised in stop-motion. Suddenly there was an unseen signal, and everybody started to walk purposefully crossways, just as they do in the Church's surreally unreal promotional videos. In another room they showed us a grown man playing with plasticine. Mr Hubbard worked out, said Tommy, that playing with clay figures helps Scientologists.

The man lumped his figures into a ball, and then rolled out his clay.

In one long room there were dozens of people, bent over their studies or playing with clay, none of whom paid any attention whatsoever to the two agents, the reporter, the four separate people behind cameras and the sound person with a very long boom. And that is weird. It is a simple constant of working for TV, everywhere on the planet, that people come up to you and say, 'What are you filming?'

and 'What's it for?' and 'When does it go out?' and 'Hello, Mum.' When people not only don't do that, but do the opposite and entirely ignore the cameras, one can reasonably deduce that they have been commanded to behave in that peculiar way, beforehand. It was like wandering around inside the set of *The Truman Show*. The reading room of the Grand People's Study House in Pyongyang felt every bit as true to life as the Church of Scientology on L Ron Hubbard Way, and that is not a compliment in this or any other galaxy.

In January 2013, Sophie Schmidt went with her father, Google founder Eric Schmidt, and former New Mexico governor and UN ambassador Bill Richardson, to Pyongyang. Sophie wrote:

> Our trip was a mixture of highly-staged encounters, tightly-orchestrated viewings and what seemed like genuine human moments. We had zero interactions with non-state-approved North Koreans and were never far from our two minders ... Ordinary North Koreans live in a near-total information bubble without any true frame of reference ... The best description we could come up with is that it's like *The Truman Show*, on a national scale. At the Kim Il-sung University e-Library, there was one problem: no one was actually doing anything. A few scrolled or clicked, but the rest just stared. More disturbing: when our group walked in – a noisy bunch, with media in tow – not one of them looked up from their desks. Not a head turn, no eye contact, no reaction to stimuli. They might as well have been figurines.[4]

Sophie and I may both be entirely wrong and the people reading at the Grand Study House and Kim Il Sung University were not

[4] http://www.thesundaytimes.co.uk/sto/newsreview/article1206351.ece

faking it. But after a few days in North Korea you become so used to questioning the evidence of your own eyes that what you see feels fake.

One day, after a particularly arduous stretch of bumpety-bump on the long empty motorway, we had an impromptu toilet stop. We tumbled out of the bus desperate for a couple of minutes of terra firma. With nothing to see for miles our minders didn't follow us, for once. After a few moments of fresh air, we were summoned back on to the bus. As I walked past Mr Hyun, I could see he was hunched over, engrossed like a little boy, reading something. I peered over and was surprised to see it was a comic book. But this was not Superman, Batman or Incredible Hulk. It was cartoon images of North Korean soldiers bayoneting, blowing up or otherwise killing the American-bastards. I realized then that Mr Hyun was more of a believer than I had thought. In his own free time he was choosing to read the regime's cartoon propaganda and by the looks of things thoroughly enjoying it. Later that same day as we zipped past endless fields I saw a woman on a chair reading a book. Nothing remarkable about it except that the image stood out. Everywhere in the West, people read: books, magazines, Kindles, newspapers. Yet over there I only saw one person reading a book. But then what are you going to read? World literature? Books on economics or philosophy? Not likely.

Marxism-Leninism back in 1945, Jucheism from the late 1950s, Kimilsungism from the 1980s, and now a hideous mutation of all three have squatted like a great toad on the North Korean mind. Dictatorships survive by enforcing ignorance, by keeping people under-educated. Gaddafi did this by making it virtually impossible for ordinary Libyans to learn English. But it strikes me that this process has been taken to a far deeper level in the DPRK.

Are North Koreans brainwashed? And if they are, how deep does the brainwashing go?

Mark Fitzpatrick is a witty American who has spent far too much of his life, first in the State Department and now at the International Institute for Strategic Studies, thinking about stopping nuclear Armageddon, triggered by the men from Pyongyang. His day job has scarred him. He does have a touch of the Dr Strangelove about him. He told me: 'It certainly would appear that the North Koreans are brainwashed. When you talk to North Koreans, you can have a normal conversation and think I'm really dealing with a human being and then all of a sudden they go into this robotic recitation of North Korean policy and you wanna shake them and say, "Come on, get real."'

The Korean civil war made the term 'brainwashing' fashionable. Thought reform has a long history, perhaps starting with the Spanish Inquisition, perhaps before; refined and darkened by Stalin's secret police, the horror of mental enslavement brilliantly told in Arthur Koestler's *Darkness at Noon*. But brainwashing per se was introduced to a wider public by Richard Condon in his 1959 novel *The Manchurian Candidate*, about a returning American ex-prisoner of war who seeks high office in the United States but is in fact controlled by the Communists, a story retold for Israeli TV viewers as *Hatufim*, which was itself picked up by US TV and retold as *Homeland*. The motor of the plot of all three is: can we trust a warrior who has been held in captivity by the enemy? Or does he still belong to them?

On brainwashing, the odd circularity of life breaks in: the world's great expert on the subject is a man called Professor Robert Jay Lifton, author of *Thought Reform and the Psychology of Totalism:*

A Study of 'Brainwashing' in China.[5] I was introduced to Lifton's work by Bruce Hines while I was investigating Scientology. Hines was at one time an auditor – Scientology's word for confessor – who used to minister to Nicole Kidman, Kirstie Alley and Tom Cruise. But he saw the light, and got out.

Lifton, an American military psychiatrist, spent the 1950s interviewing Allied ex-prisoners who had been captured during the Korean war and held in North Korea, and then Chinese and European victims of Chairman Mao's totalitarian state. He explains that the term 'brainwashing' was first used by the American journalist Edward Hunter as a translation of the colloquialism *hsi nao* (literally, 'wash brain'), which he quoted from Chinese informants who described its use after the Communist takeover.

Later, Lifton set out three defining characteristics of a cult: first, 'All cults have a charismatic leader, who himself or herself increasingly becomes the object of worship, and in many cases, the dispenser of immortality. Spiritual ideas of a general kind give way to this deification of the leader.' Secondly, in cults there is some kind of 'thought reform', popularly known as brainwashing. Thirdly, 'There is a pattern of manipulation and exploitation from above, by leaders and ruling coteries, and idealism from below, on the part of supplicants and recruits.' To sum up Lifton's definers for a cult: one, the Leader is God; two, brainwashing; three, harm. On two out of three, it's a no-brainer: North Korea is a cult. And brainwashing?

Lifton sets out eight tests for brainwashing.[6] Test number one is

[5] Lifton, *Thought Reform*, Pelican, London, 1967 (the book I keep under my pillow).

[6] Lifton's eight tests for brainwashing are examined in my book on Scientology, *The Church of Fear*, Silvertail Books, London, 2013 but the original is always better: Lifton: *Thought Reform and the Psychology of Totalism: A Study of "Brainwashing" in China*, New York, 1961.

'Milieu Control' or constriction, throttling of information. Lifton writes: 'The most basic feature of the thought reform environment, the psychological current upon which all else depends, is the control of human communication. Through this milieu control the totalist environment seeks to establish domain over not only the individual's communication with the outside (all that he sees and hears, reads and writes, experiences, and expresses), but also – in his penetration of his inner life – over what we may speak of as his communication with himself. It creates an atmosphere uncomfortably reminiscent of George Orwell's *1984*.' The most basic consequence of this information control, says Lifton, 'is the disruption of balance between self and outside world'.

Lifton's seven other tests for brainwashing are 'Mystical Manipulation' – a sense that the group ideology is beyond rational analysis; 'The Demand for Purity' – that the in-group is pure, and outsiders are impure; 'The Cult of Confession' – that self-criticism is a public good; 'The Sacred Science' – that the group's ideology is holy; 'Loading the Language' – that words mean what the group's leaders want them to mean; 'Doctrine over Person' – that the individual has no rights; and 'The Dispensing of Existence' – that the masses must be willing to surrender life for the good of the whole. The professor sums up his eight tests: 'The more clearly an environment expresses these eight psychological themes, the greater its resemblance to ideological totalism; and the more it utilizes such totalist devices to change people, the greater its resemblance to thought reform or "brainwashing".'

Quite a few people are highly sceptical that such a thing as brainwashing really exists. They cite legal precedents in the courts in the United States, which rule out 'brainwashing' as a defence. That may be sensible in a democracy, but it does not quite mean that the term has no use at all. Some prefer using the phrase 'thought reform', such as Jonathan Mirsky, one of the great experts on China, who called it 'The Auschwitz of the Mind'. I have yet to meet a North Korean defector who objected to the word 'brain-washing'. I talked to two defectors who have ended up in London's KoreaTown, New Malden, just off the A3, and asked them about their lives and whether they felt they had been brainwashed.

'Mary Lou' still has a brother inside the North – hence her transparently un-Korean name. She's in her mid-thirties, an attractive, feisty woman, lively, casually dressed with a hint of bling. She was born in an area called Shinpo Shi, which is in the middle of the eastern coast. Their house was a small two-floor apartment in a block of flats. Outside Pyongyang the flats are generally only about five storeys high because there are no elevators, or, if there are, they don't work.

I asked Mary Lou whether she ever had any doubts about North Korea when she lived there, and she said she never had an inkling. She only realized how bad North Korea was when she left it, and then convinced her parents to escape as well. She told me a story about when she was in high school; there was this good-looking, strapping young boy who was also extremely smart, perfect all round. All the girls were crazy about him, and when he went into the army all the girls cried, because they were sad to see him go. That was the last she saw of him, until many years later when she noticed him at a train station among the homeless beggars. He had lost all his weight and was only a few days from death. He had lost so much weight in the army because of the lack of food, they had sent him home, but his family couldn't look after him either. So he eventually left home, and ended up there. She bought him a sweet with what little money she had, but he wouldn't take it because he felt embarrassed, especially because she had known him in his prime. She popped it in his mouth anyway, but he couldn't even control his saliva and was dribbling. He couldn't even move to stop her, or wipe himself. She said the homeless man next to him was also bare bones, with a cut on his leg next to the knee that had become infected, and flies had laid their eggs in there. He had a little stick and was flicking the larvae that were coming out. Even seeing all this, Mary Lou said, she never thought there was anything wrong with North Korea, and that this friend was just down on his luck. It's only looking back now that she realizes how awful it was.

In 1997, at the height of the famine, her family moved by train to the sacred Mount Baekdu, where Kim Jong Il was born, according to the official scripture, although that, of course, is a fiction. 'The train was packed, people sitting on top of each other. The journey from the east coast up to a town close to the Chinese border should have taken only eight hours, but it took ten days. It was very slow. There were so many power failures. I would see people falling asleep, I would try and slap them, and discovered they were dead.'

How many died? 'I don't know. All the ordinary people died. Anyone who had energy left tried to escape to China. I saw dozens of people at stations and in market places, starving. You became used to it. So many dead it wasn't even an event . . . to see a corpse became unremarkable. Sometimes, at the railway stations, the railway workers would kick the people out . . . you could see them outside the apartment blocks . . . they would die from exposure . . . lying under plastic bags . . . in a corner away from the wind . . . you would see heaps of the dead.'

Mary Lou didn't escape because she had planned it or wanted to, but she was coerced into it by human traffickers. In 1998 she had gone to an area called Hyesan-shi, which borders China, to sell stuff at the market. On her way, all her bags were stolen. She said theft was rife because everyone was struggling. She met a friend at Hyesan-shi, who had also had all her things stolen. They had nothing to sell, no money and no way to get back home. After three days of being stuck in Hyesan, a North Korean guy came up to them and asked them to come with him to China for a day, promising that they would make more money in a day working at a Chinese farm than they would have made selling all their things. Seeing as they had no choice they decided to give it a go.

At the border, Mary Lou noticed that the land on the North Korean side of the river was barren, but on the Chinese side, full of trees. The smuggler knew where to go. They crossed the river in the dead of night, no moon shining, and the water up to her chest. How cold was it? 'I was so scared I didn't notice.' She reckoned the smuggler might have paid off the guards.

I asked what her first impressions of China were. 'In North Korea, at night the only lights you see are the ones that shine on the statues of Kim Il Sung and Kim Jong Il. I looked back, it was very dark. Ahead, I saw neon lights, red, blue. I thought it was for a show, but there were lights in every house, even tiny little villages had electricity.'

They got in a car and were driven deeper into China, further and further away from the border. They spent a night at a house, changed cars at various points, and everyone was really nice to them, saying they would get work, and that they would take them back to North Korea when they were done, never realizing that as they were changing cars, they were being handed off or sold on to other buyers.

Slowly it dawned on her that she wasn't just going to work on a farm. True enough, Mary Lou had been sold off to a farmer, a lonely ethnic Korean, the majority population in the borderlands. He'd bought her, lock, stock and barrel. 'When I went to the house of the man who bought me, I saw a whole stack of potatoes leaning against an outhouse. The spuds were shrivelled. They had frozen, then thawed, they were half rotten, but in North Korea they were good food. I was startled and said: "Why are potatoes outside? I could make potato cakes."'

The man explained: 'We don't eat that. That's for the pigs.'

'My pride was hurt. Not just the pig food, but also the fact that I had been duped into being sold off in the first place. He wasn't a bad man, this first husband, but I was twenty-one and you have dreams about the kind of man you want to marry. He was twenty-seven and already he was looking down on me. One day my father-in-law said something rude about Kim Jong Il, and I cried. I wanted to go back to North Korea.'

This last sentence suggests that Mary Lou had been profoundly brainwashed, her mind-set so narrow and forcibly blinkered that she preferred to return to North Korea than eat. But her ignorance of China, and the distance she had already travelled, made it impossible for her to go back. Slowly, she adapted, and slowly it began to sink in that everything she had learnt in her entire life so far had been a cruel lie.

Eventually, Mary Lou had to leave China, because she was ratted out and caught by the police. Although she was meant to be deported back to North Korea, her husband paid them off and got her released. Because she didn't have the right permits or paperwork, she and her husband decided to go to a bigger city, where it would be harder for them to be discovered. They did, but even there, there was a danger of being caught. So her husband eventually decided to let her leave China and go to South Korea. She left in 2002, got to Seoul, found herself a new husband, like her a North Korean refugee, and had two kids. She decided to come to Britain because she felt her children were being discriminated against in South Korea – a common complaint made by Koreans from the North. She now lives in New Malden, drives an Audi estate, and her children's English is getting better than their Korean.

Mary Lou had last spoken to her brother, who is still inside the North, via a Chinese mobile phone the previous month. He travels up to a place very close to the Chinese border, where the signal from the Chinese phone masts can reach inside North Korea, and they have a conversation. She also sends him money.

'I wire the broker in China £3,000. My brother "Richard" gets £1,500 in Chinese yuan in the North.' This is a small fortune in North Korea, and perversely makes the decision for him and his family to escape that much harder. The remaining £1,500 is split between the Chinese middleman and the North Korean broker, who smuggles the cash across and gets it to Richard and organizes the phone call. The deal takes place in a house close by the Chinese border, up a mountain where the phone signal is good. 'Without the phone call,' she said, 'I can't be sure that Richard gets the money.'

The sad thing is that much of the time on the phone they spend arguing: 'I always try and convince him to leave. It would only cost between £5,000 and £7,000 for him, his wife and the baby to get out. But he feels betrayed by the rest of his family. He has no idea what it is like outside. Our brother went into the army, placed him in a good position, but the rest of us have fled, so that is a cause of frustration and upset for him.'

Does Richard have any idea how poor North Korea is? 'He knows that North Korea is struggling because of America but he is not really aware. We argue. I say: "North Korea is poor," he says: "Don't talk like that . . ."'

Do you think your brother is brainwashed?

'Yes. Anyone who is aware gets out . . .'

Is it like locked-in syndrome? 'Yes – because no one can say anything. Everyone has been trained by the government to spy on each another. If there were three of us talking, one would be spying. I always worry that the phone is being listened in to . . . Sometimes the signal breaks or the phone crackles . . . We worry that they're spying on us . . .'

Would she ever go back?

'If I could go home without the government killing me and keep my money, then I would go back. I still dream about North Korea.

'I have nightmares, too . . .'

What kind of nightmares?

'It's always about the train journey during the famine. The people in the nightmare, their faces are formless. But they are starving, pinched, filthy. I notice they've fallen over, lying slumped on the floor. I tell a train guard . . . The bodies are covered with hessian sacks and taken away, and then the power is cut.'

Sam – obviously not his real name – picks up the defector's narrative. He was born in the early 1970s in Kil Joo, near the East Sea, not far from the area where they carry out nuclear tests. His father was in the military, a worker-peasant, a kind of North Korean version of Mao's Red Guards. His mother was a primary school teacher, one brother, one sister. They lived in a house on the edge of the city. There was an outside loo, no hot water, a pump in the basement.

'To understand North Korean society is difficult. You cannot compare it to here,' he tells me. He's sporting a pinstriped suit, sipping on a can of Coke. 'For example, we had pictures of Kim Il Sung and Kim Jong Il in the house. Everyone had the same pictures. You had to take care of the pictures, to look after them.'

The regime propaganda bolsters this up, telling mind-warping stories in which loyal citizens prefer to lose all their possessions in a fire so long as they save the pictures of Kim Il Sung and Kim Jong Il.

'Of course, I was brainwashed,' says Sam. 'From when you are born until when you die, you are told what to think. A third of the lessons you get at school are about the legends of Kim Il Sung and Kim Jong Il. You learn never to question it and no one would ever dare to mock it.'

The idea of school without mockery defeated me. He told me a story of what happened at his high school to illustrate his theme: 'There were two guys, seventeen, rivals. One borrowed a book from the other about Kim Il Sung's exploits, fighting the Japanese. He scribbles on it, gives it back, and that's the end of it. Every two or three months, ideology thought police come round to people's houses. They see the scribbles on the book about the Great Leader, and the whole family goes to the gulag. Later, the secret came out, and the guy who did it brags about it. He got away with it. No one ratted him up. Those kind of incidents happened all the time. I heard one story of a gang of kids fighting in front of a statue of Kim Il Sung. This thirteen-year-old throws a bottle and the Great Leader's ear falls off. It's plaster, painted bronze, and the whole family goes to the gulag.'

How do you know that for sure? 'There's a network of rumours, someone will have seen them taken away in trucks.' My translator

Kwon and I told Sam about the problems we had had with two North Koreans who met us, and then declined to make any criticism of the country at all, even saying that the health system in North Korea was just like the NHS. As bad as Casualty can be on a Friday night in any British hospital, I found that statement incredible.

'Even though their bodies are here in London, their minds are still in North Korea. They have nightmares, they are afraid to speak.'

Do you have nightmares? Sam said he didn't, but I didn't quite believe him.

He spent eight years in the army where, he says, he was constantly brainwashed. Sam was stationed at the DMZ for much of his time in uniform. I asked him about power supply: 'Power only works 24/7 in the Mausoleum and for the electrified fence at the DMZ' – for the dead, and the dead-to-come.

Soldiers in the army, back in the day, used to be well fed, said Sam. But once the famine hit, even in the army people suffered: one third could get by, one third starved, one third went AWOL, to go back home, just because they wanted a good meal. Sam's job was to go around the whole of North Korea, tracking down the runaways, and bringing them back to the DMZ. Such was the degree of social compliance inside North Korea that pretty much all he had to do was have a word with the soldier's parents and the runaway would meekly return with him.

Did he feel guilty? He explained that at first, at the very start of the famine years, deserters would be sent to the gulag, but as time went by the punishment became weaker. The reason they were going AWOL was hunger. Parents asked him to punish their sons quietly, hush-hush: 'I was part of a regiment, not the secret police.

I would go from place to place and bring the boys back one by one. Parents would encourage them to go back . . .'

It wasn't a difficult job, but something happened to the wall inside his head, the wall which had blocked out doubts. Not the bricks, but the mortar started to flake; in his walled-off mind, first one crack, then another. They began to spread.

'Sometimes, the parents of the soldiers would plead with me. Through my job I got to speak to a lot of people, and that is how my doubts grew. On buses everywhere, it says: "North Korea is the people's nation!" It isn't a people's nation. That was a lie. I saw the high-ups living a better life. Before, I had never questioned it: they lived that life because they deserved to live in that position, but later I did realize that it was wrong. In Pyongyang I met a woman diplomat, home for a spell, but she normally worked in the embassy in Holland: a superb job, access to the West, to money, to everything. This woman had no pity for the hungry begging for rice. When someone came to ask her for some food or money, she almost spat at them. I felt this was wrong.

'My doubts grew. But inside North Korea, there is no frame of reference. We don't know what to compare anything to . . . someone who knows, say, white and red will be able to say that's red and white but if you don't know the difference . . . you could see that people were dying . . . I wanted to leave to find the other perspective . . . as soon as I left North Korea, I saw straight away.'

The final straw was unbelievably painful for him; a life-shattering event.

'In the summer of 1999 something happened to my niece, "Janey". She was three, a toddler, but because of the famine she was the size of a one-year-old. Janey found some dried raw corn, and stuffed herself. The dried corn makes you very dehydrated so she drank too much water and her tummy expanded like a drum and she ruptured her stomach. She was a tiny kid but her stomach expanded to the size of a basketball. She looked like a bird hit by a car . . . She died. I can still see the blue veins on her tummy.'

When people came to pay their respects, they couldn't look: 'It was so gruesome . . .'

We were sitting in the back of the travel agency Kwon's parents own in New Malden. Outside, the traffic went about its business, people from Wimbledon popping in to see their mum in Surbiton, going to the local tip, to the movies. Inside, as bleak a tragedy as you ever did hear.

After a long silence, Sam continued his story: 'The death of my niece broke something inside my head. I was determined to get out. But it took me five more years to overcome my doubts. We all knew the risks, the border guards might shoot you, trouble for your family. In the summer of 2005 my job, picking up AWOL soldiers, had taken me to the far north-east, near the border with China. I rounded up seven deserters, sent them back to the DMZ, and moved closer to the Tumen river. It was August, and there was a full moon. I had to wait for three days, until clouds came, blanketing out the moon. The river is fast and deep, but not that broad up in the mountains. The problem is that in summer the level is down, so you have to crawl over 500 yards of pebbles before you get to the river proper, and the sound carries at night. If the guards hear the pebbles move, they could shoot you. I thought to myself: Do or die! I'm going to die in the gulag or die fighting . . .'

To demonstrate his pebble-crossing technique, he took off his chalk-striped jacket and laid it on the floor. He moved it ahead of him, fully at arm's length, then wriggled his body forward so that it rested on the jacket, then the process started again, all the while keeping his body as low as can be.

'To move across 500 yards of pebbles, it took me three and a half hours. The river was only 100 feet wide but the current was quite strong. It took me only half an hour to cross, if that.'

It was quiet on the Chinese side. 'Just across this river was a completely different world. I went to an apple orchard, I'd never seen one before. In North Korea an apple is eaten when it is very small.'

Did you eat one?

'I ate six.'

Sam had made it across the river but he still wasn't safe. He hid at night, he had no money, only army uniform. But after a couple of days he met a Korean Chinese, who helped him find his feet in China, and then he was on his way to freedom.

'The brainwashing,' said Sam, 'works by blocking out your mind from thinking. My brain was not wired to think critically of the regime. Only after I left North Korea, after I have seen how other cultures work, only now do I know what was wrong. People left back there may somehow sense something is wrong but they don't know for sure.'

All of the defectors from North Korea I've interviewed at length – four in South Korea, three in London – told me that they were brainwashed when they were brought up in North Korea. On Lifton's test number one, 'Milieu Control', all seven said information was constricted; they didn't know what the rest of the world was truly like until they left. On the second test, 'Mystical Manipulation', most, if not all, remembered feeling awe and veneration for the Kim dynasty, especially at school; the third test, 'The Demand for Purity' – positive, too, but this was something I did not press people on much, knowing the facts of the regime's propaganda; the fourth test, 'The Cult of Confession', everyone was familiar with; the fifth, 'The Sacred Science', is an echo of 'Mystical Manipulation', but likewise tests positive; the sixth, 'Loading the Language', positive, but again was something else I didn't press people on, knowing the lexicon of regime propaganda. The seventh, 'Doctrine over Person', and the eighth, 'The Dispensing of Existence'? How can those tests not be passed, if your country suffers a famine that kills untold numbers and yet the people remain loyal? When the stomach of a starving three-year-old bursts and no one dares deface the pictures of the fat rulers – is that not existence dispensed?

This isn't a scientific investigation. You can't do that in a tyranny. But the evidence from the defectors suggests that North Korea passes all of Lifton's tests on brainwashing, and, on that rough-and-ready basis, the Democratic People's Republic of Korea is a cult, 23-million-strong.

On the top-floor balcony of the Grand Study House we had a magnificent view of the city, looking back across Kim Il Sung Square, and beyond that the river, the Juche Tower and East Pyongyang. They were testing the public address system for the rally taking place the next day. The disembodied voice echoed out over the city empty of people, of traffic, terrifyingly loud: the sound of Big Brother.

14

God the Bad Elvis Son

For a man born on the day that the *Titanic* sank, Kim Il Sung lived a long and healthy life. But old age and then the only end of age, as the poet Philip Larkin warned, creeps up on us all. The antidote to the slide towards death was created by the Kim Il Sung Institute of Health and Longevity: the Great Leader must consume dog penises at least 3 inches or 7 centimetres long.[1] And, in the meantime, his son slowly tightened his grip on the levers of power.

Kim Jong Il is one of the most fascinating villains of history, subtle, charming, gifted, psychotic, cruel, twisted, feckless. It's nigh on impossible to see him clearly through the opaque glass of the dynasty's propaganda or the bubbling vitriol of the defectors. He kept the regime safe in power; he gave North Korea nuclear weapons; he presided over the famine which killed three million people; he became an international laughing stock. Clip-clopping around in elevator shoes and bouffant hairdo, he will go down in

[1] Martin, p196.

history as the man who tried to make himself look taller at both ends, the puppet villain of *Team America*. At times, you have to pinch yourself and remember: this comedy baddy was flesh and blood. He sent millions to their graves.

Kim the Second's story starts in confusion, with the place and date of his birth hotly disputed, the regime claiming he was born on Mount Baekdu, behind the Japanese lines in 1942; Soviet sources and Korean defectors are clear that he was born in a barracks in the Soviet Union not far from Vladivostok in 1941. No one quite knows why the regime faked not just the place but also the date of birth. His father was born in 1912, so 1942 has a pleasing echo, if you are into the wilder shores of numerology and superstition. Kim Two's mother was a vivacious but illiterate peasant, looked down on by other mothers within Pyongyang's elite as someone who knew how to butcher chickens, and not much else. Very quickly the boy-god developed a nasty reputation, biting other children, killing bugs, 'a lonely and guilty child'.[2]

By the time he was five his younger brother was dead; by the age of seven so was his mother. He was brought up by a hated step-mother, surrounded by uncles and half-brothers and nephews, all of whom had an interest in him being done down. His father was consumed with power, and had little time to spend with the boy. Against all Communist propriety, Kim Jong Il succeeded in grabbing the chalice of power, and passing it on to his least feckless son. In much else, he failed, but in that he took power and passed it on, dying in his bed, he can be counted, like his father, as a tyrant success story.

Kim Jong Il was first accused of murder when he was six years old, the victim his three-year-old brother. Young Kim was known

[2] Martin, pp205–9.

by his Russian pet name, Yura, his little brother, Shura. The three-year-old died in a swimming pool when the family were back in Pyongyang in 1947. One defector account has it that Yura killed Shura by pushing him back into the pool again and again.[3] If so, Shura would not be the last North Korean to die at the whim of the man who became the second god-king. Two years later in 1949, his mother, Vera, or Kim Jong Suk, died after complications with an ectopic pregnancy, leaving Kim Jong Il pretty much alone in the world.

The regime's official story leaves you at sea about his real upbringing. You come across stuff like Kim at the age of eight reading Lenin's *State and Revolution* and writing a commentary on it, and you know that's rubbish.[4] A few years later, during the Korean war, Kim Two became a prodigy songwriter, being rude about the Americans. This, too, is most likely rubbish. What we do know, however, is that when the war quickly went sour for the North, Kim Il Sung spirited his family out to the safety of China, where they sat out the bombing in comfort.

In the late 1960s, Kim Jong Il started working in what you could call 'Pyongywood' or, in regime-speak, the 'cultural sphere'. You get the feeling that he was a bit of a stage-door Johnny, desperately keen on impressing the actresses; very soon, of course, it would be the other way around. Early on in his career, he tapped in to the importance of knowing what the Bowibu, the secret police, knew. Towards the end of his life, he ran it. When he was a child, officials used to bow low; he started his first bespoke purges in his twenties. In 1974 he became a Politburo member. But throughout

---

[3] Martin, p206.
[4] Martin, p354. The claim is rubbish, not Martin's reporting of it, of course.

this time, he was never openly and transparently the heir apparent: he rose to power almost invisibly, just like Stalin, whose ascension to the Kremlin was described as being like that of a 'grey blur'.

Palace intrigue was the meat and veg of Kim Jong Il's life in his twenties and thirties. He had a lot against him: the biggest weakness was that he had had no experience of revolutionary struggle or the guerrilla war. How could a baby? Throughout his life, he looked small in his father's shadow.

His old man was a killer, who started a pointless war in which millions died, grew fat while his people starved, purged many entirely innocent colleagues and created a gulag of the utmost horror. But time and again witnesses say that Kim Il Sung had real class, something they hesitate to say about his son. For example, one witness said that for the first few years in power Kim Il Sung still had an 'attractive personality'.[5] Breen tells the story that during his audience with the Great Leader, someone asked what he did for leisure. The old thing replied: 'Soldiers raise bears for me to hunt, but I think that now they hide behind a tree with a tame bear and push it out when I come along.'[6] This dictator-joke against himself, writes Breen, went down well. Breen goes on to quote a Tass correspondent, comparing father tyrant and son: the old man was 'gracious as usual', the young Kim looked awkward, 'as if he had swallowed poison'.

All serious rivals to Kim Jong Il with real guts and vigour were fed into Kim Il Sung's meat-grinder. Yet Kim Jong Il played the long game, building up his father's personality cult to ludicrous levels, forever inventing new nonsense, always downplaying his own ambition.

[5] Martin, p745.
[6] Breen, p12.

Only in 1980, at the Sixth Congress of the Korean Workers' Party, was Kim Jong Il officially ordained successor to his father.[7] Long after it had become clear that the Party Centre – as Kim Two liked to style himself with typical opacity – was going to get the crown, he remained in the shadows, waiting, waiting, waiting. His greatest accolade was the near-total ignorance of Western intelligence services. People wondered whether he was a halfwit. When the South Korean President Kim Dae-Jung, an enthusiast for the Sunshine Policy, visited Pyongyang in 2000, people in the South were delighted to discover that their enemy had charm and grace. Kim Jong Il seemed to be no monster. He cracked self-deprecating jokes, was attentive to the South Korean leader, and walked slowly with him – the man from Seoul had a bad limp after a car accident. Told about his newfound popularity down South, Kim Two said: 'After I appeared on TV screens, I'm sure they came to know that I am not a man with horns on the head.'[8]

Perhaps he was. Evil hides in murk. The narratives of the people who knew him well and escaped so that they could tell the world are somehow disappointing: the picture that emerges of Kim Jong Il is incoherent, fuzzy, crepuscular. That, perhaps, is testament to his genius as a tyrant, that he made it nigh on impossible for people to read his mind. In *Team America*, the puppet Kim Jong Il feeds 'Hans Brix', the comically mispronounced nuclear weapons inspector, to the sharks. Kim is then filmed through the prism of the fish-tank containing the late Swede's skeleton, his briefcase holding nuclear secrets still chained to a skeleton wrist. The Dear Leader indulges in his melancholic song about the trials of life as a

[7] Lankov, *The Real North Korea*, p68.
[8] Breen, p77.

tyrant: 'I'm so ronery.' It turns out that the puppeteers' mix of psychotic violence and queasy sentimentality is bang on the nail.

The first and perhaps most thoughtful of our witnesses to the real Kim Jong Il is Hwang Jang Yop, the Juche theorist who became the head of Kim Il Sung University and then defected to the South in 1997, knowing that the regime would send his children and grandchildren to the gulag. Hwang had been Kim Il Sung's man, when the Great Leader was in his pomp. Under Kim the First, he rose to the fringes of power, created Jucheism, and lived a good life. As Kim Jong Il's life force slowly seeped through the corridors of power, Hwang was demoted and, first gently, then not so gently, moved aside. He is, naturally, a hostile witness.

Why did he defect? It's not clear. The sense you get from reading his essays and thoughts is that he had to, that his mind would have broken in two had he stayed any longer, genuflecting before a god he despised. It's possible to read Hwang as a materialist, out for number one, who prospered under Kim Il Sung but fell from grace under his son, and decided to quit. But that's not how I read him. Rather, he was a sincere and moral man, who had, somehow, been able to justify his actions under Kim the First, but that stance became increasingly difficult under Kim the Second. Once he decided to escape, he knew for certain what would befall his family, and a feeling of melancholy surrounds his observations. As someone who has tried to grapple with the reality of North Korea, not the fog, I feel profoundly grateful that he did defect, and spell things out to the world. At the same time, one cannot help but feel immense sorrow for his children and grandchildren, as the doors on their futures slammed shut against them.

Hwang's primary verdict is against the father, Kim Il Sung, for allowing his vanity to be the master of his judgement, and promote an obviously flawed son to take command. But few dared tell the Great Leader that his son was sly and bitter and twisted. Every single person who fell inside the Kim dynasty circle knew that their survival and that of their children, unto the third generation, depended on its continuing blessing. The mind-fuck for the Great Leader, then the Dear Leader and now the Fat Leader, is that if you tell the tyrant bad news, you risk losing your head; but if the only news you ever receive is good, you risk not knowing what on earth is going on. So power passed from Kim Il Sung to Kim Jong Il, with the father only dimly aware of who his son really was. And the handful of old warriors who dared to stand up to him were squashed flat like bugs under the thumb.

Hwang says that in the seventies, Kim Il Sung's old guard tried to fight against Kim Jong Il's succession. The vice prime minister, Nam Il, raised concerns: he was crushed to death in a road accident, when a lorry ran out of control.[9] (Author's note: there are no real road accidents in North Korea.) Four others also signalled their opposition. They were, according to Gause's report on state terror for the Committee for Human Rights in North Korea, Pak Kum Chol, secretary to the KWP secretariat; Kim Kwang Hyop, former defence minister; Ho Pong Hak, a former four-star general; and Yu Chang Sik, a former senior official. By 1982, all four, according to a defector, were in the gulag.[10]

Kim Jong Il loved a racy, capitalist version of the good things in life: fine wines, Hennessy cognac, human beds – mattress and frame constructed of entwined naked concubines. Hwang was

[9] John H. Cha, K. L. Sohn: *Exit Emperor Kim Jong Il: Notes From His Former Mentor*, Abbott Press, Bloomington, 2012, p49.
[10] Ken E. Gause, p120.

something of an old-guard puritan, and clearly disapproved. But it's one thing to enjoy a good party, another to have someone shot for dobbing you in to your old man. The story Hwang tells of one such hapless tell-tale is grim beyond belief. A woman professor at Kim Il Sung University wrote an anonymous letter to Kim Il Sung complaining about the drinking and whoring at one of Kim Jong Il's parties; she was worried about her husband's attendance. It never got to the Great Leader but was intercepted by the secret police, whose master was the Dear Leader. A gruelling investigation began to hunt down the mole. Eventually, she was caught. Her husband volunteered to shoot her, to show his loyalty, and the Dear Leader granted permission. Soon after, the husband-executioner married a new woman, selected by Kim Jong Il.[11] The lesson for everyone in the palace was simple: do not raise your hand against the Dear Leader.

Kim Jong Il became obsessed with the idea that people would not tell him 'the truth', knowing that his hangers-on only told him what he wanted to hear. Hwang's biographers tell the story of Kim Jong Il lecturing the Chief of Police and his acolytes about giving false or too rosy reports. Kim Jong Il said: 'I like accurate, true reports. All of you know Ernst Kaltenbrunner, the chief of the SS during the Nazi era. When he made his reports to Hitler, he was always simple and accurate. At times when Himmler, the number two man, exaggerated or altered any information on behalf of Hitler, Kaltenbrunner would correct his superior. I want you to be like Kaltenbrunner.'[12]

He was not, exactly, a perfect role model, as his fate suggests. Kaltenbrunner indulged Hitler's fantasies to the very end, and though less absurd than Himmler, was no less deluded. He was

[11] Cha, Sohn, p109.
[12] Cha, Sohn, p95

hanged in 1946. Odd, one might think, for Kim Jong Il to know so much about Hitler's inner circle, but tyrants are fascinated by other tyrants. One of the entries in the visitors' book for Stalin's dacha in Sochi, southern Russia, now a creepy hotel where you can sleep in Stalin's bed – I did once, and had a terrible night's sleep – was Saddam Hussein. In Baghdad, a Kurdish leader negotiating with Saddam noted that his bookshelves were full of books about Stalin.[13] But Kim Jong Il's fascination with Kaltenbrunner, the honest Nazi, speaks exactly to the primary problem of the North Korean dictatorship: information necrosis.

The caprice of the despot even extended to marriage guidance, of a kind.

In 1978, Choi Un Hee, a South Korean film actress of ravishing beauty, was lured to Hong Kong by a Chinese film executive. She was driven to Repulse Bay where there was a small white boat waiting on the beach. Suddenly, men leapt from the boat and grabbed Choi and forced her on board. The boat pushed off and headed for open sea. 'Where is this boat going?' she asked frantically. 'Madame Choi, we are now going to the bosom of General Kim Il Sung.'[14] It wasn't the old man who greeted her when she landed in North Korea, but his son: 'Thank you for coming, Madame Choi. I am Kim Jong Il.' As if she had some choice in the matter . . .

Shin Sang Ok, her South Korean ex-husband and a film director, heard about Choi's disappearance. In Hong Kong he, too, was lured to Repulse Bay in a white Mercedes. The car stopped,

[13] Simon Sebag Montefiore: *Stalin: The Court of the Red Tsar*, Weidenfeld & Nicolson, London, 2003, p25.
[14] Yoshi Yamamoto *Taken! North Korea's Criminal Abduction of Citizens of Other Countries*, Committee for Human Rights in North Korea, 2011, p27.

four men got in, threatened Shin at knifepoint, put a nylon bag entirely over him, and the goons headed off to sea with their human parcel. In the morning they transferred to a freighter, the *Sugun-Ho*. A few days later, two men in Mao tunics greeted him at Nampo, saying: 'Welcome to the Socialist Fatherland.'[15] Neither Shin nor Choi knew what had happened to each other. Shin spent five years fighting his captors. He escaped for a few hours, only to be recaptured and thrown into Prison 6, where, half starved on thimblefuls of rice and grass, he endured endless indoctrination for four years. 'Tasting bile all the time, I experienced the limits of human beings.' Eventually, he realized that cunning would be the key to unlock his gaol, and went along with Kim Jong Il's whims. He wrote reams of rubbish, praising the Dear Leader. 'What a wretched fate,' he recalled towards the very end of his life, 'I hated communism, but I had to pretend to be devoted to it, to escape from this barren republic. It was lunacy.'[16]

Eventually, after banks of security screenings, he was taken to a plush villa in Pyongyang, and ended up face-to-face with his ex-wife, who had not known until that moment that he was in North Korea. The Dear Leader said: 'Well, go ahead and hug each other. Why are you just standing there?' The marriage counsellor from hell suggested that they remarry. Why? Who knows? They did as they were told.

From their accounts, Kim Jong Il was like the psychotic character in the novel *The Collector* by John Fowles, snatching human butterflies with his net and imprisoning them in a jar.

And yet Kim Jong Il does come across in their accounts as

---

[15] *Taken!*, p29.
[16] John Gorenfeld: 'The Producer From Hell', *Guardian*, 4 April 2003.

weirdly charming. At that first dinner party in Pyongyang in March 1983, when Shin and Choi are reunited, the first thing Kim says to Shin is, 'Director, forgive my "act". I must apologize for this situation in which you have had to suffer so much,' after which Kim takes his hand and shakes it. Shin writes, 'I instinctively understood the implications behind Kim's words, "Forgive my act".'[17]

Shin doesn't explain explicitly but he implies that his imprisonment and harsh treatment have been a front that Kim has had to put up to display his authority, to others and to Shin, especially as he had tried to escape several times. The next day, there was another party, and it was at this party that Kim told Shin that the whole show was 'bogus. It's just a pretence.' Shin writes that these two 'blunt statements left a long lasting impression'.

After this night they do not see Kim for another few months, even though he has promised to meet soon after. Shin later finds out that it is because Kim had been on a trip to China. During this time Shin and Choi study North Korean, Chinese and Russian films. Shin notes that North Korean films combine songs and acting, much like operettas.

After a few months, they are invited to Kim the Second's office, and before they start their talk, Kim switches on his TV to check what's on. To Shin and Choi's surprise, Kim is watching South Korean channels, and even notes that one star on a drama show is a very good actress. It is clear that he watches a lot of South Korean TV and films from around the world.

Shin and Choi were terrified that, if they ever made it back to South Korea, no one would ever believe them that they had been

[17] Shin Sang Ok, Choi Un Hee: *Kidnapped by the Kingdom of Kim Jong Il*, Donga Ilbosa, Seoul, 1988.

kidnapped. This is long before the regime admitted to kidnapping thirteen Japanese citizens in 2002. So they secretly tape-recorded the Dear Leader, the device hidden in Choi's handbag.

Shin writes: 'First, once Kim Jong-Il opened his mouth he didn't seem to know how to stop talking. He hardly allowed us any gaps to speak at all, and he kept on talking one-sidedly. While he spoke, when we tried to say something briefly, he quickly interrupted and carried on talking. His voice was loud and high, and he spoke very fast. There seemed to be so much that he wanted to talk about, that it seemed like he could not organize his words as he spoke, so he would stutter at the end of his sentences. When I tried to transcribe what Kim had said, not one sentence he spoke can be written as a complete sentence on paper. The subject noun is normally repeated two or three times; before one sentence is even complete he will rush into another sentence, when the point he was trying to make was not clear in the first place, and there were many instances where the beginnings and ends of what he was trying to say did not connect or make sense.'

Shin transcribed word for word what Kim said. It's fairly long-winded and ranting. He talks about why the recent North–South talks broke down, why he kidnapped Shin and Choi, the state of North Korean cinema, what's wrong with it, how he wants to develop it and how he wants to take films to film festivals and even maybe set up a film festival in Pyongyang.

He comes across as bullish, the way he rants endlessly without letting Shin or Choi talk. He seems sly but naive at the same time. There does seem to be a lot going on in his mind, but it's muddled and incoherent.

On tape, Kim Jong Il says:

Eh, the first thing in the North–South relations is the cultural exchange, cultural cooperation, that's what I think. Already, people were going back and forth on their own accord, and I asked whether there was a way for you . . .'[18]

This is rubbish. No one goes back and forth between North and South Korea. The 'cultural exchange' happened by force. And Shin and Choi were not free to leave. Shin made seven films in North Korea, with Kim Jong Il his producer. The best, that is, least bad, is *Pulgasari*, about a giant metal-eating monster with a social conscience, similar to the Japanese *Godzilla*.

Film journalist John Gorenfeld summarized the dramatic ending: 'Pulgasari leads the farmers' army in an assault on the king's fortress – and against thousands of North Korean military troops who were mobilized and dressed up as extras. Ultimately, the king uses his experimental anti-Pulgasari weapon, the lion gun. But the enterprising Pulgasari swallows the missile and shoots it back at his oppressors. Finally, the king is crushed beneath a huge falling column.'

But the monster starts eating the people's tools. Gorenfeld, one of a thousand people outside North Korea who have seen the movie, carries on: 'When the blacksmith's daughter tearfully pleads with Pulgasari to "go on a diet", he seems to find his conscience, and puzzlingly shatters into a million slow-motion rocks . . . It's a terrifically bad movie.'[19]

Shin and Choi had a Mercedes, good food and a $3 million-a-year budget to make great films in the North. But they hated it.

[18] Cha, Sohn, p97.
[19] Gorenfeld, 'The Producer From Hell', *Guardian*, 4 April 2003.

Shin wrote: 'Living a good life ourselves and enjoying movies while everyone else was not free was not happiness, but agony.' In 1986, eight years after being kidnapped, Shin and his wife went to a film event in Vienna. They gave their minders the slip and hare-tailed it for the American embassy in a taxi. A minder followed in another taxi, but they managed to lose him. Free at last, the film director and his wife had endured an episode far more exciting and incredible than anything in any of their movies.

Other eyewitness testimony speaks of Kim Jong Il's subtlety and consideration, before mentioning his darker side. For example, Sung Hye Rang, Kim Two's former sister-in-law, writes:

> He is a cultured man and respects knowledge . . . He enjoys beauty . . . I think he has inherited some good points – generosity and a warm heart. He was always considerate and wanted to do well by others. His extreme, harsh personality makes him seem like a bad human being . . .[20]

In the same paragraph, two wildly different views of the same man are put forward in neighbouring sentences by someone who knew him well: 'considerate' and 'extreme, harsh'. The truth is that both are right: Kim Jong Il was like a malfunctioning television set, which, much of the time, would present a perfect picture, clear, sometimes even beautiful; and every now and then the set would flicker, then go ponk and you would see a forest of angry dots and hear a screech of white noise. Power magnifies faults or, as the old Swahili proverb has it: the higher the monkey climbs the tree, the more you can see its bottom. Mood changes, whims, paranoid

[20] Cha, Sohn, p94.

insecurity and absolute power are a bad mix. For people who had to work with him in the lower tiers of power, that mix would prove to be nightmarish.

No man is a hero to his valet. Ri Young Kuk was a palace body-guard who managed to escape to the South. He recalls of his master:

He is generally impatient and sly. There's more to him than his pleasant exterior. Inside, he is always scheming, making secret plans. And he is very clever about planning escape routes in case things go wrong. There are two sides to him, always. He is not a good listener . . . He is extremely cruel toward those who disagree with him. Many people have lost their lives trying to point out their problems to him.[21]

A courtesan in the palace describes Kim as sensitive, preferring girls of classical beauty, never taller than him, and once he got to know the girls, happy to 'pass gas' – to 'break wind' – in their company. How very attractive.

Not quite the Prince Charming was the view of some of Kim Two's old military classmates, who in 1992 were accused of plotting against him. They reportedly said that he was 'incapable' and 'bad-natured', according to Ken E. Gause's report for the Committee for Human Rights in North Korea. They lost the fight and three hundred senior officers were executed. The sound of the firing squads at work disturbed the night outside one military barracks for a month. One should note that although Kim Il Sung died in 1994, by the turn of 1990 it seems likely that the old man's powers

[21] Cha, Sohn, p96.

were waning, and that by 1992 Kim Jong Il felt secure enough to stage mass purges of his enemies, real or imagined. This 1992 plot is only one of an astonishing number of conspiracies against Kim Two, and an astonishing number of executions, cited by Gause.[22]

In 1995, officers in the Sixth Army Corps, based in the ever-suspect north-east, were found to have been plotting against the Party Centre – Kim Two – and they were executed too. In 1997, writes Gause, the regime's 'Operation Intensification' targeted Korean Workers' Party officials suspected of sabotaging food supplies. (The true cause of the famine, the folly of Kims One and Two, was not addressed.) This operation led 'to the rounding up of more than 30,000 officials and their families, many of whom were incarcerated or executed. Top secret policeman Chae Mun Tok went to the firing squad.'[23] In 1998, at the height of the famine, people stripped the Hwanghae Steelworks of machinery to sell and exchange for food: nineteen culprits were executed.

Jang Jin Seong was part of North Korea's propaganda machine. He spent his working day writing syrup in verse about Bad Elvis, before he ran away in 2004.[24] The poet met Kim Jong Il twice. The first time, in 1999, he was overwhelmed and full of emotion. 'But at the same time,' he told the BBC, 'I thought the image I had received of him – through brainwashing – was very different to how he appeared in person. He is a god-like figure. But when I met him I felt he was much more individualistic, even a bit selfish – and I was disappointed.'

Kim Two gave Jang a Rolex watch worth, he later worked out

[22] Gause, p123.
[23] Gause, p127.
[24] Jang Jin Seong: Inside North Korea: 'The day Kim Jong-il gave me a Rolex', 6 January 2012, http://www.bbc.co.uk/news/magazine-16413669

when he defected to the South, about $11,000 or £7,000. Though the population was going hungry, said Jang, Kim was using gifts as a way of buying loyalty. Once in the royal circle, Jang was protected, even from prosecution. He received the very best level of rations through-out the famine: 'I realized North Korea was the poorest country in the world, presided over by the richest king – and that's why I wrote poems that were critical of the regime while I was still there.' He got away with it because he never committed them to paper.

Selling my daughter
A poem in Korean by Jang Jin Seong

The woman was paper-thin / A sign hung from her neck / 'Selling my daughter for 100 won' / With the little girl standing next to her / The woman stood in the market place.

The woman was a mute / She gazes at her daughter / Her maternal feelings are being sold / Cursed at by passers-by / The woman stares only at the ground / The woman has no more tears.

Clutching her mother's skirt / 'My mother's dying,' cries the daughter / The woman's lips tremble / The woman knows no gratitude / The soldier gave her 100 won, saying / 'I'm not buying your daughter, I'm buying your motherly love' / The woman grabs the money and runs off.

The woman is a mother / With the 100 won she received for the sale of her daughter / She hurries back, carrying bread / She shoves the bread into her daughter's mouth / 'Forgive me,' wails the woman.

Jang Jin Seong poem; 100 won is roughly equivalent to 73 US cents or 47p.

When Jang met Kim Jong Il the second time it was shocking: 'We sat at a performance together, and he kept on crying while he watched it. I felt his tears represented his yearning to become a human being, to become an ordinary person.'

One more palace witness is a Japanese wideboy-cum-sushi-chef adopted by their majesties, Kim Jong Il and son Kim Jong Un, as an all-licens'd royal fool. Kenji Fujimoto is a thuggish, drunken but somehow charming tough, who went drinking with the boss, Kim Jong Il, the night before he was to marry a hand-picked courtesan, and woke up with his pubic hair vanished, a practical joke by the palace. Fujimoto's gift to posterity is a number of bow'n'tell books, ghost-written after he fled back to Japan, including *The Honorable General Who Loved Nuclear Weapons and Girls* and *Kim Jong Il's Cook – I Saw His Naked Body*.

Fujimoto says of Kim:

Kim Jong Il is a warm person with many hobbies, and always wears a smile. But when someone fails to report an important item, or when something goes wrong, he yells and screams into a telephone like a madman. I have often witnessed this. He has no qualms about chewing our senior officials, no matter who they are.[25]

The more his people starved, the more Kim Jong Il loved to eat and drink the finest things. Fujimoto was dispatched to the far corners of the world to track down goodies: caviar in Iran, Pilsner beer in the Czech Republic, bacon in Denmark, and regular trips to Japan to buy tuna, sea urchin, and 'toro' sushi – a prize cut of

[25] Cha, Sohn, p96.

fatty, marbled tuna. Kim Two was a night owl, and would often demand a lavish meal at two o'clock in the morning. The longest banquet went on for four days and everyone invited to it dared not fall asleep before the Dear Leader went to bed. 'It was torture for them,' wrote Fujimoto in *Kim Jong Il's Cook*.

He consumed vast amounts of alcohol, and once, reportedly, was told off by his old man for turning up to a meeting drunk. Jasper Becker reports that Soviet diplomats – the best informed, or rather, the least in the dark in Pyongyang – picked up rumours that Kim Jong Il may have picked up a drug habit too. 'Cocaine Kim' has the *Private Eye* ring of truth about it.[26] The Soviet diplomats had heard that in the mid-1980s Kim Jong Il attended several meetings in which 'he talked such a stream of gibberish that not even a personal translator could follow'.[27]

Drugs could also account for Kim Jong Il's gibberish on the secret tape recording made by Shin and Choi. At the very top of one of the most feared regimes in the world was a silly man babbling poppycock. And yet he managed to overcome his demons, alcohol- or drug-induced, and stayed in power until 2011, when he died in his bed – the only serious test of success for a tyrant.

Even so, according to these witnesses, there was also something unhinged about the man, a little boy lost, engulfed by power, something in him, perhaps, that realized that everything he did and everything he stood for was fundamentally wrong. In 2008 he suffered a stroke. A photographer captured him, scowling in his Mao casual wear, his face like a devil's, sick of sin.

---

[26] A phrase reportedly heard at a *Private Eye* lunch about a story: it may not be true, but one would like it to be.
[27] Becker, *Rogue Regime*, p43.

15

Fifty Shades of Green

I sit in a bar in Belfast, and nurse my Guinness, and listen to an IRA man tell how he spent two months in North Korea in 1988 learning how to make bombs. There are three men: the go-between; 'Len', who went to Pyongyang; and another IRA man called 'Eddie'. It's a little tense as we start. I have an Irish surname but an English accent and my employer – the BBC – could not be more British. Into this awkwardness I find myself stumbling. Eddie leans forward, deadpan: 'Before we start, John, I want you to know one thing. I'm a member of the Church of Scientology.' I replied: 'Fuck you.' After we'd stopped laughing, I thanked the Church for breaking the ice for me with all sorts of unlikely people.

Len turned out to be a soft-spoken Irishman from West Belfast with a bone-dry wit. But there is a toughness about him, too. Back then, Len was, as he saw it, a soldier in an army, his general Sean Garland, one of the great, flawed heroes of Irish Republicanism. There's an IRA ballad called 'Sean South of Garryowen' which tells the story of a doomed attack on a Royal Ulster Constabulary barracks in 1957. Three IRA men were injured in the shoot-out. Under fire, Sean Garland carried Sean South on his shoulders, in a hopeless attempt to save his friend's life. Garland escaped to the Irish Republic, but severely injured, ending up in hospital, and, once recovered, Mountjoy Gaol. The legend of Sean Garland, IRA hero, had started. Today, he is a sick and dying man. They call him Old Blue Eyes, and Len tells me he is one of the hardest men he has ever met.

Come the start of the Troubles in 1969, the IRA split into two. The nationalist wing – the Provisional IRA or Provos – set out to bomb their way to a united Ireland. The smaller, more avowedly socialist wing, the Officials or 'Stickies' or 'Sticks', after some hapless bloodshed came to believe that civil war between Nationalist and Unionist working people was a disaster. The Sticks were so called because to honour the Easter Rising in Dublin of 1916, they sported adhesive 'stick-on' lilies; the Provos used pin badges, and are sometimes called the Pin-Heads.

Ideology restrained the Sticky IRA from killing, but did not stop it completely. One estimate by the University of Ulster is that the Officials killed fifty-two people during the Troubles: twenty-three civilians, seventeen members of the security forces, eight republican paramilitaries, three of their own members and a loyalist paramilitary. The lion's share of the murders happened in the early 1970s. The single worst outrage was the bombing of the Parachute Regiment headquarters in Aldershot in 1972, a revenge attack for Bloody Sunday when the Paras shot dead thirteen unarmed Civil Rights protesters in Derry/Londonderry. Instead of the intended target, the retaliatory car bomb killed five female kitchen staff, an elderly gardener and the regiment's Catholic chaplain, Father Gerard Weston. Republican anger at the slaughter of civilians pushed the Officials to announce that they would renounce violence and give up the ghost – a claim that wasn't quite correct. But from the time of the Aldershot bomb onwards, it is true to say that whatever else the Sticks got wrong, they did not commit mass murder again. Had the Sticks joined in with the Provisional IRA's sectarianism, the story of the Troubles would have been far bloodier. Twenty-five years later, the Provos joined the Sticks in questioning whether violence could pave the way to a united Ireland. In the meantime, 1,800 lives had been snuffed out.

Garland was the king of the Sticks, officially Secretary-General of the Irish Workers' Party, which had real clout back then with the Soviet Union and its satellite states. The Soviets and their allies were wary of the Provisional IRA, but treated Garland's Workers' Party seriously. As far as the public and the media were concerned, the Official IRA had ceased to exist. In reality, they walked off into the shadows as Group B. Something of the Workers' Party's continuing paramilitary wing is told in *The Lost Revolution: The Story of the Official IRA and the Workers' Party*, a fascinating and scholarly investigation into a black hole of Irish paramilitarism by Brian Hanley and Scott Millar.[1] But Hanley and Millar didn't get to meet a volunteer like Len.

In October 1988 Len and five other Sticks – all soldiers in Group B – flew from Shannon to Moscow. Their cover story was that they were studying at Moscow University, so to make that work they wrote a series of postcards, which would be posted from Moscow while they were away. The Officials' go-between in Moscow was an Irishman, 'Fat Frankie'. He smoothed their way, and was

---

[1] Brian Hanley, Scott Millar: *The Lost Revolution*, Penguin, Dublin, 2009.

extremely well-connected in the old Soviet Union. The word is that Fat Frankie once witnessed a fist fight in the back of a limo in Moscow between a high-up in the Workers' Party and Boris Yeltsin, both of whom had enjoyed perhaps one shandy too many. Neither Russian President nor Irish rebel was a clean winner. Fat Frankie also helped organize the Sticks' rather special method of fund-raising: money-laundering fake $100 bills manufactured in North Korea, including sending a party of Irish Republican pensioners on holiday to the Black Sea, each carrying a small fortune in Pyongyang's finest US dollar fakes.

The Sticks stayed at North Korea's embassy in Moscow for a few nights, then they were driven to the airport in a Mercedes with diplomatic plates. At the check-in desk, no passports were shown. They went straight through to their seats at the very front of the plane. No security for them. The flight was fourteen hours, refuelling in Siberia and then again in Beijing. They had been told to explain to anyone who asked that they were a group from the Maltese Communist Party, 'Malta 215', preposterous cover for six hefty, white-skinned, un-tanned Irishmen, though as 'a history professor' who am I to condemn a bunch of Maltesers?

'How did you find Pyongyang?' I ask, so excited I almost shout. 'Sssh,' Len said, and looked around the bar. No one was paying any attention, but just in case I corrected myself: 'How did you find Preston?' He smiled, and told me his story.

On landing, the rest of the passengers got off before Len and his men were taken in a small procession of Ministry of Interior Mercedes to a barracks 'about 30 miles north of Preston'. Len guessed it was north of the capital, because the sunset was on the right as they were driven along dirt roads up in the mountains. They ended up somewhere near a town called 'Mariban' – Len remembered it phonetically, and there's nowhere spelt like that in North Korea. It was a military establishment, complete with a big parade ground.

Len explained what happened at the very first briefing: 'We were told through an interpreter that the North Koreans were helping with our revolution, but that we mustn't talk about our time here, ever.' They wore suits and each sported a badge with Kim Il Sung on it.

Lecture over, the boys from West Belfast found a shop which sold beer in big green bottles. 'That first night, we had a good piss-up. The food was crap. They gave us dog soup once. There was a scrap of meat and it had dog fur on it.' Len pulled a death mask face, rigid with disgust. 'And chicken. They told us it was chicken, but the legs on these chickens were so small. Once on the parade ground, one of them said, "There are your chickens," and he was pointing to a bunch of crows.'

They were given North Korean officer uniforms, billeted two to a room, and taught how to salute, North Korean-style: a kind of half-clawed gesture to the temple. 'They told us about the great revolution, how they were fighting US imperialism, the atrocities in the Korean civil war. They also took down all our personal details ... They asked us, "If ever we wanted to call on you, would you say yes?" They've used people from here as couriers.' Next came a medical examination complete with chest X-ray, taken by equipment so old-fashioned it was straight from a cartoon, recalled Len.

The North Koreans told the Sticks about Jucheism, but Len quickly came to his own conclusion: 'That was an absolute load of fuck. Your man Kim One, he was God.'

The military training started. They were taught hand-to-hand combat, a military version of Taekwondo. 'I was fit at the time, but this was way beyond me.' In a deserted, mock-up town they were given practice at firing weapons: assault rifles, pistols, belt-fed general purpose machine guns, rocket-propelled grenades, explosive ordnance, booby traps, demolition, all forms of explosives: command detonation, radio detonation.

They learnt the best way to kill a man – 'Stab a man in the back of the neck, and then twist, cutting into the cerebral cortex' – next came kidnapping techniques, but it was the explosives training that interested the Sticks the most. They worked with ammonium nitrate explosive, which looked like a bar of soap with a pre-drilled hole in it, in which Len, the engineer in the group of six, would place his detonator.

'They gave us a mathematical formula for knowing how much explosive you'd need to blow the doors off a Securicor van but it was too bloody complicated.' Gauging how much explosive to use on a job was a real problem for the Official IRA when they went ·'fund-raising', a West Belfast/North Korean echo of the moment in the film *The Italian Job* when the bullion gang blow a van to smithereens and Michael Caine complains: 'You were only supposed to blow the bloody doors off!'

The Irishmen talked about a gift for Kim Il Sung, which had been delivered to him, but they never got to meet him in person. The gift was a beautiful piece of Belleek porcelain, woven in ceramics to look like basketwork, and more than a century old. Where did you get that from? I asked, foolishly. 'It wasn't bought in a shop,' said Len. Whether the Great Leader ever realized that he was on the receiving end of stolen goods is another matter.

The Koreans thought that back home the Sticks had a full-scale army, with tanks in the mountains, waiting for the revolution.

'Garland was conning them,' said Len. The Sticks kept mum about how small their numbers were – perhaps fifty fighters, if that – and carried on with the training. Eventually, the North Koreans sent them around fifty Tokarev handguns, the Pyongyang edition of an old Soviet pistol.

They had two minders, Mr Ho and Mr Hong, whom they jointly nicknamed 'Hong Kong'. They got on with them well enough, but made time go faster by taking the mick. They realized that food and drink came best in quality and quantity when there was a banquet, so the Sticks told the Koreans that Halloween was a holy feast day for the Irish. They boosted the 'Holy Feast of Halloween' as much as they could, drank themselves silly, but Len was still conscious enough to notice that Mr Ho and Mr Hong wrapped up the leftovers from the banquet in napkins and spirited them away in their pockets.

Their living conditions were Spartan, but they knew they were well off in comparison with the North Koreans. One group of soldiers lived in a hole in the ground, with a wooden roof keeping the snow – which started to fall in late November – off their heads.

The Irishmen were not the only foreigners at the base. There were some Palestinians, too, whom the 'Maltesers' were kept well away from, and a group of Africans from the Tanzanian Air Force. Other sources say that the North Koreans have traded weapons with and/or trained a Liquorice Allsorts of terrorist organizations over the years, including Hezbollah, the Tamil Tigers and even Osama Bin Laden's moneyman 'Dr Amin' and others in the Taliban.[2] The goal appears to have been to make trouble for the West.

[2] Bruce Bechtol: *The Last Days of Kim Jong Il: The North Korean Threat in a Changing Era*, Potomac Books, Washington DC, 2013, pp113–23.

'We became bored extremely quickly,' said Len. 'Up at 6.30 a.m. running around the parade ground in pitch darkness before breakfast. We knew it was a load of bollocks.' Pretty soon, the Sticks started to mutiny. 'Getting up and running around in the dark ... we thought, Fuck this, and told Ho and Hong we weren't doing it.'

To keep morale up, they were taken to the circus – 'It was amazing, but the whole audience was in uniform.' Most comical of all was that they were taken on a merry-go-round. 'They filmed us. If that film ever comes out, it would be a disaster. The sight of the men from the IRA riding up and down on hobby-horses, we all looked like such a bunch of fucking cunts.'

There were precious few women around – they lived a monastic existence – but Len recalled one of the maids in the barracks. 'When we were served food, she always served me first. When we had apples, she would peel it for me, the whole thing coming off, so thinly peeled it was a work of art.'

A punch-up brought an end to their stay. Two Sticks got stuck into each other, hammering away. When one of the fighters was beaten, he slunk off, lay in wait in the dark, and got hammered again, almost killing him. The North Korean base commander called them in, dressed them down. The Sticks replied that their training programme wasn't working for them. After two months, Len and two others were on their way home. As he was leaving, Len gave the apple-peel lady a chocolate bar, for which she thanked him with a gracious smile. The three others stayed an extra month and then packed their bags as well.

It was wonderful getting home to Belfast after all that time. The cold, the hunger, the boredom, the power cuts, the lighting of candles in the evening, the lack of free thought, in the end Len hated it. Looking back on North Korea now, Len believes: 'It was the worst place I ever went to. The poor bastards believe they are living in Utopia.'

I met Liam, another surprisingly well-travelled Irishman, this time from the south, in a bar in Dublin. Back in the 1970s he got involved in a strike and the experience scarred him. He became a committed man of the Left, a Marxist and a member of the Irish Workers' Party, a Stick, but not an IRA man. When Liam was asked to go on a trip to East Germany, the Soviet Union and North Korea in the autumn of 1989 – one year after Len – he leapt at the chance. It turned out to be the greatest adventure and the most eye-opening experience of his life, but it ended up killing his 'faith'.

In September 1989 Secretary-General Garland and Liam flew to Moscow to attend an immense Soviet book fair. Three months before the fall of the Berlin Wall, Liam had no sense that anything very much was in the air. Soviet power seemed solid enough. But the trip didn't fuel his commitment to socialism. Far from it. 'They put us up in the Hotel Rossiya, a huge fucking dump by the Kremlin. Garland pulled some strings and we moved to a party hotel, the Octoberskaya. There, the food was excellent and we didn't have to share rooms.' Already Liam was beginning to sense that socialism, Soviet-style, was less about equality for all and more about who you knew. But the person who really knocked his faith was a beautiful young Russian woman, Elena: 'She had amber hair, green eyes, skin like the inside of an eggshell.' At first Elena just came to the Irish Workers' Party stand at the book fair to practise her English, but soon Liam had to be inventive so that he could spend more and more time with her – and less with Garland. Elena, once she realized that Liam was a true believer, was cruelly dismissive: 'She took me to GUM, the biggest store in the whole of Moscow, and threw open her arms and said: "There is nothing that we want here. You can't want this. You have no idea what it's like. We cannot breathe. You're going home to spread the gospel of bread queues."'

Their love affair was never consummated, but even now, more than twenty years later, the light in Liam's eyes grew fierce when he talked about her.

Garland and Liam flew first class to North Korea, with a stopover in Siberia. That experience, too, dented his passion: 'We got out of the plane, and had a spell in the Siberian airport. A fucking pig would have thought twice about going to the toilet. Blood lay in a pool on the floor of the duty-free shop.'

Their welcome in Pyongyang was astonishing. 'No one else was allowed off the plane until Garland and I walked down the steps. We were driven away in a great big black Mercedes Benz. I had never been in one before. There was maybe thirty police motorbike outriders, racing down these enormous empty roads.'

Liam was awe-struck by Pyongyang, at first: 'It looked magnificent, the physical structures were impressive.' The city had been dolled up to the nines in 1988, to look its best as Seoul hosted the Olympics. One year on, Pyongyang still looked smart.

Garland and Liam were given luxury villas in a compound not far from the heart of the capital. It was the absolute subservience of the staff that chilled Liam: 'If they saw you, they would freeze on the spot, eyes down, and stay frozen until you passed. They were virtually slaves. It was so servile, the bowing and scraping. I remember I said to myself: Do we really want this for Ireland?'

Liam continued: 'Sean did the political meetings, and I was not invited to them. I had a driver who spoke some English, and he drove me around, we saw the sights. One morning I spotted the workers in their black clobber going off to build the Christmas Tree' – at the Ryugyong Hotel, which does have a rough triangular symmetry – 'singing their hearts out. They worked liked ants. Jaysus, imagine waking up to that every day of your life. North Korea was the strangest place I've ever been to. Back then, Pyongyang was a beautiful city but the people, the people . . . It was like a science fiction movie, the people were the aliens. Jaysus Christ, you can't but feel sorry for them.'

They flew home via East Berlin. Liam took a deep breath: 'If Elena and the poor people of North Korea didn't do it for me, the fucking Wall did. The closer I got to it, the more horrified I became. I said: "Jaysus, no, no, no . . . for fuck's sake. Any fucking system that needs a wall needs tearing down."'

Once they got back to Ireland, Garland asked him a subtle question: would Liam know of anyone who would be willing to take a small package from Dublin to Copenhagen? 'He was really asking me to do it, of course. Denmark was then the only place with a North Korean embassy, so I kind of guessed it was something to do with them. I said no.'

Liam was wise not to play courier for Sean Garland. It hadn't been Garland's first trip to North Korea, but his sixth. The Korean Central News Agency – the mouthpiece of the North Koreans – reported Garland's first trip in 1983. Garland had told his hosts, according to BBC Monitoring at Caversham: 'The Korean people under the wise guidance of the great leader President Kim Il Sung are registering wonderful successes in the struggle to reunify the divided country . . . I firmly believe that the US and other imperialists would surely be annihilated on the globe by the struggle of the Irish people and the Korean people.'[3]

Why did Garland go to North Korea six times? It might have seemed that Garland was taken in on that first trip to North Korea in 1983. *Workers' Life*, the Workers' Party magazine, reported on his visit to the much-vaunted West Sea Barrage: 'The standard of living is quite high and the ships are well stocked . . . the people are well dressed and there were no indications of the sort of poverty that we witness in this country.'[4]

What Garland and his fellow Sticks actually thought was somewhat different. Colm Breathnach, in the Workers' Party youth wing, went with Garland on his first trip to Pyongyang. Years later, Breathnach reflected on the trip to *NK News*: 'In many ways, they [the Workers' Party] were more old-fashioned Republicans who had kind of grafted on pro-Soviet politics on to some kind of left-wing Republicanism. And they weren't fools. Of course they knew it was a load of shit.'[5]

So why did Garland keep going back? Was it the ideological twinning between the two movements, both of which were intent on uniting their divided countries? The great man himself is quoted in *The Lost Revolution* talking about the 1983 trip, which had arisen after conversations with the North Korean embassy in Denmark. Garland said: 'We had heard all these stories about North Korea but we met them anyway. It was a small country

[3] *BBC Summary of World Broadcasts*, 20 September 1983: Irish Labour Party delegation in N. Korea, North Korean Central News Agency in English, 2210 GMT, 16 September 1983. BBC summaries of KCNA reports are sources for subsequent trips by Garland to North Korea, too.
[4] Hanley, Millar, p462.
[5] Tom Farrell: 'Rocky road to Pyongyang: DPRK–IRA relations in the 1980s', *NK News*, 17 May 2013.

divided, isolated, blockaded economically, politically, militarily, and they were trying to do what they could themselves ... We pointed out to them, for instance, putting full-page ads into the *Irish Times* of Kim Il Sung's thoughts was a waste of money because nobody fucking read them. They were paying £5,000 ..."[6]

If the North Koreans were so daft they would throw away £5,000 a pop by droning on about Kimilsungism in Ireland's most conservative newspaper, would they fund the Workers' Party, and chums? That was the view of Breathnach: that the driver 'in the 1980s was funding for elections'. To that end, perhaps, dissent about North Korea was suppressed. When journalist Paddy Woodworth wrote a critical article in 1983 for the Party's magazine rubbishing the Kim dynasty, it was not published. Garland reportedly told the author: 'Ah come on, Paddy, I'm looking for support from these people.'[7]

In 1984, Garland and the President of the Workers' Party, Tomás Mac Giolla, met Kim Il Sung and Hwang Jang Yop, who subsequently defected to South Korea in 1997. The Great Leader told the Irishmen: 'Both the Korean people and the Irish people have a bitter past when they were oppressed and maltreated under the colonial rule of the imperialists ... The relationship between our two parties was established on the occasion of comrade General Secretary Sean Garland's visit to our country in September last year. Your party is vigorously struggling to get the British occupation forces out of the Northern Ireland...'

The Irishmen gave Kim Il Sung a present. The news agency did not report exactly what kind of present but added, po-faced, that

[6] Hanley, Millar, p462.
[7] Hanley, Millar, p463.

the delegation 'explained the gift to Comrade Kim Il Sung'. This may have been the Belleek porcelain, in which case it was stolen goods.

In 1986, there was no BBC Monitoring report of a Workers' Party trip but reportedly one took place. One of the delegates with Garland was Proinsias De Rossa, who later became a government minister and Euro MP. As the wheels came off the Workers' Party bus later on, De Rossa openly criticized the Pyongyang connection: North Korea was, he said, 'a completely unreal society where people were basically treated as children, not as adults at all'.[8]

In 1987, Garland was reported by the BBC, who had been monitoring the KCNA, to be back in Pyongyang; and again in the following year, 1988, for the regime's fortieth birthday celebrations, along with other European Communists, including one David Richards of the Communist Party of Great Britain. It was time to return North Korea's hospitality. Kim Yong Sun, a director of the International Affairs Department, arrived in Dublin for a fraternal visit.[9] That October Len and the boys from West Belfast arrived in Pyongyang.

Garland returned to North Korea twice in 1989, according to the KCNA, in May, when he met Kim Yong Sun for a second time, and then, with Liam, in September. On this second 1989 trip, Garland was also reported to have met Kim Yong Sun, again. Remember that name.

Sinn Féin, the political movement which marched in step with the Provisional IRA, dallied with North Korea, too. The main Sinn Féin enthusiast for Pyongyang was Gerry MacLochlainn, who

---

[8] Hanley, Millar, p483.
[9] Hanley, Millar, p489.

served two and a half years from 1981 for conspiracy to cause explosions. Once out of prison, he knocked out a pamphlet entitled *The Irish Republican and Juche Conception of National Self-Dignity are One.*[10] The pamphlet concluded, according to Martyn Frampton, a British academic and the only man I know who's bothered to read it, that the

> *Juche* concept of *Chajusong* – the notion that national pride is the foundation upon which revolutionary struggle must be based – 'expresses so clearly the aspirations and the needs of colonial and semi-colonial peoples' that its message was relevant not just to Ireland but to all 'freedom struggling peoples throughout the world'.[11]

In 1986, Sinn Féin sent a message of solidarity to the North Korean regime: 'We offer our support to the Workers' Party of Korea in its fight for the establishment of the Democratic Confederated Republic of Korea.'[12] In 1987, Sinn Féin's president, Gerry Adams, attended a reception at the North's embassy in Denmark to toast the seventy-fifth birthday of Kim Il Sung.[13] In 1989, Sinn Féin delegates MacLochlainn, Sheena Campbell – later shot dead in 1992 by loyalists – and John Doyle attended the World Youth Festival in Pyongyang.[14] Whether the IRA proper was

[10] G. MacLochlainn, *The Irish Republican and Juche Conception of National Self-Dignity*, Mosquito Press, London, 1985.
[11] Martyn Frampton: 'Squaring the Circle: The Foreign Policy of Sinn Féin, 1983–1989', *Irish Political Studies*, vol. 19, (2) 43–63, 2004.
[12] *The Blanket* e-magazine, a blog by Liam O Ruairc called 'From Havana to Pyongyang': Sinn Féin Letter to Korea, *Ireland's War*, issue 18, June 1986, p7.
[13] 'Gerry Adams visits Scandinavia', *Ireland's War*, issue 23, July 1987, p7.
[14] 'Sinn Féin Delegation at World Youth Festival', *An Phoblacht – Republican News*, vol. 11, no. 26, 29 June 1989, p14.

trained by North Korea is unknown. The evidence in the public domain suggests that Sinn Féin did not develop the same kind of traction with Pyongyang that Sean Garland and the Workers' Party did.

One man ultimately doing Garland's bidding was Hugh Todd, a South African citizen of Irish stock. In a hotel room in Birmingham, Todd boasted to one of his mates how he smuggled fake dollars through international frontiers. Little did he know that the conversation wasn't entirely private.

Oblivious to the tape silently spooling his every word, Todd told an undercover officer: 'But he wants to change the moody [crooked] dollars into different currencies. Now I have to change those back into fucking dollars. I was going to meet him in Frankfurt. I was going from South Africa to Frankfurt and Frankfurt to Moscow. I've got one hundred and eighty thousand fucking dollars, there's a big parcel like that, now I've got to go back out through those fucking customs and I'm watching, as you go, you know . . . they're putting the bag through the scanner and there's a fella the far side and the odd one he stops and searches. I had the fucking things stuffed down here, stuffed down every-where. I can feel one slipping down the fucking inside of my fucking pants . . . put my bag through, walked straight through, not searched, end of fucking story. I'm gone . . . I go into the fuck-ing Irish bar. I go out, I go into the toilet, take my bag, like that, take all my dollars out, grand, put them all into the bag, sweet, I'm through.'[15]

The tape was brought to a wider audience by BBC *Panorama*

---

[15] BBC *Panorama*: 'The Superdollar Plot', 20 June 2004, http://news.bbc.co.uk/1/hi/programmes/panorama/3819345.stm

reporter Declan Lawn and executive producer Jeremy Adams in 2004. But what Todd was explaining is the often tricky process of washing counterfeit money. The source would provide the fake dollar notes, which would then be passed off as real currency in banks and through purchases around the world. Once converted back into proper dollars, after a large cut had been taken, the banknotes would be returned to the source, so it could bank – as it were – the profit. And that meant in Todd's case returning the cash to somewhere in Moscow. Was that the original source of the 'superdollars'?

The bugged conversations between the money-laundering gang are priceless. Here's another superdollar mule, Brummie Alan Jones, bugged in a car, boasting about how the superdollars were the best fakes in the world: 'The people who handle them all the time would take them for real ones. Had every test done on them you can think of.'

Jones seemed clear there was nothing morally wrong in what he was doing: 'There's nothing to do now except earn a few quid for 'em, is there? There's nobody to kill. That's it. The FBI and that firm know about 'em. But they're called the superdollar. There's that many of them in their economy it's a fucking joke. It's been going on for twelve years. Everybody is sticking them into them. They take no notice of 'em now.'

Jones was not entirely correct about that. True, the FBI wasn't listening in. But the United States Secret Service – it guards the President, and the currency – was, along with some of Britain's best detectives.

Terry Silcock was another small-time crook who got in way over his head. He seemed particularly scared of another money-laundering conspirator, David Levin, a Russian, as he told two prospective buyers who were, unfortunately, undercover cops: 'He [Levin] turned up with these fucking five Russians. They've all got black leather jackets and dark skin, and they've got a guy in the back of the car that they've bagged and they won't let go. And they come to meet me like that!'

But who was running the operation? Silcock told the undercover officers what he knew. 'I will level with you saying that you have a perfect one hundred per cent understanding, then you can't ever come back to me. They're printed by the IRA and the KGB.'

Silcock was wrong about that. The Americans suspected that at the end of the trail beginning with the crooks from Birmingham was Room 39, the secret organization within the Kims' secret state, running the North Korean palace economy, and up to its neck in gun-running, high crimes and counterfeiting. It is also called Bureau 39, Division 39 and Office 39, but the pure Orwellianism of Room 39 is the most satisfactory translation.

The very first 'superdollar' was spotted by a bank teller in the Philippines in 1989, the very same year that Garland went to North Korea, twice. The superdollar note was a forgery of the $100 US bill of such exquisite accuracy the joke was it was more perfectly made than the US originals. The ink, the paper's manufacture, even the printing presses were virtually exactly the same as those used by the United States Bureau of Engraving and Printing. But working out who was counterfeiting these super-fakes was never going to be easy. The mock-dollars popped up in all sorts of places. When they emerged in the Lebanon, suspicion centred on Iran. But if it was the Iranians, why would superdollars pop up in Macao or Peru or Dublin or the British city with more miles of canal than Venice – Birmingham?

The source of the superdollars finally came to something

approaching daylight in 2005, when Sean Garland was arrested as he was about to address a meeting of Irish nationalists in Belfast. The United States Secret Service unsealed an indictment seeking the extradition, it read, of 'Sean Garland, also known as The Man With The Hat'. The legal papers, one reporter observed, read like a bad airport spy novel. Also wanted by the Americans was Garland's fellow Irishman Christopher Corcoran; a Russian national, David Levin, also known as David Batikovitch Batikian or Gediminas Gotautas or 'Russian Dave' or 'Doctor' of Birmingham; Todd, then sixty-eight, an Irish and South African citizen living in South Africa and also known by the names F.B. Rawling and Peter Keith Clark; and three Britons, Mark Adderley, Silcock and Jones – whose comments on tape we've already heard. The men were accused for their part in washing superdollars, taking in locations as glamorous as the Hotel Metropol in Moscow and as unglamorous as the Holyhead ferry. One boasts the scent of perfume; the other of vomit.

The US Attorney's Office making the case for the Secret Service claimed Garland had been running the superdollar racket for years. The indictment named Garland as the leader of the Official IRA, a claim he strongly denies, and stated that North Korean officials introduced counterfeit $100 bills to Ireland in the early 1990s and Garland obtained more of them in Minsk, Belarus.

The indictment claimed the notes began to appear in worldwide circulation in 1989 and were manufactured under the auspices of the North Korean government. The Americans alleged that the notes began appearing in Ireland during the early 1990s, but were eventually refused by Irish banks.

Garland – 'The Man With The Hat' – attracted the Americans' attention at around the same time, when the first 'supernotes' appeared on Dublin streets. But they had no hard evidence to nail him. Law enforcement got a break when Todd, who had a previous conviction for passing off counterfeit money, was spotted exchanging the notes in British banks. He was caught red-handed with a bundle of fake notes when he was arrested in 1994. Todd led to two Birmingham criminals, Silcock and Jones. But the Americans weren't that interested in the small fry. They wanted Mr Big – and the chain beyond him that led back to North Korea. The Americans waited a whole decade until they were happy they had the evidence they needed.

In 1996, the US redesigned its banknotes for the first time since 1928 to add additional security features, including, on the $100 bill, a winsome smile to Benjamin Franklin's face and a bigger head – the 'Bighead'. The US went to great lengths to keep one step ahead of the counterfeiters, using tiny lettering, a watermark shadow of the portrait on the bill and a security thread weaved in the paper. The real toughie to copy was their use of special Optically Variable Ink or OVI. 'Turn the bill one way, and it looks bronze-green,' explained the *New York Times*, 'turn it the other way, and it looks black. O.V.I. is very expensive, costing many times more than conventional bank-note ink.'[16]

One year later Garland travelled to Moscow. There, Garland went to the North Korean embassy to arrange, it was alleged, the shipment of new 'Bighead' fake $100 bills which the North Koreans had somehow speedily copied. Not long after Garland returned to Dublin, 'Super Bighead' notes popped up in Ireland.

Corcoran, Silcock and Adderley were said to have solicited David Levin, a former KGB agent turned British criminal, as a

[16] Stephen Mihm, 'No Ordinary Counterfeit': *New York Times*, 23 July 2006.

potential buyer for the notes. In the first six months of 1998, Garland was alleged to have travelled to Moscow three times to pick up new batches of supernotes from the North Korean embassy.

The Americans put pressure on the Russians to tell the North Koreans to stop mucking about, so Pyongyang switched operations to Minsk, the capital of nearby Belarus, and safely under the control of Europe's last dictator (if you say Europe stops at the Russian border), President Lukashenka. Team Stickie started beating a trail to Minsk, instead. Levin allegedly used his Russian contacts to arrange fake passports and fake Belarus visas to help them.

But the cracks were starting to show. The gang were becoming suspicious that they had a mole, and everyone became more paranoid. Levin explained that he was having serious problems offloading the supernotes in Russia and Germany. Garland, wary that he might be being cheated, demanded evidence of Levin's problems – and this was gold for the British crime squad and the Americans listening in the dark.

Levin got his mule Silcock to fax Garland a document in Russian showing that Russian banks had detected the 'supernotes', and a second document in German proving that the Germans had confiscated $250,000. Both faxes were read by the British crime squad. By June 1999, Levin came up with $98,000 to give to Garland, and passed it on to a courier to deliver to Dublin.

The crime squad arrested Levin the following day. He told them that he didn't know the money he received was counterfeit. A month later, he allegedly gave limited co-operation to police, telling them the whereabouts in Moscow of $70,000 in 'supernotes'. These notes were then picked up by the Russian authorities as evidence.

The same day, Silcock was arrested at a Birmingham boozer, the White Swan, also known, more suitably, as the Mucky Duck. Jones was picked up a few days later.

In 2002, Levin, Silcock and Adderley were jailed for nine, six and four years respectively for what police said was the largest counterfeit dollar operation ever seen in Britain. Silcock alone handled $4.2 million in counterfeit money, the court heard, and the whole operation was worth $29 million. What the North Koreans made of these events, we'll never know.

After the superdollar convictions in 2002, the Americans waited another three years before they pounced on Garland. He made the mistake of leaving the Irish Republic and going to Northern Ireland for a Workers' Party conference. Once arrested, he pleaded ill-health, was released from British custody, and slipped back over the border to the Irish Republic, not for the first time.

Ireland, some say, doesn't like extraditing old IRA men anywhere, and Garland was no exception. Irish TDs, that is, members of parliament, and artists such as Pete Seeger, Christy Moore, Alabama 3 and John Spillane campaigned against an old and sick man being sent to America to stand trial. Just before Christmas in 2011, an Irish judge decided that Garland was staying in Ireland. In the United States, the other men indicted have never been brought to court.

There is no doubting the extraordinary technical achievement of the North Korean counterfeiting operation. The world's most vocally anti-capitalist state made a killing out of Uncle Sam. Two North Korean defectors told *Panorama* what the North had got up to. One said: 'When I defected I brought some of these counterfeit notes to South Korea and I showed them to the experts in the South Korean Intelligence Agency. They said: "These are not fake notes, they are real." These are the people who are supposed to be professionals. I thought to myself: You have no idea. I'm the professional here, this is what I used to do. The counterfeiting was all done at government level. We had a special plant for doing it in.'

A second defector said: 'We bought the best of everything, the best equipment and the best ink, but we also had the very best people, people who had real expertise and knowledge in the field. Then, when government officials or diplomats travelled to South-East Asia, they distributed the counterfeit notes mixed in with the real ones at a ratio of about fifty–fifty.'

Two more defectors told the *Daily NK* website in 2005, after the US indictment against Garland had emerged, of the location of the secret counterfeiting plant. The third defector, who smuggled himself out of the North in 2000, said he had lived in Pyongsung, north of Pyongyang, where many locals knew that they printed fake dollars at the Trademark Printery in Samhwa town: 'It is an open secret to the residents of Pyongsung. I directly heard about it from the workers of the Party Centre and of the National Security Agency.' He described the Trademark Printery as a small concrete building, not entirely anonymous, with signboard, surrounded by barbed wire and patrolled by soldiers.[17] The fourth defector explained that his sources, state-licensed traders who worked for the regime, were permitted to smuggle old, used Japanese cars into North Korea and then sell them on in China. (The direct used-car trade route from Japan to China is barred by Chinese import controls.) The defector explained: 'The Chinese smugglers who bought the used cars also wanted to buy forged US dollar bills from us. Forged bills are sold for half of their face value. Trade workers

---

[17] *Daily NK* website, Seoul, in English, 4 December 2005.

of the central party mix forged US dollar bills with genuine bills when they circulate them in volume. They take the forgeries from Pyongsung.'

The State Department's point man cracking down on the counterfeiting was David L. Asher. In a speech, Asher accused North Korea of counterfeiting, manufacturing drugs, money laundering, arms sales and illicit trade in sanctioned items, such as conflict diamonds, rhino horn and ivory. 'Under international law, counterfeiting another nation's currency is an act of casus belli, an act of economic war. No other government has engaged in this act against another government since the Nazis under Hitler. North Korea is the only government in the world today that can be identified as being actively involved in directing crime as a central part of its national economic strategy and foreign policy.' And that made it, he said, 'The Soprano state'.[18]

My Irish friend, Liam, after his adventures in the Soviet Union, North Korea and East Germany, stayed connected to the Workers' Party for another ten years but his passion for the cause was slowly dying. It was a case, he thought, of not knowing that to do next. After he left, other members questioned him at funerals: 'Why weren't you at the party meeting?' Soon, he was shunned, he said, 'like the Amish'.

And what of Kim Yong Sun? The North Korean who met Garland twice in 1989 came to a sticky end in 2003 – not that long after the British trial when the superdollar mules were convicted. Kim died in yet another North Korean 'car accident', most likely executed by the state for failure.

---

[18] Bill Gertz, *Washington Times*: 'N. Korea charged in counterfeiting of U.S. currency', 2 December 2005.

The North Koreans had their official say in 2005, shortly after Garland was arrested. The BBC reported that the North's KCNA news agency in Pyongyang had struck back, declaring: 'The United States has recently escalated its smear campaign against the DPRK [Democratic People's Republic of Korea]. Typical of this is its fiction about a "deal in counterfeits" floated by the US this time. The US is claiming that the DPRK is massively issuing highly sophisticated false 100 US dollar notes known as "super money" and spreading them worldwide. In order to verify this, no sooner had [Sean] Garland, leader of the Irish Workers' Party, been arrested than the US Department of Justice released on 7 October a "written indictment" which it has long prepared. The "written indictment" characterized by extreme nature of politicization and selection said that there was a "deal in counterfeits" between the DPRK and Garland. Nothing is clumsier than what was invented by the US, a past master at lies, fabrication, disinformation and plot.'

The accused – North Korea – doth protest too much. I say that with confidence because, apart from the American indictment against Garland, the British court convictions and all the other evidence cited above, Len the Stick told me that he had counted some of the cash in Belfast, after it had been converted from the moody North Korean bills into pounds sterling. 'I would count £30,000, just in one day. And remember we had only one team and there were five teams working. Men were sent around Europe. I had a contact in the United States, and he moved $700,000 in the fake bills.' What was his cut? I asked. 'Remember, I was fighting for a cause. So I got paid around £40 a day to count £30,000.'

Today, Len realizes that the Sticks were little more than Sean Garland's private army – 'I woke up in around 1996' – but like all the Sticks he remains grateful that his version of the IRA didn't go in for twenty-five years of mass murder. I had to ask one last thing. I'd heard a story that one Stick got to go to the DMZ and managed to look at a US Marine through the sights of a sniper rifle. Did you do that? No, said Len. It was Fat Frankie who did that, on Christmas Eve.

I shook Len's hand and he walked out of the bar, one of the Irishmen kicked out of North Korea because of bad behaviour.

16

Empty Bellies

Day Six: and our coach left Pyongyang for the east coast resort of Wonsan. We were crossing the spine of the country, going up and up, through terrifying tunnels, entirely unlit with dripping wet walls, where the danger came from oncoming lorries with poor or no lights, and then out again into the fresh air, birds of prey spinning in thermals far below us. At lunch, we stopped for a picnic at what promised to be a magnificent waterfall. We could hear the Ullim waterfall, but we couldn't see it. Stiff after three hours in the coach, we all wanted to walk towards the falls, but for some reason our guides held us back.

And then it came to me in a brainwave. 'They're switching on the waterfall' – a joke that had Miss Jun bent double with laughter. Even Mr Hyun may have raised a wintry bank manager's smile, but I might have been mistaken.

Bizarrely, there were two roads to the waterfall, a wholly un-necessary waste of tarmac. The road on the right of the river flowing down from the falls was beautifully asphalted and rested on concrete stilts, elegantly constructed. The road on the left was far simpler. I started walking up the posh road – nothing is too good for ordinary people – and was quickly ordered by one of the guides to get back on the simple road.

Only when the waterfall hove into view did the reason for the two roads become obvious. The road to the right ended at a Bond-villain style chalet, with a prime view of the falls. We were asked not to take photos of the chalet, but everyone did anyway. The special road and the chalet had clearly been created for the Leaders, Great, Dear and Fat. From this, you could get some sense of the colossal waste of resources the demands of the palace economy create for the whole country. It is hard to imagine anything more economically unproductive than a duplicate road: one for the scum, one for their majesties.

The walk uphill made me fancy a swim. This might have been an eccentric decision. Mr Hyun, Miss Jun and the Continentalists looked on, aghast, as the only British student, 'Fred', and I stripped down to our underpants and waded in. On the bank, a great block of unfrozen ice lay, a warning unheeded. It was testicle-shrivellingly cold, and I wanted to go back the moment I had stuck my toe in. But thankfully Fred gave me a playful shove and I collapsed into the ice-water. Once in, it seemed only proper to swim towards the falls a bit. On the way out, I stood up and posed for the cameras, arms akimbo, in prize-fighter mode. But this was fakery. On leaving the water I was shivering so much I could barely stand up, and Mr Hyun, wearing a full-length black overcoat and frankly creepy black gloves against the cold, steadied me while I put my socks and trousers back on.

Only at the end of the tour did Mr Hyun point out that other tour groups had gone for a dip but later in the year, in the summer.

This was the earliest, and coldest, swim ever. As Fred and I basked in the warm glow of his praise, Mr Hyun unsheathed his dagger: 'Next time you go swimming, Professor, no holes in your underpants.'

I blushed then. I blush now.

Our picnic in the cold sun was a pleasant break from the torture of long-drawn-out meals in the fanciest restaurants in North Korea. While we were messing about, a North Korean child came out from nowhere and started fishing for frogs. He used a long stick with a dead frog speared on the end of it. The moment a live frog would grip the dead frog, he upended the stick and dropped the frog into a bucket. It was only when we got close up that we realized he wasn't a child at all, but a tiny adult, with a wizened face, maybe fifty years old. Outside of Pyongyang, people we saw were generally shorter. This man, from the mountain country, looked like a pygmy: evidence of famine written in bone.

The hotel/restaurant affair where our coach was parked had not yet opened for what passes as the tourist season, so we had to pee behind it. There, we saw our first dog in our whole time in North Korea, a miniature Alsatiany-thing, cute, fluffy but filthy, covered in dusty mud. No one dared touch him. The absence of things dulls the mind quite quickly, but it is worth reporting that even here, far away from the city, there were no ducks, chickens or birds to be seen; no wildlife of any kind, apart from the stray dog and frogs being remorselessly hunted by the child-man.

Next stop was the Wonsan Agriculture University. As ever, our tour started with an introduction by the local guide dressed in traditional garb. As ever, she said that the university had been founded thanks to the wisdom and inspiration of the Great Leader Kim Il Sung and the Dear Leader, Kim Jong Il. We were taken to the main entrance of the university, a grey monstrosity boasting a large portrait of Kim Il Sung with gleaming, Doris Day teeth. Inside, there was yet another exhibition of the great and happy moments when Kims Major and Minor had visited the university. There were no students in sight.

Jais and Fred were dawdling at the back and somehow took a wrong turning and ended up in a courtyard. There, they found a drum-set. Jais, who fancies himself as a Moroccan Charlie Watts, takes up the story: 'I decided to jam on the drum-set for about five minutes, only to find out at the end of my jam that forty North Korean students had emerged from nowhere and were staring in awe at the performance. When I finished, they were all clapping. Mr Hyun appeared, infuriated since I had strayed off with Fred for my little performance. It was one of the most surreal experiences ever. I was like an alien to the North Korean students. It was probably the weirdest thing they'd seen: a foreigner from Morocco who couldn't communicate with them, who just started playing on their drum-set while another filmed with his iPhone, and then just left, dragged away by his angry minder.'

The tour, like the struggle, continued. We came upon a fair-sized greenhouse complete with ripening tomatoes and orchid-like flowers. I zoned out, but I may well have been shown Kimilsungia and Kimjongilia – two flowers specially made to honour the great men. Kimilsungia is a purple orchid; Kimjongilia, as the Hitch, ever the one to spot small gradations of class differentiation, even in horticulture, points out, a low-rent begonia. Everard, the former British ambassador, is especially funny about the fuss the regime made when it came to floral respects to the Leaders, Great and Dear. He writes: 'Ambassadors were routinely invited to see the displays of flowers by different units from around the country. This unusual form of political flower arrangement was fiercely competitive ... An official from a central government ministry once invited me to come and look at the ministry's display – and it was indeed impressive. Then she took me to see the display of another government department, a much less elaborate offering. "I think they tried quite hard," she said, oozing *schadenfreude*.'

Everard goes on: 'I worked out that in one year we had spent longer debating the EU presence at the flower show than discussing human rights in North Korea.'[1] The former ambassador adds a footnote, mildly enfeebling his point; whether the footnote was his own idea, or something suggested by a desk wallah at King Charles Street before copy approval for his book was given, is not entirely clear.

To be fair to the European florist-diplomats, the regime addresses any attempt to discuss human rights of its own people with a wall of marble, as Senator Macaluso observed way back in 1969. But, for example, in the late 1980s at least some of Europe's diplomats did stick it to Ceausescu's tyranny. Arranging flowers nicely should not, perhaps, be a primary occupation of European diplomacy in Pyongyang.

Our tour continued along a concrete path on which were marked two green crosses, indicating where the hallowed feet of Kim Il Sung had stopped, the better to give 'on-the-spot guidance': yet more evidence that visiting North Korea is like being inside an enormous cult.

To rub the point home was a large painting of Kim the First sporting a white hat, in grey business suit and tie, shielding his eyes from the sun, with Kim the Second standing a few yards back, in blue Mao suit and holding a stalk of wheat in his hands; behind

[1] Everard, p73.

him a Korean farmer and his wife stand, smiling appreciatively, in a field bursting with wheat. He's holding a book, presumably Juche's line on planting wheat. The sun is shining but there are some sweet fluffy clouds in the sky. The reality, of course, is entirely different: that the first two Kims wrecked North Korean agriculture, and the people starved because of their folly. The painting is a monstrous deceit.

The true cause of the famine which gripped the land from 1996 to 1999 is a non-subject in North Korea. It happened, according to famine expert Jasper Becker, because of a long-term collapse in agriculture under Kim the First which no one could articulate: 'The leadership never grasped the extent of the unfolding disaster because no one dared tell Kim Il Sung the truth.'[2]

The great economist Amartya Sen, whose native Bengal suffered too often from famine during centuries of British imperial rule, noted: 'A free press and an active political opposition constitute the best early-warning system a country threatened by famines can have.' In North Korea, journalism, the job of telling the stories power and money do not want told, of giving a voice to the voiceless, does not exist.

Kim Il Sung died before the famine turned critical in 1994, to mass mourning, apart, that is, from the embalmers in Moscow who reportedly charged the DPRK $1 million for turning him into a waxwork. But the failure of North Korean agriculture over time, created by the state's diktat forbidding a free market, is the responsibility of Kim Il Sung. His son is to blame for following slavishly in his father's footsteps.

How many people died? Foreign experts dispute the numbers.

[2] Becker, *Rogue Regime*, p102.

There feels something wrong, obscene even, about arguing about how many people died in a famine. Once the numbers go beyond a few thousand, that's too many. But the lowest credible estimate according to one of the best, most humane and drily cynical Pyongyangologists in the world, Andrei Lankov, is around 500,000, or 2.5 per cent of the population: 'This is roughly equal to the ratio of Chinese farmers who perished from starvation during the Great Leap Forward of the early 1960s. In other words, it was the largest humanitarian disaster East Asia had seen for decades.'[3]

Others say it was far, far worse than Lankov's estimate. The most highly placed defector from the regime believes the number of dead was three million. This dispute cannot be satisfactorily resolved until the regime falls.

Big numbers dumb the mind. In Seoul, we met a defector, a man with a plastic hand. He gave me some sense of what that word 'famine' meant. Ji Seong Ho saw dead bodies piled up in the streets, near railway stations and in parks. Family and friends wilted under the hunger; many died.

I think I lost my mind from dizziness, sleep deprivation and hunger. My grandmother and my neighbours died of starvation. It wasn't just where I lived. When you went into the cities, train stations, markets and alleyways, you found lots of dead bodies. I do not know the exact number but countless people died. Countless.[4]

He was so hungry he risked stealing coal from a train. One of the railwaymen pulled the wrong lever, and the train was suddenly

[3] Lankov, *The Real North Korea*, p80.
[4] BBC *Panorama*: 'North Korea Undercover'.

side-tracked, towards policemen on a platform. Ji jumped and fell between the concrete of the platform and the train's wheels. When Ji came to, his hand and leg were hanging off. They amputated both without anaesthetic.

The moment Ji told me about corpses piling up near the railway stations, I knew he was telling the truth. People dying of starvation don't want to die on their own. They seek out a public place, perhaps in hope of some last-minute salvation. I'd heard that several times from Russian and Ukrainian survivors of Stalin's Great Famine in 1933. Some ironic souls even dared to die in front of statues to Stalin and Lenin.[5] Malcolm Muggeridge wrote of Stalin's famine in 1933: 'One of the most monstrous crimes in history, so terrible that people in the future will scarcely be able to believe it ever happened.'

Back then in the Soviet Union, while George Bernard Shaw proclaimed there was no famine, people were eating each other. A ninety-three-year-old Ukrainian lady remembered one of her neighbours being taken away after a child's arm was found in her stove. Cannibalism came to North Korea in the late 1990s. This famine, like Stalin's, is a monstrous crime people scarcely believe ever happened.

What could be worse than fear of starving to death? Why didn't people rebel? The man with the plastic hand explained: 'In North Korea, if you say the wrong thing you will die. You will be sent to a political prison camp. Even if one knows, sees or hears something one must pretend to be ignorant. Disagreement isn't an option. Disagreement means death.'

Fear of the regime is greater than fear of starving to death. That is a formidable tribute to the force of the tyranny.

[5] R. Redlich: *O Staline I Stalinizme*, Frankfurt, 1971, p217.

At no time throughout the famine did the secret police let up. One defector is quoted in Gause's pamphlet on the Bowibu and other state organs of control, reporting on the state's demand that each urban household had to produce 30 kilograms (66lb, or more than 4 stone) of dried human excrement mixed with soil, to help fertilize the countryside: 'It was a battle for people to produce 30 kg of compost per family in a severe winter. People frantically scratch the floor of their conventional toilets to collect the meagre excrement there, meagre because it is the discharge of people who are nearly starving.' If you are suffering from famine, human excrement resembles rabbit droppings. 'All residential areas were filled with the smell of human excrement that was being dried. To make things worse, Dong [the district sub-divisions of the Bowibu secret police] offices had Inminban compete with one another by preparing "Charts of Competition for Securing Excrement".'[6]

International organizations are not good at working out what is happening behind the scenes inside dictatorships. While some Westerners were saying there was no problem, North Koreans were eating one another. The famine peaked in the late 1990s, but many were starving long before that. Kim Yong was a lieutenant colonel in the North Korean National Security Agency before he was arrested in 1993, when his father's work during the Korean war as a translator for the Americans emerged in a background check. In *Long Road Home*, he tells the story of a police investigation into the deaths of thirteen people in Kim Il Sung's birthplace, close to Pyongyang. A doctor saw fresh meat on sale in the market at an unusually low price, and, with horror, realized

[6] Ken E. Gause, p47.

that he was looking at human flesh. The police investigated and discovered that thirteen people had been killed by the butcher and his family, and resold as meat.[7] The former officer recalls two more stories of cannibalism: of an old man going to a cemetery, digging up the freshly buried and marinating the meat before eating it; of a grandmother, driven mad by hunger, boiling her grandchild alive. These stories seem incredible but I have heard something similar from people in the Ukraine, people with no reason whatsoever to lie.

In 1998, at the height of the famine Kim the Father and Kim the Son had created, they did what they do best. Blame somebody else. One September day in Unification Square a crowd of thousands saw a score of officials shot, including the minister for agriculture, So Kwan Hi. They went one better, and dug up his predecessor, long-dead, and shot the corpse of Kim Man Kum, too.[8] In the Zombie state, you can't be too careful about the dead.

The response from the West to this slow-motion tragedy was dire. For a long time, the famine was denied or down-played by some Westerners, who spouted North Korea's official line. Kim Jong Il threatened nuclear proliferation, then offered nuclear talks, then went back to threats. In this atmosphere, the famine victims became pawns in a chess game about the nuclear threat. Andrew Natsios was, then, running World Vision, one of the biggest NGOs in the world. He wrote a piece in the *Washington Post* criticizing the Clinton administration for its overly political response to the

[7] Kim Yong: *Long Road Home*, Columbia University Press, New York, 2009, p57.
[8] Kim Kwang In: 'NK Exhumes and Decapitates Body of "Traitor"', *Choson Ilbo*, 5 October 2002.

famine, putting Western 'geo-strategy' over humanitarian con-
siderations. But the great problem for people like Natsios was that
the regime denied famine, and powerful evidence of the death of
millions was lacking, so therefore, the fashionable logic went, it
was not happening.

In his book, *The Great North Korean Famine*, Natsios quotes an
NGO worker on the nightmare of working out what was what
inside North Korea:

> I can identify with a recent visitor to North Korea when he said he
> couldn't sleep – not due to jet lag, but because of the difficulty in
> sorting through the ever-present and strong ideological message . . .
> A Norwegian UNICEF official told us that he had served in
> Uganda after Obote took over, worked in Afghanistan, and worked
> in Zaire, but 'this is the most difficult location – not because of
> physical safety, but because of a sense of not knowing what is going
> on.'[9]

Natsios' uncle had died in Greece due to the famine caused by
the Nazi occupation of his homeland. This family tragedy must
have been at the back of his mind as Natsios ignored the official
denials of famine. Natsios went to Pyongyang, was stone-walled by
the regime's officials, and saw a comfortable, if eerily strange,
capital city with no one starving. Not believing the non-evidence of
his own eyes, he went up to the Chinese border and interviewed
defectors. They told him the truth: that North Korea was gripped
by a great famine. One eyewitness was twenty-seven, whose

[9] Andrew Natsios: *The Great North Korean Famine*, US Institute of Peace,
Washington DC, 2001, p41.

harrowing description of a train journey to the Chinese border reminded Natsios of trains packed with Jews on the way to the Holocaust. Train carriages with 120 seats carried seven hundred people, squeezed into every space imaginable, many of them the starving *Kochibis* or wandering swallows – the Korean term for internally displaced people.

At the height of the famine, fear of the regime weakened and much of North Korea degenerated into a state of anarchy. The rules forbidding movement inside the country were swept aside as the hungry became more and more desperate. The *Kochibis* would climb on the roof of a train, hang off the sides, hold on underneath and crowd into the toilets. As a result, people urinated where they stood. The stench was sickening. The train would stop, due to power cuts. Natsios' eyewitness continued:

Dead bodies were taken off at train stations. Some riding on the rooftop would die accidentally when they stood up and touched the electrical lines above the train. Altogether I saw 20 dead bodies during my trip . . . Some people riding between the train carriages were trapped [and squeezed] to death because of a sudden train stop. Some hanging over the train car entrance fell to their death.[10]

But this evidence of famine was dialled down by some, including a few NGO workers, who said that because it came from defectors it was suspect. The greater problem was that Kim Jong Il continued to play the nuclear chess game, leaving the West sacrificing pawn after pawn for no gain. The dismal drift of Western policy changed when Pyongyang itself admitted that yes, there was a famine, and

[10] Natsios, p79.

they needed help. In the spring of 1997, North Korean diplomats at the United Nations met with Natsios and other big NGO officials and asked for food aid. The Americans replied yes, but said that they needed a media campaign, to alert people to the famine, and that would help push the American government to act. The North Koreans pulled a face, writes Natsios: 'Their government would never agree to any media coverage and we should forget about it. They were particularly insistent about not allowing any photographs of any kind, which is exactly what we most needed.'

No photos, as Mr Hyun would put it.

Eventually, in the late 1990s, food aid from the United States, China and Europe arrived in abundance. The regime took it, gave it to the army, the secret police and the Party cadres, and the hungry carried on dying.

Natsios is scathing about the West's failure to act effectively when the evidence of famine was overwhelming:

> The clash of these geostrategic interests with the humanitarian imperative to stop the famine caused the worst paralysis I have witnessed in any major relief effort since the close of the Cold War. Although food aid was pledged in the summer of 1997, and did arrive, it was two years too late, was sent to the wrong regions of the country, and had no rigorous controls on its internal distribution to prevent the elites from stealing it.[11]

Not everyone starved, of course.

The phone call came in the middle of the night. For Ermanno Furlanis, Italian pizza chef, raconteur and lover of life, it was the

[11] Natsios, p163.

start of the most surreal adventure of his life. Two weeks later, in the summer of 1997, Furlanis, his wife, another chef from the southern Italian city of Bari, Antonio Macchia, and his wife, flew to Berlin. At Tegel airport the two couples were given tickets for a flight to Pyongyang that did not exist. Leastways, there was no mention of it on the departures board. The Air Koryo jet was all but empty when it took off, destination North Korea.

On arrival the two chefs were hurried through the city to a brand new clinic, entirely empty of patients. And then the tests started: blood and urine samples were taken, X-rays, an electro-cardiogram and, thanks to a large magnetic resonance imaging machine, a brain scan. 'I was by now worried out of my mind,' said Furlanis. 'Here was proof that we were completely in their power, and they could do with us as they pleased.'[12] They had gone out of curiosity, forgetting what it had once done to the cat.

The Italians waited for the results of the medical tests, and waited and waited. Bored to distraction in their empty, gilded cage – they were put in a luxury villa, but deprived of contact with ordinary North Koreans – they begged their minder, Mr Om, could they go to a club and dance. Mr Om went away and came back. The answer was yes. But they didn't exactly end up in a nightclub. The Italians were taken to Kim Il Sung Square, where they found themselves in front of a sea of 30,000 people. After the master of ceremonies gave a signal, the crowd began to dance in uncannily precise formations. First, the mass formed thirty perfect squares, and as the music picked up tempo the squares became stars, then circles. It was dancing for robots.

[12] 'Making Pizza for Kim Jong Il', BBC Radio 3, 12 August 2004, http://news.bbc.co.uk/1/hi/3559266.stm

They were witnessing the anniversary celebrations for the end of the Korean war. But Ermanno and his wife wanted to dance, not merely play the audience in yet another North Korean propaganda show. 'Join them,' said Mr Om. Furlanis and his missus took to the floor and began whirling around with the North Koreans, who joked with them when they got their steps wrong. It meant a break from the boredom, but it wasn't what they had been hoping for.

Suddenly, the test results came through – all clear – and they were on the road. The Italians were shocked by the poverty they glimpsed as their motorcade sped through the countryside. They saw people washing their clothes in the river and then waiting around naked for them to dry: 'It was like the Middle Ages,' said Furlanis.

The further they travelled, the more they realized that the country was strictly parcelled up, with frequent military check-points blocking people from travelling from one district to another. The couple witnessed scenes of mass desperation, with people screaming and begging the soldiers to let them through on either side of the checkpoints, with little or no chance of success. Travel was only allowed with a special permit issued by the Korean Workers' Party. As day turned into night, they drove on, coming across people appearing to sleep on the road itself. One man with a bicycle seemed to have nodded off on the tarmac, but with his legs either side of the bike frame, as though he was still riding it in his sleep. 1997 was the worst year of the famine, and it's possible that what the Italian couples were actually seeing was people so worn down by hunger they had collapsed on the road. Furlanis said: 'We were scared a number of times. We thought we would end up running someone over.'

They ended up at a military base near the beach. To begin with, all the two chefs had to do was teach three North Korean chefs, who also seemed to be soldiers, or at least behaved as if they were under military discipline, how to cook pizza. Ingredients were not a problem. Capers from Pantelleria and trout from San Daniele were amongst the delicacies that were rushed in from Italy, shipped along with several cases of Barolo from Piedmont.

Furlanis said: 'While I worked, my pupils, pen and notebook in hand, took down every detail while the rest of the staff, a dozen people or so, gathered round to watch the proceedings in an absorbed silence.' Furlanis said that one of the students even asked to count the olives he used and to measure the distance between them. 'I don't know if he was just pulling my leg, but he looked totally serious.'

After several days of tuition, the chefs and their pizza ovens and other clobber were moved to a pontoon, tied to a large yacht. The mysterious client remained invisible, not on the pontoon, nor the yacht. Furlanis glimpsed through the yacht's windows something amazing: a man-made floating island which, he said, 'Fellini could not have imagined.'

The floating island boasted a magnificent villa three storeys high, a large terrace out front, and gigantic fun slides that ended up in the water. Some soldiers later told him that the island also boasted its own racing track. No one ever discussed the kind of people who lived on that platform, but it could only have been Kim Jong Il. Suddenly, there was huge agitation on board. Crossing the gangplank to the ship was Kim Jong Il himself. Furlanis missed him, but, he said, 'Our chef, who had no reason to fib, was, for the space of several minutes, utterly speechless. He said he felt as if he had seen God, and I still envy him this experience.'

Furlanis raised the contrast between the leaders' obscene levels of luxury and the plight of the people. Mr Om replied: 'Ermanno, my good friend, man is the same all over the world.'

Only once did the Italians witness something resembling a protest against the regime. Every day, early in the morning, a crowd of cleaners would enter the compound gates as Furlanis's limousine drove past them, bound for where the yacht was docked. One morning the gates opened to let the car in, but an elderly woman stood in front of it, placing her fists on the front of the car, shouting something. Furlanis asked for a translation but Mr Om ignored him. It was as if the scene did not exist. After a moment of hesitation, the driver weaved out of her way and accelerated off.

Trivial interactions with the locals were not welcome. Marilu, Furlanis's wife, once walked past an open door on the first floor of their residential complex where some young North Koreans were playing videogames and eating sweets. In broken English, they invited her to join them, seemingly enjoying the company of the exotic guest. Glad to have finally made some friends away from the tight supervision of Mr Om, Marilu left them after fifteen minutes to go back to her apartment. At around one o'clock in the morning, there was a knock on the door. Guards announced: 'We are leaving now. Pack your bags.' The Italian couple had no choice but to obey.

They were taken to a second villa by the beach, even more secluded than the first. They had the entire first floor, while the ground floor was reserved for Mr Om. While the men worked, the women had next to nothing to do. One day they were invited on a trip. Not realizing where they were going, they took no bathing costumes. When they ended up on a private beach very close to the villa, they stripped down to their underwear – not topless, entirely correct, but not acceptable for ultra-conservative North Korea. On the second day, they were taken to a small room where they were encouraged to borrow swimsuits straight out of the fashion pages of 1953.

On the beach, the wives were monitored, their environment totally controlled. The sand was raked to the point of obsession, leaving it as hard as cement. Access to the sea was permitted, but only via a small pier covered in green velvet. Walking down the beach was not allowed. At the end of their narrow strip was an anti-aircraft gun position, made up of heavy machine guns and rockets. Marilu once put her feet in the shallows – an area not officially designated for bathing – which resulted in two young soldiers popping up, rifles at the ready, screaming their heads off. It wasn't exactly Capri.

Furlanis and Macchia and their wives were rewarded for their hard work with very generous tips and the occasional trip to North Korean holiday sites. They were once taken to a supposedly uninhabited island, where expensive food and bottles of Barolo and Rémy Martin were laid out for the Italian guests to enjoy. When their guide fell asleep after one too many glasses of wine, Furlanis set out to explore the island. After walking for a few minutes he saw two men with bare chests and military fatigues fishing in the distance. He waved at them; they ran into the undergrowth.

Puzzled, Furlanis decided to follow the two men, and as he walked further towards the centre of the island he saw two goats and a small kitchen-garden with a few onions and tomatoes. As the other Italian guests joined him, they were soon encircled by other North Koreans. The mood turned sour. The Italians were scared. Two armed guards they knew arrived and ordered the Furlanises and the Macchias to return to the yacht they had arrived in. A football came out of nowhere. Being tipsy, the Italians told the guards to forget about Mr Om and to join them in a game of football. The global magic of football did its trick. The North Koreans scored three early goals but the Italians ended up winning 4–3, avenging the notorious 1–0 loss of the 'Azzurri' in the 1966 World Cup at Middlesbrough. No one ever explained what the young men were doing on the supposedly deserted island.

After three weeks, and with very little notice, the North Korean adventure was at an end. A Pakistani chef had already arrived, renowned for cooking the best chicken curry in the world. Their passports magically reappeared and the Italian party prepared to be driven back to Pyongyang. As they left the military base, their students ran after the car for as long as they could, waving goodbye and lobbing them sweets through the windows.

Once back at home in Italy, Furlanis hit the scales. In the middle of famine, he had managed to put on several kilos.

Back in Wonsan, we caught a train to nowhere. An old-fashioned waiting room complete with cruelly thin wooden benches led us to a splendid black steam engine with great black wheels and a carriage or two painted blue with red stripes. Dylan sat by a carriage window and did a brilliant impression of Celia Johnson in *Brief Encounter*, waving to a disconsolate Trevor Howard, a hilarious moment unwittingly captured by the KITC cameraman. The train was the magical vehicle that took Kim Il Sung from the port of Wonsan to Pyongyang on 20 September 1945. Again, the date was not given in Juche Time because the propagandization of the magical train journey took place long before 1997. Back in 1945, of course, Kim Il Sung was only a contender for power. That autumn, he rose to become top cherry for the Soviets, but he certainly didn't arrive at Wonsan as the chosen one. I left the museum and popped out into the fresh air, looking for the railway station proper. It wasn't there. They had created a mock-railway station, simply for the purpose of falsifying history on wheels.

Next, off to the Wonsan Children's Camp. There were no children. Well, no flesh-and-blood children anyway. There was a bronze statue of Kim Il Sung in a Western suit with his arms around a little boy with a trumpet in his hand and a slightly taller girl. Half hidden by a pine tree but clearly visible on the KITC video is a security camera, watching over the statue from behind. To the left and right were two more CCTV cameras, which we filmed. None of us had ever seen a security camera in North Korea and it could only have been placed there for one reason: fear of vandalism. It's possible that at least some of the international students from places like Russia, Vietnam, Burma and Africa who have ended up in this camp dared show disrespect to authority. Even more shocking, it could be North Korean kids. We asked Mr Hyun: 'Why the CCTV?' He asked the local guide. He translated that the CCTV was there to prevent a plot by the South Korean secret agents to blow up the statue. It was perhaps the most preposterous explanation he gave in our whole trip.

The statue was the centrepiece of a bleak square, surrounded by Sovietische accommodation blocks. Further off was a funfair and a water slide. The local guide explained that the rooms the students used were closed, so we couldn't see them, but we could look at the children's gulag, sorry, centre. The whole place had a hang-dog air of neglect about it. It looked as though it had been knocked up in the 1980s, possibly for the Student Games. The external walls were streaked with damp. A series of flagpoles stood barren, no flags flying.

Inside, the lights being off, the facilities looked even bleaker in the gloom. A large vestibule was dedicated to photographs of the Kims: older black-and-white shots of Kim the First, then, in colour, Bad Elvis being weird here, there and everywhere. Hey, look, kids, here's a picture of Dr Evil opening a factory – just what a twelve-year-old wants on holiday. Further on, there were snaps of Kim Three in the rocket control room, urging his technicians on to Armageddon. I can't imagine any youngster looking at these photographs and being able to sleep at night. The comedy of the inappropriateness of the regime's propaganda drivel as something young teenagers might enjoy got to the group, and we started giggling. Our trepidation of the first day was long gone. Had we been invited to bow in front of the statue of Kim Il Sung and kids, CCTV and all, I doubt whether a single one of us would have done so.

We walked past a large mosaic map of the world, with North Korea picked out in red, and we entered a great, empty theatre, a forum for plays illustrating the excellence of Jucheist internationalist thought, no doubt. Now that Kim Jong Un has been threatening thermo-nuclear war, it seems hard to imagine how the children's camp is going to compete with other attractions. On the way out, there was a plaster goose pulling down the trousers of a plaster pig. Disneyland can rest easy.

17

The American Who Went to North Korea and Stayed

On 15 August 1962, Private James Joseph Dresnok of the US Army walked across the DMZ and defected to North Korea. More than half a century later, he's still there, the father of three children. In the case against the North Korean regime, Dresnok is a disturbing witness for the defence, an American who quotes Kim Il Sung, condemns his old country for its military occupation of the South and weeps at how his food ration remained good throughout the 'Arduous March'. He mouths the rhetoric of Pyongyang in a Virginian accent.

A giant haystack of a man, 6 foot 5 inches, Dresnok was seventy-two years old at the time of writing in 2013. His bulk and metal fillings remind one of Jaws. In a documentary about his life, Dresnok drawls in his southern, quaintly old-fashioned speech – because his American has been uncorrupted for fifty years – by proclaiming: 'I will give you the truth. I've never told anyone before.' The last sentence may be true.

Dresnok's story is told in *Crossing the Line*,[1] made by two Britons,

[1] *Crossing the Line* was broadcast on the BBC in 2007. It's available on YouTube in six parts: https://www.youtube.com/watch?v=okeL5Xk1qz4

Nicholas Bonner, the impresario behind Koryo Tours, one of the very few travel companies licensed to do business in North Korea, and Daniel Gordon, formerly of Sky TV. Bonner and Gordon are the leading Western lights in 'Pyongywood', the North Korean movie industry. Their first film, *The Game of their Lives*, 2001, tells the story of the North Korean football team which beat Italy in the 1966 World Cup. *A State of Mind*, 2005, is a subtle and beautifully observed film about two young girls training to take part in the Pyongyang Mass Games. *Crossing the Line*, 2007, is the most political of their films. All of their work is fascinating because they get extraordinarily good access to North Korea. But that very access raises questions about how far you go in a trade-off with a totalitarian state. Bonner, as boss of Koryo Tours, believes in working with the North Korean regime. *Observer* travel writer Carole Cadwalladr was allowed to go to North Korea. She wrote: 'I have a special, rare dispensation as a travel writer because Nick Bonner, the founder of Koryo Tours, believes that the more the world engages with North Korea, the more North Korea will engage with the world. And because I've agreed in advance that I shan't write about North Korea's human rights record or in any way insult the Dear Leader.'[2] None of Bonner's films do.

Bonner has been asked whether he has been at best wilfully naive in promoting North Korea as anything less than a bizarre and oppressive tyranny. He replied: 'We believe very strongly in engagement. Since 1945 the West has worked on very few policies to engage with North Korea on a cultural level. If being naive represents lack of experience, well we have more experience than most, and as for lack of wisdom, or being duped, I think the projects we have worked

[2] Carole Cadwalladr, *Observer*, 14 February 2010: 'The strange innocence of the "axis of evil"'.

on with our Korean colleagues are testament to the effectiveness of engagement and understanding.[3]

Dresnok's story, officially, runs like this. He was born into a poor family in Virginia, in 1941. His father abandoned the family before he was ten. After a broken upbringing, in and out of foster homes, he enlisted in the US Army when he was seventeen. His first marriage broke up after he returned from a two-year tour in Germany: 'I'm just thankful we never had any kids, because I swore I would never leave my children,' he says in the film, tears pouring down his face. Dresnok re-enlisted and went to South Korea. He found discipline unbearable, was caught with prostitutes and faced court martial. One summer's day in 1962, while cleaning his army shotgun, he upped sticks and walked across 'the Zee': 'I was fed up with my childhood, my marriage, my military life, everything. I was finished. There's only one place to go. On August 15th, at noon in broad daylight when everybody was eating lunch, I hit the road. Yes, I was afraid. Am I gonna live or die? And when I stepped into the minefield and I seen it with my own eyes, I started sweating. I crossed over, looking for my new life.'

The Korean People's Army took him prisoner, but treated him correctly, the story goes. Soon, he was introduced to another American deserter: 'I opened my eyes. I didn't believe myself. I shut them again. I must be dreaming. I opened them again and looked and, "Who in the hell are you?"' His name was Larry Abshier, another GI defector who had crossed the line three months before Dresnok. Two more US Army defectors would join them in the next two years, Jerry Parrish and Sergeant Charles Robert Jenkins.

[3] Interview with Nick Bonner: 'Touring North Korea', Worldhum website: http://www.worldhum.com/features/travel-interviews/interview-with-nick-bonner-head-of-koryo-tours-to-north-korea-20090807/

All four were running away from internal torment; they had no idea what they were getting into. Dresnok recalled what it was like being an American in North Korea a decade after the civil war: 'The uneasiness of the way people look at me when I walk down the street. "Oh, there goes that American bastard."'

In 1966, the four Americans sought asylum in the Soviet embassy in Pyongyang. The Russians said sorry, but handed them straight back. Dresnok set his mind to making a go of his new life. Or so he says: 'They might be a different race. They might be a different colour. But God damn it I'm gonna sit down and I'm gonna learn their way of life. I did everything I could. Learning the language. Learning the customs. Learning their greetings. Their life. Oh, I gotta think like this, I gotta act like this. I've studied their revolutionary history, their lofty virtues about the Great Leader.'

His devotion was rewarded in 1978 with a starring role in one episode of a North Korean TV series, *Unknown Heroes*. Dresnok plays Lieutenant Colonel Arthur, a psychotic American commander of a POW camp, in shades, Zapata moustache and matching handgun.[4] *Unknown Heroes* makes a bad Spaghetti Western look like *The Searchers*. It is 'the Yankee soldiers took out their bayonets and sliced through the women's breasts like bean curd' on acid, on tape. Dresnok told Bonner and Gordon: 'I don't consider it a propaganda movie. I took great honour in doing it.'

Orwell's clock just struck thirteen. One is compelled to wonder whether Dresnok's lost his marbles or whether he is a captive who has to say what his gaolers want him to say. Having been inside North Korea for more than fifty years, that may come fluently, but

---

[4] For clips of *Unknown Heroes*, watch *Crossing the Line* or look at CBS's short news item which features Dresnok's role: http://www.cbsnews.com/video/watch /?id=2405878n

one should not mistake fluency for truth.

Crossing the Line does 'not cross the line by asking simple questions of the regime. Gordon has said: 'We have taken an apolitical viewpoint.' The assumption that you can be apolitical in a totalitarian dictatorship like North Korea is a big fat one.

Over pictures of soldiers running into battle, American bombers dropping their payloads on the North, flaming houses and refugees running from the inferno, the commentary voiced by Christian Slater of *Vampire Chronicles* fame intones: 'In 1950, Korea experienced at first hand the brutal realities of the Cold War, a clash of ideologies that would devastate the peninsula. The Korean war was one of the most vicious of the century.' Nowhere does *Crossing the Line* make clear that this war was started by the North. Is that apolitical? Or mucking about with history?

As well as being a Pyongywood star, Dresnok helped translate the Great Leader's wisdom into vernacular English and taught English at the spy school, er, sorry, Pyongyang University of Foreign Languages. In the film, he tells how he met a beautiful brunette: 'I thought I was the happiest man in the world. I went completely crazy.' But her name, identity and origin remain a mystery for the viewer. Dresnok says: 'I'd get her drunk and ask her, and she'd say: "Shut up, don't ask that question."'

The mystery European woman and Dresnok had two sons, Ted Ricardo Dresnok and James Gabriel Dresnok. His wife died, and he married the daughter of an African diplomat and a Korean woman; she and Dresnok have a boy, now eleven years old.

Dresnok's second son, James Gabriel, is a real catch for Pyongywood: a handsome blue-eyed strapping young man, who looks 100 per cent American but speaks English with a halting, heavily Korean accent. He doesn't just speak like a North Korean, he acts like one too. If you were to do a twenty-first-century remake of *The Manchurian Candidate*, James Gabriel would be the star. Funnily enough, he too is studying at the elite foreign language university. 'My father is American and I've got American blood. But as I was born here I consider myself as Korean,' James Gabriel told Bonner and Gordon. James Gabriel is a living fossil from the Cold War, a human coelacanth.

Crossing the Line's director, Gordon, told CBS: 'His best friend, who's Korean, says, "All the Korean girls love him." They love him. He's got blond hair and blue eyes.'

In the film, James Gabriel says: 'I start to learn English to become a diplomat. I'd like to make the world which has no war at all. And no terror at all.' James Gabriel seems unaware of the Kim dynasty's track record on terrorism: the bomb on Korean Air Flight 858, killing 115 people in 1987; the training camp for the IRA men; the kidnapping of foreign nationals. On that very issue, he could have asked his mother.

Was she Doina Bumbea, the Romanian artist who vanished in 1978? That question haunted her family back in Romania when they heard about the film and got to watch it, and with mounting horror realized that James Gabriel looked astonishingly like their daughter, missing for almost three decades. Had Doina ended up in North Korea?

Doina's tragedy is as black as can be. On Facebook, there is a page dedicated to her memory.[5] The photographs are heart-breaking, showing a young woman of real beauty, dark-haired, elfin. Born in 1950, the daughter of a Romanian officer and a Russian woman, she became an artist. One photograph shows her cuddling her much

[5] https://www.facebook.com/photo.php?fbid=365015986896971&set=
a.364364606962109.86128.215937755138129&type=1&theater

younger brother, what looks like a self-portrait in the background; a second, the cocky artist on the make, sporting a black hat, leopard-skin coat and jeans, standing by one of her paintings – she had real talent, her work reminiscent of Modigliani; a third, Doina in a floral-patterned dress, eyeing the camera, self-confident, poised, happy to take on the world. She married an Italian, moved to Rome, fell pregnant, had a miscarriage, and got divorced. Looking for fresh adventure – and who doesn't at the age of twenty-eight? – she was approached by an Italian man who offered her exciting prospects of working in the art scene in the Far East. She jumped at the chance. Her family last had contact with Doina when she called from Italy to say she was travelling to Tokyo and promised to call immediately after she arrived. That was in 1978. The family never heard from her again. Doina's promise, her future, was robbed from her; instead she entered a world of worry.

None of Doina's story is clear or easy to tell. Instead, there are scraps of dog-eared information here and there, which float down over the decades. After her trip to the Far East, no one hears of her for nigh on thirty years. We know what happened next thanks to another kidnapping, on the far side of the world.

In 1978, the same year that Doina vanished, Hitomi Soga lived on a small island off the west coast of Japan. One August evening she went for a walk at dusk with her mother, enjoyed an ice cream, and was only a few hundred yards from home when her life changed forever. Three men grabbed her from behind, tied her hands, stuffed a gag in her mouth, bundled her into a big black plastic bag and carried her to a skiff. The skiff went out to sea, then she was dumped in the hold of a ship. She never saw her mother again; it is most likely that she resisted and her kidnappers murdered her. The ship sailed for a whole day until it arrived at the port of Chongjin.

The next morning, they told Hitomi: 'Maybe it would be fun for you to go to the beach and look for some clams' – evidence, to the man who became her husband, 'of how strange the North Korean cadres are, how out of touch they are with the emotions normal people have.'

Hitomi was bereft, afraid, sick to the bottom of the heart. And then one day she was introduced to a small, wiry American, who became the great love of her life.

Charles Robert Jenkins, one of the four soldier-defectors like Dresnok. Dreading the thought of being sent to Vietnam, unhappy and insecure, Jenkins ran across the DMZ in 1965, a decision he was to regret. He owes his liberty to the regime's obsession with racial purity, the feckless incompetence of Kim Jong Il, and the power of Hitomi's love for him.

The kidnapping of foreigners began in 1977, as Kim the Second's sway in the regime grew. But Kim Il Sung had survived in Manchuria in the late 1930s by kidnapping the family members of rich farmers, demanding ransoms. Kidnapping was old Kim family business. Thirteen of the known kidnap victims were Japanese, plucked from ordinary lives, walking home at night, going for a stroll on the beach, then suddenly pinioned by strangers, forced into a small boat and down the hatch of a North Korean submarine or fishing boat, only to reappear in Pyongyang, to start a new life in absolute terror. Some were from Lebanon, Thailand, ordinary people engulfed by a power acting with no accountability.

Why kidnap foreigners? The most likely explanation is the regime's obsession with espionage. Professor Yoichi Shimada of Fukui University in Japan told a US Congress Human Rights sub-committee in 2006: 'North Korean defectors have told us that in 1976 Kim Jong Il issued a secret order to use foreign nationals more systematically and thereby improve the quality of North

Korean spy activities. He dubbed it "localization of spy education".'
The professor suggested six reasons for the kidnapping: 'North
Korea appears to abduct foreign citizens in order to eliminate
hapless witnesses who happened to run into North Korean agents
in action; steal victims' identities; force abductees to teach their
local language and customs to North Korean agents; brainwash
them into secret agents; use abductees' expertise; use abductees as
spouses for defectors or other abductees.'[6]

Thanks to its belief in racial purity, the foreigners could not marry
North Koreans. But if the defectors and the kidnapped women
could have children together, then their progeny might be useful as
agents – this, sick as it is, might also be part of the regime's logic.

In 2002, in a thaw in relations between the old colonial power,
Japan, and North Korea, the Japanese prime minister Junichiro
Koizumi visited Pyongyang. On offer was a big deal: billions of aid
money from Japan in return for North Korea burying the hatchet.
One irritant for the Japanese were the persistent rumours that a score
of their people had been kidnapped. To smooth things along, Kim
Jong Il blithely admitted the regime had abducted thirteen Japanese
citizens in the 1970s and '80s, and released the names of a handful of
Japanese who were still alive, including Hitomi. The irony is that she
was not on any Japanese list of abductees, her disappearance and that
of her mother had been all but forgotten. It took the Japanese
media less than twenty-four hours to stand up the story: she and
her mother vanished in 1978, and the immensely hostile reaction
from the Japanese public to the kidnaps smashed the proposed deal

---

[6] Yoichi Shimada, Professor of International Politics, Fukui Prefectural
University, Committee on House International Relations, Subcommittee on Asia
and the Pacific, Subcommittee on Africa, Global Human Rights and
International Operations, 27 April 2006.

to pieces. Kim Jong Il, with no sense of what public opinion can do, was at sea. Soon, the Japanese abductees were on their way home. Hitomi never gave up on her man, and eventually, after pressure from the Japanese, Jenkins was allowed to leave too, escaping after forty years from what he describes as 'a giant, demented prison'.

He tells his story in *The Reluctant Communist*.[7] Read it.

Jenkins paints a bleak and wholly convincing picture of four decades inside the DPRK. He describes the freezing cold; the hunger that lasted for year after year; the petty corruption of the cadres detailed to look after them; the boredom; the emotional anguish of realizing his treachery against the United States was an unrecoverable mistake; the brainwashing; the 'gibberish' and 'horse-shit' of Jucheism; the time they found a cat's cradle of microphones in the loft of one of their houses, listening in to their every word.

Initially, the four Americans shared a house. Nearby, there were some houses which they had been told were off-limits. In the same area they had seen the army digging a hole in the ground. A while later, the hole had been filled in, leaving just a bald spot of earth. A dog was digging up the fresh dirt: 'That's when we saw them: two dead human feet sticking right up out of the ground. We didn't believe what we were seeing, but we took a closer look, and sure enough, there was no mistaking it. From the size of the grave, about two by five yards, it could have held five to ten people . . . A few days later, however, we saw a woman running down a hill from where the grave was. She was screaming her head off, and we knew exactly what it was all about. A little while later, people from the army came around and killed every dog in the neighbourhood.'[8]

[7] Charles Robert Jenkins with Jim Frederick: *The Reluctant Communist: My Desertion, Court-Martial and Forty-Year Imprisonment in North Korea*, University of California Press, London, 2008.

Jenkins says Dresnok became a stooge, a loyal and faithful servant of what Jenkins calls in his book, 'the Organization', that is, the regime, the Party, the secret police, whatever. Jenkins says Dresnok tortured him on the orders of their minders, habitually beating him to a pulp.

Dresnok in *Crossing the Line* calls Jenkins 'a liar' and says of his fellow American: 'Bye-bye, baby! Who cares?' CBS asked Gordon was there any sense of the government ordering Dresnok to beat Jenkins? The Pyongywood director replied: 'We never got that sense from Dresnok. He just denied and denied and denied that he was the North Korean strong arm ... From what we can gather there was a lot of times when it was drink oriented. They went out and they drank and they drank and they had a fight.'[9]

Dresnok says in the film: 'One day he tried to push me around with his so-called rank and there was two blows. [Jenkins had been a sergeant, Dresnok a private.] I hit him and he hit the ground. I think you know *Alice in Wonderland*. Well, I just wonder if it's not Jenkins in Wonderland.'

Crossing the Line does reflect Jenkins's version of events, but the star of the film is Dresnok, not Jenkins. Nick Bonner, at a Q&A after a screening of the film in Beijing, faces the question, which of the two men does he believe? He answers it by imitating Dresnok's southern drawl, mocking Jenkins's claims that he was tied up, then beaten: 'Tie him up? Why would I need to tie him up? I could hold him in one hand and beat him with the other.' The audience laughs. Perhaps they haven't been to North Korea.[10]

The detail of Jenkins's account in his book of Dresnok beating

[8] Jenkins, p53.
[9] http://www.cbsnews.com/8301-18560_162-2398580.html
[10] Nick Bonner, talking about *Crossing the Line* at a Q&A in Beijing at 22 minutes in: http://www.youtube.com/watch?v=zu8s_zf59e4

him up is compelling. For example, Jenkins specifically recalls the date on which Dresnok's attacks on him began: 9 September 1972, the anniversary of the foundation of the Workers' Party. Jenkins angers his minder, whom he calls the Tall Cadre. The Americans are held under loose house arrest because they know that they stand out a mile in racially pure North Korea. The Tall Cadre ties Jenkins up and orders Dresnok to hit him. Jenkins is small and compact, Dresnok a much bigger man:

> The sick bastard enjoyed it. He took solid, square-knuckled cracks at me across my face, one after another … My nose began to gush blood after the first few swings. By the time he had finished, my top lip had split in two places, and my bottom teeth were sticking out of the skin between my lower and my chin … Why was he always an eager torturer? He had become a stooge.[11]

So who to believe? If Jenkins is a liar, as Dresnok insists, then his information about Doina cannot be relied upon.

The fine detail of Dresnok's military record does not feature in *Crossing the Line*. His old local paper, *The Virginian*, dug it up: on 26 January 1960, Dresnok stole a Volkswagen valued at $715 from its owner, Franz Schuhmann, and threatened a second German with a bayonet. He was court-martialled, but got a suspended sentence. In South Korea, he made a poor impression: one report described him as 'a chronic complainer, lazy' and 'defiant to authority'. In July of 1962 he faced a second court martial over a forged pass, drinking, indebtedness and promiscuity.[12] A few days before the hearing, he crossed 'the Z'. None of the above

[11] Jenkins, p64.
[12] Earl Swift: 'Why seek solace in N. Korea?', *The Virginian*, 7 September 2004.

makes Dresnok out to be a bad bad man, but it is evidence of a weakness of character the Organization could play on.

In the film Dresnok does not come across well. One newspaper reviewer in the States found Dresnok unconvincing: 'Although a curious study in political exploitation for most of the film – snippets of the Kim Jong Il-directed propaganda epic "Nameless Heroes," starring Dresnok as a sinister American, are fascinating – by the end, his sallow, corpulent frame has settled into stooge-like, Kool-Aid-drunk offensiveness.'[13]

What about Jenkins the man? His ghost-writer, *Time* journalist Jim Frederick, says: 'Robert [Jenkins] tells the truth. There have been numerous times when Robert told me something that either sounded insane, trumped up, or nonsensical only to have my doubts shattered by the realization that he was absolutely correct ... Although Dresnok recently denied to a documentary film crew in North Korea' – Bonner and Gordon – 'that he ever beat up Robert in anything more than a single fair fist fight, it seems to me to be such an odd thing to fabricate, and a thing that reflects poorly on Robert.' Frederick asks: 'What soldier would want to admit that he couldn't defend himself against another? I can't imagine why he would make a story like that up.'

To this day, the regime does not admit that it abducted anyone else apart from the thirteen Japanese they have already confessed to kidnapping. But there are seriously evidenced reports that South Korean, Thai and Lebanese women were also kidnapped. And, perhaps, too, one Romanian.

Jenkins in his book touches on an eastern European woman who ended up marrying Dresnok. He calls her 'Dona'. Her story, says

[13] http://articles.latimes.com/2007/oct/12/entertainment/et-capsules12

Jenkins, was that she met this Italian 'big shot' art dealer, who was in retrospect a North Korean sympathizer or paid agent. He invited her to 'Hong Kong'. She didn't have an Italian or Romanian passport at the time, but the Italian supplied her with North Korean papers. On the way to Hong Kong, they stopped over in Pyongyang: there, she faced hostile interrogation, that her papers were fake. The trap was sprung. There was no way out.

Is the woman Jenkins calls Dona the Romanian artist Doina who disappeared in 1978? Ceausescu's former interpreter, Izidor Urian, is haunted by Doina's story. He sounded wretched when he explained that he went through all of the old Romanian archives, trying to find any mention of her case. There was nothing there. But if Doina's kidnap was a black operation by the North Koreans, the absence of evidence in the Bucharest archives does not mean much.

Jenkins gets one detail wrong, saying that the Italian who kidnapped her promised her work in the art scene in Hong Kong, not Tokyo, where she told her family she was going. But people often mistake small details of a story like that. There are two more facts the old sergeant does remember. The first is that Jenkins says of Dona: 'She was one hell of an artist . . . she could draw like she knew what she was doing.'

Dona's second boy, James Gabriel, the blue-eyed star of *Crossing the Line*, was known as Gabi to Jenkins. Doina's younger brother, the one she is seen cuddling in the photograph when he was around three, is called Gabriel.

'It's the same woman,' Gabriel Bumbea told me. 'She is my sister. I am 100 per cent convinced. Jenkins and Hitomi lived with my sister for nineteen years.'

After the film was aired, Gabriel flew to Japan in 2007 and met Jenkins and Hitomi. Jenkins gave Gabriel a much fuller picture of

Doina than he set out in his book, written in 2004. Jenkins said that Doina told him about the mystery Italian, how they had stopped off in Moscow but ended up in Pyongyang. First, in 1978, she was sent to a paramilitary training camp, which sounds pretty much like one described by Len the IRA man. There, she was taught Kimilsungism, martial arts and that, in North Korea, to eat, you had to obey. No one in the outside world knew where she was. She had no hope of escape; no hope at all.

The marriage with Dresnok was arranged by the Organization. Jenkins recalls meeting Doina just after the birthday of Larry Abshier's son: 'She was beautiful and intelligent.' In 1981, she still dreamed of escape back to Italy. At the birthday party, Doina asked Jenkins: 'When will I be free?' Jenkins replied: 'Never.' Jenkins said that the marriage with Dresnok was not happy: there were endless rows, beatings too. Doina ran away from home at times; but in North Korea, where any Caucasian stands out a mile, she had no chance.

The four couples lived in a compound not far from Pyongyang, Dresnok and Doina and their two boys, known as Ricardo and Gabi; Jenkins and Hitomi and their two daughters; Abshier and his wife, who Dresnok in *Crossing the Line* claims was a Korean, but Jenkins says is a Thai, Anocha Panjoy, also kidnapped; and Jerry Parrish and his wife, Siham Shrieteh, originally from the Lebanon, and their three sons. Siham says in *Crossing the Line* that she is happy to stay in North Korea. The film does not point out the strong likelihood that her three boys are effective hostages and that Siham may have been rehearsing her gaolers' script; as she talks her face looks unbearably strained.

They did not make for 'Happy Families'. Jenkins says that was because of Dresnok. Jenkins says that as well as being violent towards him and Doina, Dresnok beat up Abshier, 'a simple, sweet, good hearted soul who was more than a little dumb and easy to take advantage of'.[14] At one point, on Jenkins's illicit radio, they heard a dramatization of Steinbeck's *Of Mice And Men*, after which Dresnok and Parrish would mock Abshier as 'Lennie', the dumb giant. Abshier died of a heart attack in 1983. On his tombstone, it was written his place of birth was Pyongyang. That should have read Urbana, Illinois.

Doina sold a gold necklace she'd managed to keep from Italy for a sewing machine. An excellent seamstress, she made clothes for all of the children, and she was a good cook too, magicking fine-ish meals out of miserable ingredients. Her speciality was a Russian salad, and when they had meat she knew how to grill it to perfection. She even cultivated a piece of land, growing corn, potatoes and onions.

Their two sons grew up. Ricardo, the oldest, was more rebellious. Aged twenty, he sneaked out to a party thrown by children of some diplomats in Pyongyang. For this crime, he was sentenced to six months in prison. He pops up in *Crossing the Line* but is not interviewed, unlike his younger brother, James Gabriel, the student at the spy school, although the film does not call it that. It's possible that the older brother is less compliant, less brainwashed.

Doina died of cancer in 1997, Hitomi giving her shots of morphine to ease the pain. Back in Romania, her family continued to know nothing of her fate for another decade.

Jenkins said: 'Doina told both of her boys that she is Romanian and she was kidnapped.' All of this makes Dresnok's statement in *Crossing the Line* that he did not know where the mother of his two

---

[14] Jenkins, p46.

boys was from – 'Shut up, don't ask that question' – incredible.

Gabriel Bumbea told me: 'I dream of my nephews getting out of North Korea and coming home to Romania. My mother, Petra, who is now eighty-four, only lives for the day when she can see her grandsons. The two boys are all that's left of my sister and we want to meet them.'

To lose the blue-eyed, blond-haired James Gabriel Dresnok would, of course, be a disaster for Pyongywood. It's only because of *Crossing the Line* that Doina's Romanian family know what happened to her, and for that they are grateful to Bonner and Gordon. But that happy consequence appears to have been unintended. A film setting out North Korea's version of the Americans who crossed the DMZ ends up revealing, by mistake, a hitherto unknown and monstrous case of kidnapping. Pyongywood's Dream Factory screwed up, big-time.

Crossing the Line's emotional crescendo comes when Dresnok weeps at the thought that the regime made sure he was supplied with enough food at the height of the 'Arduous March' – the regime's Newspeak for the famine – while so many perished. Dresnok is moved to tears by the graciousness of the Dear Leader. Thinking about the tragedy of the four Americans who made the long mistake of defecting to North Korea and the crueller fate of the kidnap victims they ended up being married to, one could imagine a different ending. Rather than giving the stage to the regime stooge, better, surely, to use a line from Jim Frederick, Jenkins's ghost-writer, that they were all consumed by 'an almost unbearably understated evil'.

And, if Doina's two boys remain in North Korea, an evil that continues to this day.

18

The Hospital that Has Patients, but Only in the Morning

In the half-light of the morning Wonsan was revealed to us. The sea was calm, the sun shone, but it's not exactly San Tropez. The North Korean Riviera has some way to catch up. My father was a ship's engineer and he ingrained in me the habit of wandering around harbours, checking out the seaworthiness of the craft. The most striking thing about Wonsan was the absence of small fishing boats, presumably because if any fisherman had the option, he would be on his way to the South as quickly as possible. One of the few vessels in view was an old rust-bucket of a tub, maybe 70 feet long, which looked as though it had not been out to sea for a very long time. One could imagine that with North Korea's fuel crisis, diesel for domestic consumption would be very hard to come by; the alternative, allowing the market to fund commercial fishing, is not an option. Yet again, the often-voiced commitment to improve the economy is in conflict with North Korea's core policy of regime security. So ordinary people are denied the opportunity of reaping the sea.

We headed back on the long, bumpy drive to the Big Zombie.

There, we had lunch at the Koryo Hotel, far grander than our own hotel, in its revolving restaurant – a fashion trend from the 1970s which has finally arrived in Pyongyang. The restaurant did rotate, but creakily so. Inch by inch, the whole demented city crawled by: the Juche Tower, the Three Prongs, the Grand People's Study House. It felt like we had been there a lifetime. After lunch, Hoe-Yeong spotted a piano in the restaurant and went over to tinkle. Mr Hyun found some scores of North Korean songs, mostly of the patriotic variety. Seeing Hoe-Yeong could play the piano, Mr Hyun said: 'I'll sing and you play.' Hoe-Yeong did as he was told: 'It was real fun engaging with our tour guide in music making.' But at the end when he told Hoe-Yeong that they had just performed a very well-known song that told of the greatness of Kim Il Sung, Hoe-Yeong had difficulty stifling his dismay. As a form of redemption, he started playing 'The Star Spangled Banner' in the softest of pianissimos. It was certainly within earshot of Mr Hyun. Then again, he might not have known what the tune was, just as Miss Jun had explained to us that the Statue of Liberty was in Paris.

In the basement of the hotel we found a casino, entirely empty of customers, complete with CCTV, slot machines and washed-out croupiers who never see the light of day. As North Koreans of the wrong sort would never dare enter a hotel for foreigners, and foreigners with any sense wouldn't play here, it seemed hard to divine how the casino could ever make any money. That mystery, like many other, was left unsolved.

They took us to the Metro, one of the great sights of Pyongyang. It was profoundly deep, at least a hundred feet below the ground, perhaps deeper, because it doubles up as a nuclear shelter. There are no advertisements so you descend into the bowels of the earth looking at nothing very much. However, that sensory lack is more than made up for once you arrive at platform level by a giant statue of the Great Leader offering OTSG to commuters. The station halls have a faded grandeur, great echo chambers ill-lit with enormous chandeliers, the tunnel walls decorated with murals depicting amazing wheat harvests and belching factory chimneys, the exact opposite of everything we had seen with our own eyes. The Metro might have looked impressive when first built, but a quarter of a century on the effect is Miss Havisham, not Paris Hilton: dowdy, old-fashioned, down-at-heel. The green and red trains do not look special but once inside the carriages the unique selling point of the Pyongyang Metro becomes apparent. Not only does every carriage have two portraits, one of the Great Leader, the other of the Dear Leader, but tinny loudspeakers blare out the latest regime propaganda, barely audible over the clickety-clack of the tube tracks. The newspaper stuck inside a glass case for the benefit of commuters was full of talk of war: 'The artillery of the sacred mountain will show its power'; the commuters looked no less miserable than they do on London's Northern Line.

In 2012, Tomiko, then in her last year at LSE, led a group of mainly international relations students from the university to North Korea for a similar trip. The weather was colder, the students more rebellious, but the tour was much the same, apart from the hospital visit. They went to Pyongyang's maternity hospital, a huge Stalinist concrete block. It smelt, not of disinfectant, but of musty neglect. On the top floor, she was shown two sets of triplets lined up in a row of metal cots. 'Ahh,' she cooed, then asked where the worn-out mothers were. 'Oh, they are not necessary,' was the reply.[1]

When triplets are born, the state takes them away. In exchange,

[1] Tomiko Newson: 'Journey into the heart of North Korea', *Independent*, 13 April 2012.

parents are given gifts, a ring for girls and a silver knife for boys. They say the state looks after them for the first four years but there is no way of checking that – it could be forever. The official logic behind this bizarre behaviour is that triplets are expensive so the state eases the parents' burden by looking after them. But there may be a darker reason: Kim Jong Il was reported to have feared an astrologer's prediction that a triplet would assassinate him.

The maternity hospital seemed like a living museum. They gave the 2012 trip a demonstration of a 1960s machine which, the guides said, could cure infertility. It looked like a bad confidence trick. The hospital's take on patient care was medieval. Mothers have to give birth alone and aren't allowed to meet with any family or even their husbands for at least a week after. The only contact they have is through little booths with phones like the ones in American prison dramas, except the mothers aren't behind glass but on a TV screen. The explanation for this isolation is to prevent infection, yet rubber gloves, disinfectant or hand soap did not seem to be deemed necessary.

In the maternity hospital Tomiko saw no disabled children. A doctor told her they are cared for in special homes, and no, they were not allowed to visit them. In 2006 Dr Ri Kwang Chol, who defected from the North to the South, claimed that babies who were born with physical defects were put to death and buried. Handicap International and the Red Cross do work with disabled people in North Korea, but there have long been concerns about how much effective monitoring of such aid work takes place. Also, people can become disabled in work accidents. In 2012, Tomiko's party of fifteen students, Britons, Italians and others, saw no disabled people at all. One year on, we saw two: a man on crutches and a woman in a wheelchair, close to the hospital.

That there are disabled adults in North Korea does not rule out the possibility of a policy of infanticide of disabled babies. Dr Ri's claim of state infanticide does not seem far-fetched, and tallies with what we know about its far-right ideology of racial purity. David Hawk's 'The Hidden Gulag' (a report written for the Committee for Human Rights in North Korea) details more evidence of infanticide, in particular the killing of babies and, more common, the forced abortions of North Korean women who have been impregnated by Chinese men.[2] This, too, conflicts with racial purity. Hawk writes: 'The women impregnated by Chinese men were routinely punished and their babies killed, accompanied by racial slurs and refusal to accept children who were part Han Chinese.' Hawk's witnesses include a midwife who saw three babies killed immediately after they were born in 2000 at a prison camp in the north-west of North Korea, close to the Chinese border; a former prisoner who helped deliver seven babies who were killed in a police detention centre in the same area, also in 2000; another witness on the north-east side of the country near the Chinese border who helped deliver four babies who were then killed in 1999; a former nurse in the North Korean army who saw multiple forced abortions by injection of the drug ravenol into the womb of pregnant women. North Korean guards cursed the women, reportedly, as 'bitches who got Chinese sperm and brought this on themselves'. The report cites one woman in a detention centre who refused to have an abortion: 'Guards compelled male prisoners to jump on her stomach until the woman aborted on the floor. The woman was then taken to hospital where she died.'[3]

[2] David Hawk: *The Hidden Gulag: The Lives and Voices of 'Those Who Are Sent to the Mountains'*, Committee for Human Rights in North Korea, Washington DC, 2012, http://www.hrnk.org/uploads/pdfs/HRNK_Hidden Gulag2_Web_5-18.pdf

[3] Hawk, p154.

The hospital we were taken to in 2013 is famous in North Korea. The 'local guide' was a senior doctor, who popped up again on the video boasting about the nation's medical achievements played on the plane leaving Pyongyang. The doctor went through the usual motions, proclaiming that the hospital was created thanks to the wisdom of Kim Il Sung and Kim Jong Il, in front of a painting of the two men, walking by the bank of the river that runs through Pyongyang, the Taedong. In the painting, Kim Two is in a black Mao jacket and Kim One in a Crombie overcoat, both men's shadows faintly reflected in a puddle beneath their feet.

As we listened to the standard lecture in front of the painting, one of our party darted forward and glimpsed in the distance a great crowd of patients and sick people being hurried out of the way down a corridor, lest we capture them on video. The doctor said the hospital looked after 1,300 patients. Once inside the hospital proper, it was freezing, so cold I buttoned up my coat. But at least the lights were on. And then they went out. After a bit, the power came back on, and they showed us a series of fancy machines, a CT scanner, UV lights, but something was missing. We hadn't been shown a single patient. I asked a doctor, or, at least, a lady in a white coat: 'There are no patients today?' She replied: 'Mostly, the patients come and get treated in the morning, because in the afternoon they go to work, or have social activities. They were here and they left.'

In South Korea, I asked a doctor who had defected from the North, anonymous for fear of reprisals by the state, what would have happened if she had said, 'We need more money for medicines for the patients'.

She replied: 'They would kill me the next day or even that same day. They would kill you regardless of your rank. Even a high-ranking official would be killed. Everyone knows that.'

Bill Gates does not know that. One of the richest men in the world is giving some of his billions to help North Korea's health service back on its feet. Raelyn Campbell of the Bill and Melinda Gates Foundation told a conference in 2013: 'Relative to other countries, the health situation is not that bad in North Korea.' Campbell cited World Health Organization (WHO) statistics revealing high vaccination rates, dramatic reductions in infectious diseases, decreasing child mortality rates, and several other positive health indicators based on WHO data. The North Korean health system, she said, is accordingly 'dysfunctionally functional'.[4]

The same message, that things are better than people think they are inside North Korea, was echoed by Dr Hazel Smith, professor of resilience and security at Cranfield University.[5] Dr Smith told *NK News* some startling statistics on public health in North Korea. For example, she said the rate of severe malnutrition in the North, at 5 per cent, is significantly lower than the 17 per cent average in Asia, and much lower than India at 20 per cent and Indonesia at 14 per cent. These statistics, says Smith, say: 'You've got a society that hasn't collapsed, for a start. Most of all, it tells you terms of poverty indicators, when you've got child mortality, infant mortality and maternal mortality, they're a lot better than lots of other Asian countries. If you look at the data on TB and malaria from the 2000s, you see that with the help of the WHO and the Gates Foundation, they've shot down. If you compare the data, you find

[4] Raelyn Campbell of Bill and Melinda Gates Foundation: http://www.asanplenum.org/programme_detail/sessionSketchesDetail.asp?x=y&seq=660
[5] Matthew McGrath: *NK News* website, 29 August 2013.

that North Korea is actually doing pretty well in getting these diseases under control, with help of course but pretty well.' Dr Smith added: 'Of course the North Korean government is not a good government . . . What we do know is that North Korea is by no means one of the worst-off countries in Asia.'

Dr Smith is relying on statistics published regularly by the WHO. She puts down exaggerations of the North's malnutrition to 'lazy scholarship . . . Or else it's more sinister than that, but I'll put it down as lazy scholarship to be kind.'

Are the Bill and Melinda Gates Foundation, the WHO and experts like Dr Smith right? Finding people who will openly criticize the Gates Foundation, one of the major benefactors in the world, is not easy. I asked one expert on North Korea if the Gates people speak Korean, had done on-the-spot checks, and have done lots of upcountry visits. He replied: 'No, no, and no. These numbers are likely fed to them by the North Korean authorities. They are not reliable.'

In Saddam's Iraq, I came across the same thing, of the WHO parroting Saddam's numbers, as if, in a corrupt and totalitarian state, mass murder is acceptable, but faking health statistics not so. If I was a betting man, I'd bet Bill Gates a pint of beer and a packet of crisps that, come regime change in Pyongyang, the Ministry of Health will admit that it made statistics up, big-time; that it prevented foreigners from seeing the worst provinces; and that doctors who did complain on behalf of their patients were silenced.

Mary Lou is not an expert in health statistics, still less a billionaire. But she is a North Korean defector who speaks to her brother on the phone and knows what conditions are really like in North Korea, even though she now lives in south-west London. We showed her our filming inside the hospital. Like the majority of defectors, she had never been to the big city, and had spent her whole life in the north-east of the country, not permitted to visit Pyongyang. It's hard to get across to Western readers the chasm in wealth and opportunity between the Big Zombie and the rest of North Korea. Perhaps the way to understand it is recalling the awe with which Dorothy and friends first see the gleaming emerald city in *The Wizard of Oz*.

Mary Lou said: 'You only get hospitals like that in Pyongyang. Hospitals in other areas are nothing like that. There are small hospitals with doctors, but no medicine, because the doctors sell it all on the black market. They are given medicine from the government, but very little, and what they do get is just sold. Very few go to hospital, because they know there is no medicine, and only go as a last resort. Women give birth and have cesareans without anesthetic.'

It's the end of our tour of the hospital, which has been quite the most depressing visit of our eight-day tour, where the authorities have been openly contemptuous, it seemed to me, of civilized standards. You need heat and light in a hospital. How come the dead kings enjoy that in their mausoleum but ordinary people must do without? And where were the 1,300 patients? On the tarmac apron at the entrance to the hospital, the doctor explained that we could not see patients without their – the patients' – permission. But we couldn't ask for that without seeing them. Catch-22.

Through Mr Hyun I told the doctor what I thought of his display of the North Korean public health service: 'Tell the doctor we're not fools. We haven't seen any patients. Please don't treat us in this way.'

On the basis of what we saw with our own eyes, the power cut, the absence of patients, and felt with our skin – the cold – the grave charges made by defectors against the public health system seem valid, that it is a monstrous lie.

19

The Gulag Circus

The most arresting thing about our trip to the State Circus in Pyongyang wasn't the clowns, creepy and unfunny as ever, or the high-wire act or the juggler atop five wibbly-wobbly chairs or the sequinned lady acrobat whizzing around above the audience inside a cardboard inter-continental rocket, but the audience itself. Ten thousand saw I at a glance, tossing their heads in sprightly dance, clapping in terrifying unison: officers of the Korean People's Army, brown-uniformed, obedient to the core. Our minders had kept us away from the parade, but our trip to the circus was a healthy reminder of the power of the regime over the masses. Mad and bad and sad and silly as the government of North Korea is, it didn't feel like a regime in imminent danger of self-destruction. Not once inside the DPRK did we see an indication of dissent, a suggestion that people were not enthralled with the regime. In North Korea everything stays the same.

Or does it? As the soldiers clapped in step and roared their approval when the acrobat lady popped out of the toy rocket, one couldn't help wondering: What do they really think? Do they buy it all?

The counter-argument is invisible and inaudible to us. But that does not mean, like Bishop Berkeley's tree falling in the forest, that it doesn't exist. That argument would be: a big number of people hate the regime with a passion; they know it tells lies about itself; they know that it stuffs itself with the finest food and wines while millions starve. And the proof of the existence of that counter-argument? The people in the gulag.

Satellite technology is a wonderful thing. From space, we can stare down and look at perimeter fences, huts, mine entrances and even sites of mass graves. To me, they look like fuzzy, small jagged-edged indications on a computer screen, but to a North Korean defector who served time in the gulag, it's home.

The best overall guide to the punishment state inside the North Korean state is 'The Hidden Gulag', written by David Hawk for the Committee for Human Rights in North Korea.[1] Hawk details an enormous gulag system, with satellite photographs and testimony from former prisoners and guards. His latest, August 2013, estimate is that around 100,000 are locked inside the Kwan-Li-So, the political prison camp system. The phrase means 'management place'. A second set of prison camps for 'ordinary criminals' – many of whom would never be imprisoned in the West – is called the Kyo-Hwa-So, literally 're-education facility', more like a penitentiary. Jimmy the Gold-Smuggler ended up in the latter; the former sucks in political enemies of the regime.

The Kwan-Li-So gulag is hell on earth. Here, political prisoners

[1] Hawk's 'The Hidden Gulag' report for HRNK is available in printed format or as a PDF: http://www.hrnk.org/uploads/pdfs/HRNK_HiddenGulag2_Web_5-18.pdf An update was released in August 2013: http://www.hrnk.org/events/announcements-view.php?id=10

who have gone through the mockery of a trial or no trial at all live behind barbed wire and electrified fences in the shivering cold of the mountains of north or north-central North Korea. Some starve to death; some are worked to death; some are tortured; some commit suicide. This leads to what Hawk calls 'exorbitant rates of deaths in detention'. His estimate of the political gulag population has come down from around 200,000 a decade ago to 100,000 in 2013. This may be because of a relaxation of political persecution; or that a big fraction of that 200,000 are now dead. No one knows. The Red Cross is not allowed into the gulag; officially, the regime does not admit it exists.

Unluckily for the Kim dynasty, there are now around 20,000 defectors from the North in South Korea and around the world. Three defectors have written astonishing stories about their time in the worst layers of the gulag: *The Aquariums of Pyongyang*, *Escape from Camp 14* and *Long Road Home*.[2]

The Aquariums of Pyongyang is the story of a boy who enters the gulag in 1977, when he is nine years old. When the lorry arrives at the camp, Kang Chol Hwan's reaction to his fellow inmates is one of disgust: 'How frightfully filthy they all were, dressed like beggars, their hair caked and matted with dirt.' His grandfather had been a successful businessman in Japan of Korean origin; the family are lured home, and then their troubles begin. It's a harrowing story of public executions, horror, insane cruelty and beatings. The grimmest is Kang's description of a schoolmate arguing with their bully of a teacher. The teacher, clearly psychotic, beats him savagely and then dumps him into the septic tank.

[2] Kang Chol Hwan, Pierre Rigoulot: *The Aquariums of Pyongyang*, Basic Books, New York, 1995; Blaine Harden: *Escape from Camp 14*, Pan Macmillan, London, 2012; Kim Yong with Kim Suk-Young: *Long Road Home*, Columbia University Press, New York, 2009.

The boy, half unconscious, cannot save himself and dies in the excrement.

Escape from Camp 14 tells the story of Shin Dong Hyuk, the only person born in the gulag for the invisibles, the lowest of the low, to escape. He survived by betraying his mother and older brother to the Bowibu. He watches them hang. You might think it is hard to sympathize with this monster, but his story is so harrowing, you do. *Long Road Home* is the story of Kim Yong, a North Korean lieutenant colonel in the National Security Agency who falls from grace and ends up in Camp 14, too. He manages to get out, then escapes to the South. Along the way, you read more than you might prefer about cannibalism. At Camp 14, Kim Yong worked more than 2,000 feet below ground, in a state of permanent hunger; the air was foul, the light a feeble glow-worm. One day a cave-in buried five prisoners alive. When the others managed to dig through to them, they were dead. The guards ordered the bodies to be wrapped in straw mats and removed, but two prisoners hacked off a leg and hid it in a shaft. 'They came back to eat the raw flesh the following day.' They were discovered, and shot.[3]

All three books provide such intricate detail they build an un-answerable case that the gulag does exist.

Torture is routine, and has been a consistent feature of the gulag, from Ali Lameda's experience in 1967 to the present day. But the number of would-be defectors has shot up in recent years, and so, consequently, has the savagery of the regime's gaolers.

Accounts of women victims suffering extreme torture are uncommon; accounts of them suffering rape and forced abortions, as set out in Chapter 18, all too common. There is an ocean of this stuff out there; I have only selected a few cases, virtually at random.

[3] Kim Yong, p89.

In 2005, Kim Seong Cheol ended up in the Bowibu prison in Onsong, in the far north-east of the country, bang next to China, and stuffed to the gunnels with 'border-crossers', either caught on the North Korean side or sent back from China. The detention cell was so crowded there was nowhere to sit. If a prisoner did not comply with 'exercise' drills, sitting down and standing up, repeatedly, they would make him stick his arms through the cell bars, tighten the handcuffs, and beat his hands with the iron rods used to clean their guns. The guards were wary of leaving bruises on faces. Once, Kim Seong was kicked in the eye. The bleeding was bad, so the guards sent him back to his cell. Receiving medical care or medicine was unimaginable.

While detained by the Inminboanseong, the People's Safety Agency, the lower-ranking and theoretically less nasty security agency to the Bowibu, he witnessed a prisoner subjected to the strappado, a torture first used by the Spanish Inquisition, in which the victim's hands are tied behind their back and then suspended in the air by ropes tied around the wrists. 'Anyone,' he said, 'who would come back to the cell after having it done on them would be unable to speak and nearly dead.'[4]

In South Korea I met Jung Gwang Il, a shy, diffident man. He was born in Yanji, China, of Korean-Chinese stock. His family moved to North Korea when he was seven. Following military service in the North Korean army, Jung became a trader, selling high quality mushrooms to China. But he went one better, and sold his fungi directly to South Korean traders, skipping the Chinese middlemen. In China, he rubbished the Kim dynasty to someone who turned out to be a North Korean snitch. On his return in July

---

[4] 'Survival Under Torture, Briefing Report on the Situation of Torture in the DPRK', Citizens' Alliance for North Korean Human Rights, 2009, http://www.nk humanrights.or.kr

1999, he was arrested at Hoeryong and ended up in an underground Bowibu torture interrogation. There, they tortured Jung to confess to spying for South Korea. He was beaten with a stick, they broke his teeth, scarred the back of his head. Tortures include the 'sit/stand torture' – where you ceaselessly have to stand and sit until you collapse – and the 'reading the newspaper torture', where a person is forced to maintain a position like he is reading a newspaper but without a chair. The worst was the 'pigeon torture'. The victim's legs and arms are tied together behind his back; the man's chest is thrust outwards like a pigeon's, the whole body locked, almost entirely immobile. After suffering this for hours, the muscles seize, and people fear permanent paralysis. During his time in the underground cells, two fellow prisoners died in detention. Jung's weight fell from 75kg to 38kg (165lb to 84lb, from 11 stone to 6). Underground, 'no matter how much you scream, no one can hear you'.

In early 2002, he was transferred to Camp 15, Yodok. We looked at it through Google Earth.[5] Yodok has sixty-five fake reviews on Google Maps, from punters having a playful poke at tyranny. Even so, comments like: 'Certainly not for the work shy and if you want to lose weight, this is the place', fail to raise much of a smile.

In September 2013 Andrei Lankov made a bold and provocative claim, that human rights in North Korea had recently shown an improvement, moving from 'being disastrous to being really bad.'[6] Lankov argued: 'It seems clear that in the last fifteen or twenty years the general trend has been a lessening of repression.' The rule of three generations of state revenge was over, he said, as the 'family responsibility principle' had been abandoned. He noted,

[5] Dial 'Yodok' into Google Earth and it comes up as Yodok Concentration Camp.
[6] http://www.nknews.org/2013/09/how-human-rights-in-north-korea-are-gradually-improving/

too, David Hawk's research that indicates the number of detainees in the gulag has dropped. Lankov's claim prompted a strong rebuttal from Greg Scarlatoiu of the Committee for Human Rights in North Korea, who argued that, contrary to Lankov's view, the fall in inmates may be due to fresh atrocities committed under Kim Jong Un. If the decline is true, he wrote: 'The main reason for the decline was the staggeringly high rate of death in detention, due to executions, severe malnutrition and concomitant disease, and work accidents. This hardly qualifies as indication of improvement of the human rights situation in North Korea.'[7] In the absence of any independent inspection of the camps it's impossible to come to a conclusion on this matter, but the continued absence of scrutiny does not make one optimistic. A young dictator is more vigorous, and more unpleasant to live under, than an old dictator. Scarlatoiu notes the one statistic that the world can subject to scrutiny; the number of defectors arriving in South Korea fell from 2,706 in 2011 to 1,502 in 2012. That's almost 50 per cent and that's not a sign that life inside North Korea is improving under Kim The Third.

I asked Jung, how do they bury the dead in the winter when the ground is so cold? He replied: 'No, we don't bury them. We leave the dead bodies in a warehouse till April. We bury them in April. When we go to bury them, they are already rotten and totally decomposed. So they are shovelled like rubbish and buried.'

How many bodies in one hole in the ground?

'Up to eighty people.'

That's a big mass grave. One day, it can be dug up again, and, perhaps, the people responsible will answer to justice. That would be a circus well worth turning up to. One day . . .

[7] http://www.nknews.org/2013/09/are-human-rights-really-improving-in-north-korea/

20

God the Fat Boy Kim

Will he, won't he, blow the world up?

At a restaurant one day, the television was on and viewers were treated to a series of colour photographs of the world's youngest head of state. There was plump-cheeked Kim Jong Un in his trademark short sides and floppy top haircut, sporting a long-length blue coat. The Young Leader was being shown around a military facility by three generals wearing flat circular hats, a little like the kepis worn by the French Foreign Legion but without the white flap at the back. Kim the Third gave OTSG while he inspected a funny large box and bits of machinery. 'Military equipment,' explained Mr Hyun, 'so we can strike the White House with one blow.'

That was Mr Hyun's catchphrase. He always delivered it with a swing of his fist and a smile on his chops. The next photograph was utterly bizarre. Two generals looked on as Kim Jong Un checked out two children's slides, one blue, one red. The 'Military-First' policy has created a parallel economy, where manufacturing children's play equipment is as much a job for soldiers as guarding the DPRK from the American-bastards. The incongruity of a military inspection of children's slides didn't seem to bother the Young Marshal. Maybe he is the future, but on the basis of his generals showing him kiddy slides, he, too, looks locked in the past.

During our stay in North Korea, we bumped into some foreign diplomats and I asked them whether, since the switchover in power from Kim the Second to Kim the Third, they had observed any serious changes. 'It's been very disappointing,' said one. 'Not that much change.'

On the ground, there are a few signs of something new. It was hard not to spot the Chinese bank slowly growing up outside our hotel window; kids roller-skated across Kim Il Sung Square with expensive-ish Chinese-made roller skates where before only tractors towing ballistic rockets were allowed; the Pyongyang traffic jam-ettes seemed to get longer during our stay. Middle-class North Koreans, I heard, these days were watching Tom Cruise star in *Mission: Impossible*. Life was too short to explain the Church of Scientology to my interlocutor, so I gave up.

The augurs for Kim Jong Il did not seem so bad. Kim Jong Un was schooled in Switzerland, where he must have picked up a few odds-n-sods of Western civilization. Well, the cuckoo clock, perhaps, and a taste for chocolate. Everything is a bit fuzzy because he was there at roughly the same time as a slightly older brother, and no one is quite sure which Kim did what. Kim Three is the youngest of Kim Jong Il's three sons, but clearly the savviest. The oldest, Kim Jong Nam, also seems to be the most sensible. He's on the record as saying that the North Korean economy is bust, but fixing it would be regime suicide. Kim Jong Nam told a reporter: 'Taking North Korea's unique position into account, there is a fear that economic reforms and openness will lead to the collapse of the present system . . . The North Korean leadership is stuck in a bind. Without reforms the country's economy will go bankrupt, but reforms are fraught with the danger of systemic collapse.'[1] Lankov commented wryly: 'This is a remarkably forthright – but completely reasonable – admission.'

Kim Jong Nam was groomed for the top. In 1998, he joined the Ministry of Public Security, the key organization in the police state. But administering the gulag and running the state's torture machine must have paled. Leastways, the oldest of the trio lost the keys to the throne in May 2001. Kim Jong Nam was arrested in Japan, travelling with two women and his four-year-old boy. He had forged a Dominican Republic passport using a Chinese alias, Pang Xiong, or 'Fat Bear'. The Pyongyang wannabe dauphin told interrogators that he wanted to visit Disneyland. Big mistake. He now lives in Macao, where he takes well-aimed pot-shots at the regime from afar.

Fujimoto, the Japanese thug-cum-chef, had been Kim Jong Un's nanny for a while, a little like Nana the Newfoundland dog-nanny in *Peter Pan*. He neatly skewered the succession chances of middle brother Kim Jong Chol when he said that Kim Jong Il preferred his youngest boy. Fujimoto reported that Kim the Second had said in front of top officials: 'The big one [Jong Chol] has a weak heart and is feminine, but the young one is manly.' Fujimoto explained: 'To a first-time observer, it looked like Jong Un was the older brother and Jong Chol the younger.'[2]

[1] Lankov, *The Real North Korea*, p117.
[2] 'Kim Jong Un "Loves Nukes, Computer Games and Johnny Walker"', *Chosun Ilbo*, 20 December 2010, http://english.chosun.com/site/data/html_dir/2010/12/20/2010122001136.html

As the Young Pretender entered his teens, Fujimoto played Falstaff to Kim Jong Un's Prince Harry, it seems. Kim Jong Un liked Johnny Walker whisky and secretly smoked Yves Saint Laurent cigarettes with the naughty sushi chef. He drove a Mercedes, listened to South Korean pop and played Super Mario and Tetris. Had he been an ordinary North Korean, any single thing on that list of conspicuous Western consumption would have meant trouble.

The old man dies in 2011, Kim Three takes power and all that normality ends up in the spring of 2013 with the crazy rhetoric that thermo-nuclear war is on the cards. In the summer of 2013, a story breaks in China that Kim Three has had an old lover machine-gunned on framed charges of being a porno star. Are we happy that this man has a finger on a nuclear trigger? Not very.

It's hard to assess the truth of the matter but Chinese sources, cited in the South Korean daily *Chosun Ilbo*, say that Kim Jong Un's former lover, pop star Hyon Song Wol, and a dozen friends in the North Korean music scene, were machine-gunned by firing squad.[3] The Chinese sources said that Hyon and Mun Kyong Jin, head of the Unhasu Orchestra, had been arrested for violating North Korean laws against pornography. Three days later, Hyon, Mun and ten or so band members, singers and dancers in the Unhasu Orchestra and the Wangjaesan Light Music Band were executed in public. Officially, they were accused of making porn videos. It seems hard to see why that justifies the death sentence. 'They were executed with machine guns while the key members of the Unhasu Orchestra, Wangjaesan Light Band and Moranbong

[3] 'Kim Jong Un's ex-girlfriend "Shot by Firing Squad"', *Chosun Ilbo*, 29 August 2013, http://english.chosun.com/site/data/html_dir/2013/08/29/2013082901412.html

Band as well as the families of the victims looked on,' the source said. Surviving family members have been sent to the gulag, the source added.

Hyon's band were famous in the North, knocking out smash hits like 'Footsteps of Soldiers', 'I Love Pyongyang', 'She is a Discharged Soldier' and the pop-pickers' favourite, 'Excellent Horse-like Lady'. Actually, that's a lousy translation: it's a song about a woman who completes a five-year plan in three years or something like that, and could be better rendered as 'Hard-working Woman'. A video on YouTube, with more than a million hits so far, shows Hyon in fine form, running around a clothing factory with an orange headscarf, sticking cotton reels on bobbins.[4] It's impossible to reconcile this silly innocence with her being murdered.

Chinese whispers started in China. The story may be entirely untrue. The sources, clearly relying on information coming out of Pyongyang, say Kim Three and Hyon had been lovers, but Kim Jong Il did not approve. She married someone else and had a child with him, but the pair kept on seeing each other. Kim Jong Un's wife, Ri Sol Ju, was also a member of the Unhasu Orchestra before she married him. Whether she had any hand in the spilling of blood is not clear. In democracies, this kind of stuff ends up in the tabloids, not in the mortuary. If they are indeed dead – and, this being North Korea, the dead do sometimes pop back up again, very much alive – Kim Three's old girlfriend and her friends may have been victim of some terrible palace intrigue. Perhaps they were taped speaking disloyally or plotting revenge against Kim Three. Perhaps they had porn tapes of Kim Jong Un behaving in a way

[4] 'Excellent Horse-like Lady', sung by Hyon Song Wol, https://www.youtube.com/watch?v=v5tkXgw2OMY

that might embarrass him. If someone was trying to blackmail him, that could explain the extent of the bloodbath. The easiest way for the regime to deny the allegations is a big concert, with the alleged corpses headlining the bill. In the event of this not happening, that is not a good sign for them, and, because it reflects on the mental stability of North Korea's new ruler, the entire world.

When the machine-gunning story surfaced in the Japanese media, the regime fired back in the language it alone holds dear: 'These days the South Korean authorities let reptile media run the whole gamut of vituperation hurting the dignity of the supreme leadership of the DPRK.'[5] The Korean Central News Agency, the voice of Pyongyang, proclaimed that Marshal Kim Jong Un had been slandered, 'an unpardonable hideous provocation hurting the dignity of the supreme leadership of the DPRK and thrice-cursed crime which can be committed only by the confrontation maniacs. No matter how mad the puppet group goes with confrontation with compatriots, there is the red line of recklessness it should not cross . . . This is barbarism and thrice-cursed treason which can hardly be imagined by human beings.'

In plain English, Fat Boy Kim is pissed off. But the bluster means little. What the world needs to see is the alleged dead brought back to life. If proof of life of Hyon and others is not forthcoming, then we may be forced to conclude the worst, that the Young Leader is like his grandfather and father before him, a gangster running, not a racket, but a state. The difference is that in the twenty-first century, the dynasty can no longer annihilate an ex-lover and no one notice. Hyon exists forever on YouTube,

[5] KCNA, Pyongyang, 22 September, 2013: 'Those Who Hurt Dignity of DPRK's Supreme Leadership Will Pay Dearly: KCNA Commentary' http://leonidpetrov. wordpress.com/category/north-korea-news/

singing 'Excellent Horse-like Lady'. This particular snuffing out of innocent life may come to haunt the murderer. Further evidence of Kim Jong Un's brutality concerns the fate of former vice minister of the army, Kim Chol, who was reportedly executed with a mortar round in October 2012. He had been caught by the Bowibu drinking and carousing during the official mourning period after Kim Jong Il's death. Kim Jong Un ordered that 'no trace of him should be left behind, not even his hair'. Kim Chol, according to the South Korean media, was forced to stand on a spot that had been zeroed in for a mortar round and be 'obliterated'.[6] This killing, and the purge of other old generals, suggests that Kim Jong Un was using 'mourning period' breaches – surely a fault in etiquette, not conduct requiring obliteration – as an excuse to get his father's cronies out of the way and put in his own people. But the purge, and what appears to have happened to his ex-girlfriend and her band, shows that Kim Three is happy to continue the family tradition of mass murder. We have been warned.

Kim Jong Un might think he can get away with Armageddon unscathed. North Korea is the gruyère state. Defectors have been telling stories for decades of great tunnels under the earth, housing fake South Korean streets, the better for spies to practise on, and secret bunkers for the regime's leaders, and secret nuclear and chemical weapons factories in the bowels of the earth.

'Kim Jong-il builds "Thunderbirds" runway for war', was a smashing headline in the *Sunday Times* in 2008.[7] The story's source

---

[6] 'Kim Jong Un's ex-lover "executed by firing squad"', *Daily Telegraph*, Julian Ryall: 29 August 2013, http://www.telegraph.co.uk/news/worldnews/asia/northkorea/10272953/Kim-Jong-uns-ex-lover-executed-by-firing-squad.html
[7] Michael Sheridan, Uzi Mahnaimi: 'Kim Jong-il builds "Thunderbirds" runway for war', *Sunday Times*, 27 April 2008.

was a North Korean air force defector, who said that the dynasty had built three underground fighter bases, part of an extraordinary troglodytic world below ground. Just as in the *Thunderbirds* TV puppet show, tunnel doors would open and aircraft would shoot out to strike the Americans with one blow, etc., etc. What is so silly about these underground airfields and the rest is that the information from the defectors is hoovered up by the spy agencies in South Korea, Japan and, of course, the United States. A secret base your enemies know about is not a secret but a target.

North Korea has certainly exported this tunnelling know-how to its friends in Syria, Iran and Hezbollah, making life difficult for the makers of bunker-busting bombs. The North has also been caught exporting chemical weapons technology to countries like Syria. In 2009 Greek authorities seized 14,000 anti-chemical weapons suits from a North Korean ship most likely headed for Syria.[8] In 2013, a Japanese newspaper, *Sankei Shimbun*, reported that a Libyan-registered vessel, the *Al En Ti Sar*, out of North Korea bound for Syria, was stopped by Turkish authorities. Turkish officials seized 1,400 rifles and pistols, 30,000 bullets and anti-chemical weapons gas masks.[9]

Nate Thayer, a brilliant investigative journalist whose first great scoop was tracking down Pol Pot in languid internal exile in Cambodia – the Khmer Rouge killed the ex-tyrant off, Nate once told me over a beer, before he could get a proper interview – investigated a peculiar train accident in North Korea in 2004.[10] A

[8] 'Greece seizes N. Korea chemical weapons suits', AFP, 16 November 2011.
[9] http://www.iol.co.za/news/world/north-korea-tried-to-send-gas-masks-to-syria-1.1568595#.UiMvrLxM_fN
[10] http://natethayer.wordpress.com/2013/08/27/the-violent-consequences-of-the-north-korea-syria-chemical-arms-trade/

blast, measuring 3.6 on the Richter scale and detected at international earthquake monitoring stations in Russia and the United States, blew up a train in Ryongchon as it headed to the port of Nampo, the site of the West Sea Barrage. The explosion was so big Pyongyang appealed for emergency international help. The Red Cross counted 160 people killed and 1,300 injured; the blast left a crater 60 metres (196 feet) deep. That's a big hole in the ground. The regime said the explosion was caused by fertilizer. Ha ha, good joke. Thayer speculates that the true cause was a remote-detonated bomb which blew up the train, loaded with rockets and rocket fuel, destined for Syria. The bomber may have been a Mossad agent. Thayer says that amongst the dead were a dozen Syrians, and that North Koreans wearing chemical weapons suits worked on the clean-up.

The traffic of chemical weapons technology to Syria over the years suggests it is not unlikely that the North Koreans had some hand in the nerve gas attacks on rebel areas in Damascus which President Obama contends were the work of the Assad regime. A photograph of two North Korean military attachés paying their respects to injured regime fighters in a military hospital in Damascus hardly allays the world's suspicions.[11]

Chemical weapons, grim as they are, kill thousands. Nuclear bombs kill millions. In a wine bar off Fleet Street I asked one of the best Dr Strangeloves in the business, Mark Fitzpatrick, the 'will he, won't he?' question at the start of this chapter. Mark explained that the regime's threats of lobbing rockets all the way to mainland United States were so much hot air. Their most reliable rocket, he said, could hit South Korea in minutes, Japan easily and possibly

[11] *Chosun Ilbo*, 18 September 2013, http://english.chosun.com/site/data/html_dir/2013/06/11/2013061101459.html

one of the American bases in the Pacific. Possible, but unlikely. The two challenges of nuclear warmongery are having the right missile, he explained, and making the bomb small and lightweight enough to be carried on it. Thus far, the North Koreans have proved that they can lob a missile over Japan, a distance of around 1,000 kilometres, but they have yet to stick a bomb on top. Bombs aren't feathers; a one-kilotonne bomb weighs so much that it would considerably reduce the range of a rocket.

So, phooey, Mr Kim, I asked. Mark pulled a face. It's still dangerous, he said. The thing that worries people like him is that if North Korea sinks a South Korean warship or shells a South Korean island, as it did in 2010, then the South will not be so easygoing this time. They've given orders for commanders to react on the spot, an eye for an eye, so that if the North shells the South, the South will fire back. Instantly, this raises the problem that the South, with all its twenty-first-century firepower, will shatter the North's fragile bellicosity. From then on in, the North has only its shiny nuclear button to press. Mark had to go. He had a vegetable garden to attend to in south London. Life must go on.

But will Kim Jong Un, won't Kim Jong Un, blow up the world? Three words: I don't know. If he does, he is dead, along with the regime his grandfather built. My guess is, he won't, but that does not mean that we can rest easy for a long, long time to come. It could last fifty years, said Izidor, Ceausescu's interpreter. I hope he's wrong. In the meantime, it seems sensible not to fall for their bluffs, and right to press the regime on human rights, and wait.

The government of China is in the best place to put effective pressure on the Kim dynasty. Far from helping the ordinary people of North Korea, defectors say the Chinese authorities are sending more and more people back – a plain breach of their international obligations towards refugees. The highly critical interim report on human rights in North Korea by the United Nations, reporting 'unspeakable atrocities' in September 2013, was attacked by North Korea, and its allies Belarus, Syria and China. A Chinese diplomat said: 'Politicized accusations and pressures are not helpful to improving human rights in any country. On the contrary they will only provoke confrontation and undermine the foundation and atmosphere for international human rights cooperation.'[12] That issue may not get much traction inside the Chinese Communist Party, but North Korea's behaviour is generating security worries for China. If Kim Jong Un keeps on messing about with rockets flying over Japan and staging nuclear tests, then the Japanese Right may argue it is time for them to have nuclear weapons – leading to a regional nuclear arms race in east Asia. For the moment, it seems that change in Pyongyang will follow, not precede, change in Beijing.

On our last night it was Mr Hyun's birthday. He blew out the candles on his cake with one blow, just like the White House will fall. We then all watched the KITC video of our trip, Alex seldom more than two feet from me, in paroxysms of laughter. At times like this it is hard not to feel great affection for the people of North Korea. They are locked inside the madhouse, slaves to Zombie and Sons, at home in the craziest nation on earth.

Suspecting I'd struggle to find a copy there, I took Orwell's *Animal Farm* with me to North Korea. In Wonsan, I re-read his great introduction to the Ukrainian edition – they, too, know a thing or two about famine, and brainwashing. Orwell wrote: 'If I

[12] 'North Korean inmates starved and tortured, abuse widespread': U.N., Reuters, 17 September 2013, http://www.reuters.com/article/2013/09/17/us-korea-north-crimes-idUSBRE98G0B920130917

had to choose a text to justify myself, I should choose the line from Milton: "By the known rules of ancient liberty."' As it happened, I finished *Animal Farm* whilst in North Korea and left my copy behind, thinking perhaps someone there might find it useful.

One thinks of the people shivering in the gulag, and wonders: how can we accelerate change? In Tom Stoppard's play *Night And Day*, about journalism and drinking and freedom and tyranny, the hero Wagner listens to the lover of a dead journalist attack the whole damn thing as a waste of time: the heartbreak beauty queen, the classified ads, the editorial. He half agrees but then replies: 'People do awful things to each other. But it's worse in places where everybody is kept in the dark. It really is. Information is light. Information, in itself, about anything, is light. That's all you can say really . . . What's the name of the hotel?'

Information is light. Shine a light into North Korea. The BBC *could* think seriously about calls to start a North Korean service, specifically staffed with people who speak with heavy, rural North Korean accents. My South Korean translator in New Malden often had difficulty in understanding what the defectors from the North were saying. Likewise, North Koreans, listening to their secret radios at low volume lest the Bowibu catch them, might struggle with Seoul accents. Perhaps they could consider broadcasting *1984*, *Animal Farm* and the books on the North's gulag. Second, perhaps some smart South Koreans could take apart the Orascom mobile phones used in North Korea and work out whether there is a simple modification that can be done that would enable ordinary people in the North to do more with their phones. Third, build the world's biggest mobile phone masts all along the northern border of the South. Information is light.

On the way to the airport we overtook an oil train, a camouflage net draped over the engineer's cab, leaving the two hundred wagons somewhat naked to the sky. The engineer waved to us as if he was in a North Korean version of *Thomas the Tank Engine*.

When I got back to Heathrow, I got down on my knees and kissed the revolting plastic jetty. It was good to be back in England, drizzle and all. Leaving North Korea is not an option for its people. They will probably only be free to come and go as they wish when the Kim dynasty is dead, and on that day I shall go to 'Excellent Horse-like Lady' on the internet, and press play, and raise a glass to poor Hyon, dead or alive, and Ali and Doina, long dead, and all the others condemned to exist inside North Korea's living death.

Acknowledgements

Tomiko Newson returned from North Korea in 2012, passionate that the world should know more about the continuing tragedy of its people. Without her, this book would never have been written. Thanks, too, to Alex Niakaris, for his great good humour inside the North, and thanks to all the students who went on Tomiko's trip in 2012 and the trip in 2013. For their observations, special thanks to Hoe-Yeong Loke, 'Fred', 'Herta', 'Dylan', Jais and the Russian goddesses.

At the BBC, thanks to all my colleagues at *Panorama*, but especially Tom Giles, Clive Edwards, Karen Wightman and Howard Bradburn. Thanks, too, to James Jones and Owen Phillips for beer and cheer.

Long ago at the LSE, Professors Leonard Schapiro, Geoffrey Stern – he led a trip to Hoxha's Albania, packed to the gunnels with journalists pretending to be academics – and Wolfgang von Leyden helped frame my views about tyranny and free speech. I will always remember von Leyden's aside about the Nazis: 'They were churlish and ill-bred.'

Thanks to Ludovico Tallarita for his work on the Italian section, Sorana Stanescu for her help in Romania, Carlos David with his help on the tragic case of his uncle, Barbara Demick, Gerry Gregg, Hugh Jordan and my two sources in West Belfast, and, in Washington DC, Andrew Natsios and Greg Scarlatoiu of the Committee for Human Rights in North Korea.

Jang Ho Kwon did sterling work tracking down North Korean defectors in New Malden. All of the defectors I met in South Korea, Washington DC and London have helped me understand their old country. One day, I hope, they will be able to return.

At Transworld, thanks to Henry Vines. No book would have happened without my agent, Humfrey Hunter.

Lastly, to Tomiko, Sam, Molly and Bertie: tyranny trembles in the face of mockery and laughter, for which much thanks.

Picture Acknowledgements

The author would like to thank Alexander Niakaris and Georgia Short for their photographs. All other images have been supplied courtesy of the author unless otherwise stated. Every effort has been made to trace copyright holders. We apologize for any omissions in this respect and will be pleased to make the appropriate acknowledgements in future editions.

Section One
Page 1: Kim Jong Un © AP/Press Association Images. Page 2: North Koreans walk past a portrait of their late leaders © Wong Maye-E/AP/Press Association Images. Page 3: both images © AP/Press Association Images. Page 4: the Pyongyang Arc de Triomphe © Getty Images. Page 6: North Koreans parade in Kim Il Sung Square © AP/Press Association Images; troops marching © Jon Chol Jin/AP/Press Association Images.

Section Two

Page 10: Kim Jong Un waves to a crowd © Ng Han
Guan/AP/Press Association Images; North Korea's Unha-3 rocket
lifts off © AP/Press Association Images. Page 12: satellite image
© DigitalGlobe/Getty Images. Page 14: James Dresnok ©
Kino/Everett/REX features. Page 15: North Korea at night ©
NASA/NOAA. Page 16: South Korean protestors © Ahn Young-
joon/AP/Press Association Images; defaced banner © Kin
Cheung/AP/Press Association Images; young men using mobile
phones in Pyongyang © AP/Press Association Images.

Index

ABOUT THE AUTHOR

John Sweeney is a reporter for BBC *Panorama* who became a YouTube sensation when he lost his temper with a senior member of the Church of Scientology. Before joining the BBC in 2001, Sweeney worked for twelve years at the *Observer*, where he covered wars and revolutions and unrest in more than sixty countries from Algeria, Bosnia, Chechnya to Zimbabwe.

Over the course of his career John has won two Royal Television Society prizes, an Emmy, a Sony Gold award, the *What the Papers Say* Journalist of the Year Prize, an Amnesty International prize and the Paul Foot Award.

He is the author of eight books, including most recently *The Church of Fear: Inside The Weird World of Scientology* and his first novel, *Elephant Moon*. His hobby is falling off his bike on the way back from the pub.